GLENCOE LANGUAGE ARTS

Teacher's Annotated Edition

Grammar and Language Workbook

GRADE 6

Glencoe McGraw-Hill

New York, New York   Columbus, Ohio   Woodland Hills, California   Peoria, Illinois

Glencoe/McGraw-Hill

*A Division of The **McGraw·Hill** Companies*

Send all inquiries to:
Glencoe/McGraw-Hill
8787 Orion Place
Columbus, Ohio 43240-4027

ISBN 0-07-820542-5

Printed in the United States of America

7 8 9 10 11 009 10 09 08 07 06

Contents

Handbook of Definitions and Rules

SUBJECTS AND PREDICATES

1. The simple subject is the key noun or pronoun that tells what the sentence is about. A compound subject is made up of two or more simple subjects that are joined by a conjunction and have the same verb.
   The **lantern** glows.   **Moths** and **bugs** fly nearby.

2. The simple predicate is the verb or verb phrase that expresses the essential thought about the subject of the sentence. A compound predicate is made up of two or more verbs or verb phrases that are joined by a conjunction and have the same subject.
   Rachel **jogged** down the hill.
   Pete **stretched** and **exercised** for an hour.

3. The complete subject consists of the simple subject and all the words that modify it.
   Golden curly hair framed the child's face.
   The soft glow of sunset made her happy.

4. The complete predicate consists of the simple predicate and all the words that modify it or complete its meaning.
   Lindy **ate a delicious muffin for breakfast.**
   The apple muffin **also contained raisins.**

5. Usually the subject comes before the predicate in a sentence. In inverted sentences, all or part of the predicate precedes the subject.
   (You) Wait for me at the corner. (request)
   Through the toys **raced** the **children.** (inverted)
   Is the **teacher** feeling better? (question)
   There **are seats** in the first row.

PARTS OF SPEECH

Nouns

1. A singular noun is a word that names one person, place, thing, or idea.
   aunt   meadow   pencil   friendship

   A plural noun names more than one person, place, thing, or idea.
   aunts   meadows   pencils   friendships

2. To help you determine whether a word in a sentence is a noun, try adding it to the following sentences. Nouns will fit in at least one of these sentences:
   He said something about _____.   I know something about a(n) _____.
   He said something about **aunts.**   I know something about a **meadow.**

3. A common noun names a general class of people, places, things, or ideas.
   sailor   city   holiday   music

   A proper noun specifies a particular person, place, thing, event, or idea. Proper nouns are always capitalized.
   Captain Ahab   **Rome**   **Memorial Day**   *Treasure Island*

4. A concrete noun names an object that occupies space or that can be recognized by any of the senses.

leaf   melody   desk   aroma

An abstract noun names an idea, a quality, or a characteristic.

loyalty   honesty   democracy   friendship

5. A collective noun names a group. When the collective noun refers to the group as a whole, it is singular. When it refers to the individual group members, the collective noun is plural.

The **family** eats dinner together every night. (singular)

The **council** vote as they wish on the pay increase. (plural)

6. A possessive noun shows possession, ownership, or the relationship between two nouns.

Monica's book   the **rabbit's** ears   the **hamster's** cage

Verbs

1. A verb is a word that expresses action or a state of being and is necessary to make a statement. A verb will fit one or more of these sentences:

He _____.   We _____.   She _____ it.

He **knows.**   We **walk.**   She **sees** it.

2. An action verb tells what someone or something does. The two types of action verbs are transitive and intransitive. A transitive verb is followed by a word or words—called the direct object—that answer the question *what?* or *whom?* An intransitive verb is not followed by a word that answers *what?* or *whom?*

Transitive: The tourists **saw** the ruins.   The janitor **washed** the window.

Intransitive: Owls **hooted** during the night.   The children **played** noisily.

3. An indirect object receives what the direct object names.

Marcy sent **her brother** a present.

4. A linking verb links, or joins, the subject of a sentence with an adjective or a noun.

The trucks **were** red. (adjective)

She **became** an excellent swimmer. (noun)

5. A verb phrase consists of a main verb and all its auxiliary, or helping, verbs.

We **had been told** of his arrival.

They **are listening** to a symphony.

6. Verbs have four principal parts or forms: base, past, present participle, and past participle. Form the past and past participle by adding -ed to the base.

Base: I **talk.**   Present Participle: I am **talking.**

Past: I **talked.**   Past Participle: I have **talked.**

7. Irregular verbs form the past and past participle in other ways.

PRINCIPAL PARTS OF IRREGULAR VERBS

Base Form	Past Form	Past Participle	Base Form	Past Form	Past Participle
be	was, were	been	lead	led	led
beat	beat	beaten	lend	lent	lent
become	became	become	let	let	let
begin	began	begun	lie	lay	lain
bite	bit	bitten *or* bit	lose	lost	lost
blow	blew	blown	put	put	put
break	broke	broken	ride	rode	ridden
bring	brought	brought	ring	rang	rung
catch	caught	caught	rise	rose	risen
choose	chose	chosen	run	ran	run
come	came	come	say	said	said
do	did	done	see	saw	seen
draw	drew	drawn	set	set	set
drink	drank	drunk	shrink	shrank *or* shrunk	shrunk *or* shrunken
drive	drove	driven			
eat	ate	eaten	sing	sang	sung
fall	fell	fallen	sit	sat	sat
feel	felt	felt	speak	spoke	spoken
find	found	found	spring	sprang *or* sprung	sprung
fly	flew	flown			
freeze	froze	frozen	steal	stole	stolen
get	got	got *or* gotten	swim	swam	swum
give	gave	given	take	took	taken
go	went	gone	tear	tore	torn
grow	grew	grown	tell	told	told
hang	hung	hung	think	thought	thought
hang	hanged	hanged	throw	threw	thrown
have	had	had	wear	wore	worn
know	knew	known	win	won	won
lay	laid	laid	write	wrote	written

8. The principal parts are used to form six verb tenses. The **tense** of a verb expresses time.

Simple Tenses

Present Tense: She **speaks.** (present or habitual action)
Past Tense: She **spoke.** (action completed in the past)
Future Tense: She **will speak.** (action to be done in the future)

Perfect Tenses

Present Perfect Tense: She **has spoken.** (action just done or still in effect)
Past Perfect Tense: She **had spoken.** (action completed before some other past action)
Future Perfect Tense: She **will have spoken.** (action to be completed before some future time)

9. **Progressive forms** of verbs are made up of a form of *be* and a present participle and express a continuing action. **Emphatic forms** are made up of a form of *do* and a base form and add emphasis or ask questions.

   Progressive: Marla **is babysitting.**   The toddlers **have been napping** for an hour.
   Emphatic: They **do prefer** beef to pork.
   We **did ask** for a quiet table.

10. The **voice** of a verb shows whether the subject performs the action or receives the action of the verb. A sentence is in the **active voice** when the subject performs the action. A sentence is in the **passive voice** when the subject receives the action of the verb.

   The robin **ate** the worm. (active)
   The worm **was eaten** by the robin. (passive)

Pronouns

1. A **pronoun** takes the place of a noun, a group of words acting as a noun, or another pronoun.

2. A **personal pronoun** refers to a specific person or thing. **First-person** personal pronouns refer to the speaker, **second-person** pronouns refer to the one spoken to, and **third-person** pronouns refer to the one spoken about.

	Singular	Plural
First Person	I, me, my, mine	we, us, our, ours
Second Person	you, your, yours	your, your, yours
Third Person	he, she, it, him, her, his, hers, its	they, them, their, theirs

3. A **reflexive pronoun** refers to the subject of the sentence. An **intensive pronoun** adds emphasis to a noun or another pronoun. A **demonstrative pronoun** points out specific persons, places, things, or ideas.

   Reflexive: **Nikki** prepares **himself** for the day-long hike.
   Intensive: **Nikki himself** prepares for the day-long hike.
   Demonstrative: **That** was a good movie! **These** are the files you wanted.

4. An **interrogative pronoun** is used to form questions. A **relative pronoun** is used to introduce a subordinate clause. An **indefinite pronoun** refers to persons, places, or things in a more general way than a personal pronoun does.

   Interrogative: **Whose** are these?   **Which** did you prefer?
   Relative: The bread **that** we tasted was whole wheat.
   Indefinite: **Someone** has already told them. **Everyone** agrees on the answer.

5. Use the subject form of a personal pronoun used as a subject or when it follows a linking verb.

   He writes stories.   Are **they** ready?   It is **I.** (after linking verb)

6. Use the object form of a personal pronoun when it is an object.

   Mrs. Cleary called **us.** (direct object)   Stephen offered **us** a ride. (indirect object)
   Sara will go with **us.** (object of preposition)

7. Use a **possessive pronoun** to replace a possessive noun. Never use an apostrophe in a possessive personal pronoun.

   Their science experiment is just like **ours.**

8. When a pronoun is followed by an appositive, use the subject pronoun if the appositive is the subject. Use the object pronoun if the appositive is an object. To test whether the pronoun is correct, read the sentence without the appositive.
We eighth-graders would like to thank you.
The success of **us** geometry students is due to Ms. Marcia.

9. In incomplete comparisons, choose the pronoun that you would use if the missing words were fully expressed.
Harris can play scales faster than **I** (can).
It is worth more to you than (it is to) **me**.

10. In questions use *who* for subjects and *whom* for objects.
Who wants another story?
Whom will the class choose as treasurer?

    In subordinate clauses use *who* and *whoever* as subjects after linking verbs, and use *whom* and *whomever* as objects.
These souvenirs are for **whoever** wants to pay the price.
The manager will train **whomever** the president hires.

11. An antecedent is the word or group of words to which a pronoun refers or that a pronoun replaces. All pronouns must agree with their antecedents in number, gender, and person.
Marco's **sister** spent **her** vacation in San Diego.
The huge old **trees** held **their** own against the storm.

12. Make sure that the antecedent of a pronoun is clearly stated.
UNLCLEAR: Mrs. Cardonal baked cookies with her daughters, hoping to sell **them** at the bake sale.
CLEAR: Mrs. Cardonal baked cookies with her daughters, hoping to sell **the cookies** at the bake sale.
UNLCLEAR: If you don't tie the balloon to the stroller, **it** will blow away.
CLEAR: If you don't tie the balloon to the stroller, **the balloon** will blow away.

Adjectives

1. An adjective modifies, or describes, a noun or pronoun by providing more information or giving a specific detail.
The **smooth** surface of the lake gleamed.
Frosty trees glistened in the sun.

2. Most adjectives will fit this sentence:
The _____ one seems very _____.
The **handmade** one seems very **colorful.**

3. Articles are the adjectives *a, an,* and *the.* Articles do not meet the preceding test for adjectives.

4. A proper adjective is formed from a proper noun and begins with a capital letter.
Tricia admired the **Scottish** sweaters.
Our **Mexican** vacation was memorable.

5. The comparative form of an adjective compares two things or people. The superlative form compares more than two things or people. Form the comparative by adding *-er* or combining with *more* or *less*. Form the superlative by adding *-est* or combining with *most* or *least*.

POSITIVE	COMPARATIVE	SUPERLATIVE
slow	slower	slowest
charming	more charming	most charming

6. Some adjectives have irregular comparative forms.

POSITIVE:	good, well	bad	far	many, much	little
COMPARATIVE:	better	worse	farther	more	less
SUPERLATIVE:	best	worst	farthest	most	least

Adverbs

1. An adverb modifies a verb, an adjective, or another adverb. Adverbs tell *how, where, when,* or *to what extent.*
   The cat walked **quietly.** (how)
   She **seldom** misses a deadline. (when)
   The player moved **forward.** (where)
   The band was **almost** late. (to what extent)

2. Many adverbs fit these sentences:

   She thinks _____.   She thinks _____ fast.   She _____ thinks fast.
   She thinks **quickly.**   She thinks **unusually** fast.   She **seldom** thinks fast.

3. The comparative form of an adverb compares two actions. The superlative form compares more than two actions. For shorter adverbs add *-er* or *-est* to form the comparative or superlative. For most adverbs, add *more* or *most* or *less* or *least* to form the comparative or superlative.
   We walked **faster** than before.
   They listened **most carefully** to the final speaker.

4. Avoid double negatives, which are two negative words in the same clause.
   INCORRECT: I have not seen no stray cats.
   CORRECT: I have not seen any stray cats.

Prepositions, Conjunctions, and Interjections

1. A preposition shows the relationship of a noun or a pronoun to some other word. A compound preposition is made up of more than one word.
   The trees **near** our house provide plenty **of** shade.
   The schools were closed **because** of snow.

2. Common prepositions include these: *about, above, according to, across, after, against, along, among, around, as, at, because of, before, behind, below, beneath, beside, besides, between, beyond, but, by, concerning, down, during, except, for, from, in, inside, in spite of, into, like, near, of, off, on, out, outside, over, past, round, since, through, till, to, toward, under, underneath, until, up, upon, with, within, without.*

3. A **conjunction** is a word that joins single words or groups of words. A **coordinating conjunction** joins words or groups of words that have equal grammatical weight. **Correlative conjunctions** work in pairs to join words and groups of words of equal weight. A **subordinating conjunction** joins two clauses in such a way as to make one grammatically dependent on the other.

I want to visit the art gallery **and** the museum. (coordinating)
Both left **and** right turns were impossible in the traffic. (correlative)
We go to the park **whenever** Mom lets us. (subordinating)

COMMON CONJUNCTIONS

Coordinating:	and	but	for	nor	or	so	yet

Correlative:	both...and	neither...nor	whether...or
	either...or	not only...but also	

Subordinating:	after	as though	since	when
	although	because	so that	whenever
	as	before	than	where
	as if	even though	though	wherever
	as long as	if	unless	whether
	as soon as	in order that	until	while

4. A **conjunctive adverb** clarifies a relationship.
Frank loved the old maple tree; **nevertheless,** he disliked raking its leaves.

5. An **interjection** is an unrelated word or phrase that expresses emotion or strong feeling.
Look, there are two cardinals at the feeder.   **Good grief!** Are you kidding?

CLAUSES AND COMPLEX SENTENCES

1. A **clause** is a group of words that has a subject and a predicate and is used as a sentence or a part of a sentence. There are two types of clauses: main and subordinate. A **main clause** has a subject and a predicate and can stand alone as a sentence. A **subordinate clause** has a subject and a predicate, but it cannot stand alone as a sentence.

            main   sub.
She became a vegetarian because she loves animals.

2. There are three types of subordinate clauses: adjective, adverb, and noun.

   a. An **adjective clause** is a subordinate clause that modifies a noun or pronoun.
   The wrens **that built a nest in the backyard** are now raising their young.

   b. An **adverb clause** is a subordinate clause that often modifies the verb in the main clause of the sentence. It tells *when, where, how, why,* or *under what conditions.*
   Before they got out, the goats broke the fence in several places.

   c. A **noun clause** is a subordinate clause used as a noun.
   Whatever we do will have to please everyone. (subject)
   The prize goes to **whoever can keep the squirrels away from the feeder.** (object of preposition)

3. Main and subordinate clauses can form several types of sentences. A **simple sentence** has only one main clause and no subordinate clauses. A **compound sentence** has two or more main clauses. A **complex sentence** has at least one main clause and one or more subordinate clauses.

                      main

Simple: The apples fell off the tree.

                main   main

Compound: The dancers bowed, and the audience clapped.

                     sub.   main

Complex: Because they turn to face the sun, these flowers are called sunflowers.

4. A sentence that makes a statement is classified as a **declarative sentence**.
My dad's favorite horses are buckskins.

An **imperative sentence** gives a command or makes a request.
Please close the door on your way out.

An **interrogative sentence** asks a question.
When will the mail carrier arrive?

An **exclamatory sentence** expresses strong emotion.
Watch out!
What a view that is!

Phrases

1. A **phrase** is a group of words that acts in a sentence as a single part of speech.

2. A **prepositional phrase** is a group of words that begins with a preposition and ends with a noun or pronoun, which is called the **object of the preposition**. A prepositional phrase can act as an adjective or an adverb.
The house **on the hill** is white. (modifies the noun *house*)
Everyone **in the house** heard the storm. (modifies the pronoun *everyone*)
The geese flew **toward warmer weather**. (modifies the verb *flew*)

3. An **appositive** is a noun or pronoun that is placed next to another noun or pronoun to identify it or give more information about it. **An appositive phrase** is an appositive plus its modifiers.
Our sister **Myra** is home from college. Her college, **Purdue University**, is in Indiana.

4. A **verbal** is a verb form that functions in a sentence as a noun, an adjective, or an adverb. A **verbal phrase** is a verbal and other words that complete its meaning.
   a. A **participle** is a verbal that functions as an adjective. Present participles end in *-ing*. Past participles usually end in *-ed*.
   The **squeaking** floor board gave me away.   The **twisted** tree was ancient.
   b. A **participial phrase** contains a participle and other words that complete its meaning.
   Moving quickly across the room, the baby crawled toward her mother.

c. A gerund is a verbal that ends in *-ing.* It is used in the same way a noun is used.
Sailing is a traditional vacation activity for the Andersons.

d. A gerund phrase is a gerund plus any complements or modifiers.
Walking to school is common for many school children.

e. An infinitive is a verbal formed from the word *to* and the base form of a verb. It is often used as a noun. Because an infinitive acts as a noun, it may be the subject of a sentence or the direct object of an action verb.
To sing can be uplifting. (infinitive as subject)
Babies first learn **to babble.** (infinitive as direct object)

f. An infinitive phrase contains an infinitive plus any complements or modifiers.
The flight attendants prepared **to feed the hungry passengers.**

SUBJECT-VERB AGREEMENT

1. A verb must agree with its subject in person and number.
The kangaroo **jumps.** (singular)   The kangaroos **jump.** (plural)
She **is leaping**. (singular)   They **are leaping**. (plural)

2. In inverted sentences the subject follows the verb. The sentence may begin with a prepositional phrase, the word *there* or *here,* or a form of *do.*
Into the pond **dove** the *children.*
Does a *bird* **have** a sense of smell?
There **is** a *squeak* in that third stair.

3. Do not mistake a word in a prepositional phrase for the subject.
The **glass** in the window **is** streaked. (The singular verb *is* agrees with the subject, *glass.*)

4. A title is always singular, even if nouns in the title are plural.
Instant World Facts **is** a helpful reference book.

5. Subjects combined with *and* or *both* need a plural verb unless the parts are of a whole unit. When compound subjects are joined with *or* or *nor,* the verb agrees with the subject listed last.
Canterbury and Coventry have famous cathedrals.
A **bagel and cream cheese is** a filling snack.
Either two short **stories** or a **novel is** acceptable for your book report.

6. A verb must agree in number with an indefinite pronoun subject. Indefinite pronouns that are always singular: *anybody, anyone, anything, each, either, everybody, everyone, everything, neither, nobody, no one, nothing, one, somebody, someone,* and *something.*
Always plural: *both, few, many, others,* and *several*
Either singular or plural: *all, any, most, none,* and *some*

Most of the snow **has** melted.   **All** of the children **have** eaten.

USAGE GLOSSARY

a lot, alot Always write this expression, meaning "very much" or "a large amount," as two words.
The neighbors pitched in, and the job went **a lot** faster.

accept, except *Accept,* a verb, means "to receive" or "to agree to." *Except* may be a preposition or a verb. As a preposition it means "other than." As a verb it means "to leave out, to make an exception."
I **accept** your plan.   We ate everything **except** the crust.

all ready, already *All ready* means "completely prepared." *Already* means "before" or "by this time."
They were **all ready** to leave, but the bus had **already** departed.

all together, altogether The two words *all together* mean "in a group." The single word *altogether* is an adverb meaning "completely" or "on the whole."
The teachers met **all together** after school.
They were **altogether** prepared for a heated discussion.

beside, besides *Beside* means "next to." *Besides* means "in addition to."
The sink is **beside** the refrigerator.
Besides the kitchen, the den is my favorite room.

between, among Use *between* to refer to or to compare two separate nouns. Use *among* to show a relationship in a group.
The joke was **between** Hilary and Megan.
The conversation **among** the teacher, the principal, and the janitor was friendly.

bring, take Use *bring* to show movement from a distant place to a closer one. Use *take* to show movement from a nearby place to a more distant one.
You may **bring** your model here.
Please **take** a brochure with you when you go.

can, may *Can* indicates the ability to do something. *May* indicates permission to do something.
Constance **can** walk to school.
She **may** ride the bus if she wishes.

choose, chose *Choose* means "to select." *Chose* is the past participle form, meaning "selected."
I **choose** the blue folder.
Celia **chose** the purple folder.

fewer, less Use *fewer* with nouns that can be counted. Use *less* with nouns that cannot be counted.
There were **fewer** sunny days this year.
I see **less** fog today than I expected.

formally, formerly *Formally* is the adverb form of formal. *Formerly* is an adverb meaning "in times past."
They **formally** agreed to the exchange.
Lydia **formerly** lived in Spain, but now she lives in New York City.

in, into Use *in* to mean "inside" or "within" and *into* to indicate movement or direction from outside to a point within.
The birds nest **in** the trees.
A bird flew **into** our window yesterday.

its, it's *Its* is the possessive form of the pronoun *it*. Possessive pronouns never have apostrophes. *It's* is the contraction of *it is*.
The dog lives in **its** own house.   Who is to say whether **it's** happy or not.

lay, lie *Lay* means "to put" or "to place," and it takes a direct object. *Lie* means "to recline" or "to be positioned," and it never takes an object.
We **lay** the uniforms on the shelves each day.
The players **lie** on the floor to do their sit-ups.

learn, teach *Learn* means "to receive knowledge." *Teach* means "to give knowledge."
Children can **learn** foreign languages at an early age.
Mr. Minton will **teach** French to us next year.

leave, let *Leave* means "to go away." *Let* means "to allow" or "to permit."
I will **leave** after fourth period.
Dad will **let** me go swimming today.

loose, lose Use *loose* to mean "not firmly attached" and *lose* to mean "to misplace" or "to fail to win."
The bike chain was very **loose**.
I did not want to **lose** my balance.

many, much Use *many* with nouns that can be counted. Use *much* with nouns that cannot be counted.
Many ants were crawling near the anthill.
There was **much** discussion about what to do.

precede, proceed *Precede* means "to go or come before." *Proceed* means "to continue."
Lunch will **precede** the afternoon session.
Marly can **proceed** with her travel plans.

quiet, quite *Quiet* means "calm" or "motionless." *Quite* means "completely" or "entirely."
The sleeping kitten was **quiet**.
The other kittens were **quite** playful.

raise, rise *Raise* means "to cause to move upward," and it always takes an object. *Rise* means "to get up"; it is intransitive and never takes an object.
Please **raise** your hand if you would like to help.
I left the bread in a warm spot to **rise**.

sit, set *Sit* means "to place oneself in a sitting position." It rarely takes an object. *Set* means "to place" or "to put" and usually takes an object. *Set* can also be used to describe the sun going down.

Please **sit** in your assigned seats.   **Set** those dishes down.
The sun **set** at 6:14.

than, then *Than* is a conjunction that is used to introduce the second element in a comparison; it also shows exception. *Then* is an adverb meaning "at that time."
Wisconsin produces more milk **than** any other state.
First get comfortable, **then** look the pitcher right in the eye.

their, they're *Their* is the possessive form of the personal pronoun *they*. *They're* is the contraction of *they are.*
The Westons returned to **their** favorite vacation spot.
They're determined to go next year as well.

theirs, there's *Theirs* means "that or those belonging to them." *There's* is the contraction of *there is.*
Theirs is one of the latest models.
There's another pitcher of lemonade in the refrigerator.

to, too, two *To* is a preposition meaning "in the direction of." *Too* means "also" or "excessively." *Two* is the number that falls between one and three.
You may go **to** the library.
It is **too** cold for skating.
There are only **two** days of vacation left.

where at Do not use *at* in a sentence after *where.*
Where were you yesterday afternoon? (*not* Where were you at yesterday afternoon?)

whose, who's *Whose* is the possessive form of *who*. *Who's* is the contraction of *who is.*
Do you know **whose** books these are?
Who's willing to help me clean up?

your, you're *Your* is the possessive form of *you*. *You're* is the contraction of *you are.*
Please arrange **your** schedule so that you can be on time.
If **you're** late, you may miss something important.

CAPITALIZATION

1. Capitalize the first word of every sentence, including direct quotations and sentences in parentheses unless they are contained within another sentence.
   In *Poor Richard's Almanack,* Benjamin Franklin advises, "**W**ish not so much to live long as to live well." (This appeared in the almanac published in 1738.)

2. Capitalize the first word in the salutation and closing of a letter. Capitalize the title and name of the person addressed.
   Dear **P**rofessor **N**ichols:
   Sincerely yours,

3. Always capitalize the pronoun *I* no matter where it appears in the sentence.
Since **I** knew you were coming, **I** baked a cake.

4. Capitalize the following proper nouns:

   a. Names of individuals, the initials that stand for their names, and titles preceding a name or used instead of a name

Governor **C**ordoba	**A. C. S**hen
Aunt **M**argaret	**D**r. **H. C. H**arada
General **D**iaz	

   b. Names and abbreviations of academic degrees, and *Jr.* and *Sr.*
   Richard Boe, **Ph.D.**
   Sammy Davis **Jr.**

   c. Names of cities, countries, states, continents, bodies of water, sections of the United States, and compass points when they refer to a specific section of the United States

Boston	**D**ade **C**ounty	**N**orth **C**arolina	**A**ustralia
Amazon **R**iver	the **S**outh		

   d. Names of streets, highways, organizations, institutions, firms, monuments, bridges, buildings, other structures, and celestial bodies

Route 51	**C**ircle **K S**ociety	**T**omb of the **U**nknown **S**oldier
Golden **G**ate **B**ridge	**C**oventry **C**athedral	**N**orth **S**tar

   e. Trade names and names of documents, awards, and laws

No-**S**neez tissues	the **F**ourteenth **A**mendment
Golden **G**lobe **A**ward	the **M**onroe **D**octrine

   f. Names of most historical events, eras, holidays, days of the week, and months

Boston **T**ea **P**arty	**B**ronze **A**ge	**L**abor **D**ay	**F**riday **J**uly

   g. First, last, and all important words in titles of literary works, works of art, and musical compositions

"**I A**sk **M**y **M**other to **S**ing" (poem)	*Giants in the Earth* (book)
Venus de **M**ilo (statue)	"**A**merica, **T**he **B**eautiful" (composition)

   h. Names of ethnic groups, national groups, political parties and their members, and languages

Hispanics	**C**hinese	**I**rish	**I**talian	**R**epublican party

5. Capitalize proper adjectives (adjectives formed from proper nouns).

English saddle horse	**T**hai restaurant	**M**idwestern plains

PUNCTUATION, ABBREVIATIONS, AND NUMBERS

1. Use a period at the end of a declarative sentence and at the end of a polite command.
Mrs. Miranda plays tennis every Tuesday.
Write your name in the space provided.

2. Use a question mark at the end of an interrogative sentence.
When will the new books arrive?

3. Use an exclamation point to show strong feeling and indicate a forceful command.
Oh, no!   It was a terrific concert!   Don't go outside without your gloves on!

4. Use a comma in the following situations:

a. To separate three or more words, phrases, or clauses in a series
A tent, sleeping bag, and sturdy shoes are essential wilderness camping equipment.

b. To set off two or more prepositional phrases
After the sound of the bell, we realized it was a false alarm.

c. After an introductory participle and an introductory participial phrase
Marveling at the sight, we waited to see another shooting star.

d. After conjunctive adverbs
Snow is falling; however, it is turning to sleet.

e. To set off an appositive if it is not essential to the meaning of the sentence
Mr. Yoshino, the head of the department, resigned yesterday.

f. To set off words or phrases of direct address
Micha, have you called your brother yet?
It's good to see you, Mrs. Han.

g. Between the main clauses of compound sentences
Whiskers liked to watch the goldfish, and she sometimes dipped her paw in the bowl.

h. After an introductory adverb clause and to set off a nonessential adjective clause
Whenever we get careless, we always make mistakes.
Spelling errors, which are common, can now be corrected by computer.

i. To separate parts of an address or a date
1601 Burma Drive, Waterbury, Connecticut
She was born on February 2, 1985, and she now lives in Bangor, Maine.

j. After the salutation and close of a friendly letter and after the close of a business letter
Dear Dad,   Cordially,   Yours,

5. Use a semicolon in the following situations:

a. To join main clauses not joined by a coordinating conjunction
The house looks dark; perhaps we should have called first.

b. To separate two main clauses joined by a coordinating conjunction when such clauses already contain several commas
After a week of rain, the farmers around Ames, Iowa, waited hopefully; but the rain, unfortunately, had come too late.

c. To separate main clauses joined by a conjunctive adverb or by *for example* or *that is*
Jen was determined to win the race; nonetheless, she knew that it took more than determination to succeed.

6. Use a colon to introduce a list of items that ends a sentence.
   Bring the following tools: hammer, speed square, and drill.

7. Use a colon to separate the hour and the minute in time measurements and after business letter salutations.
   12:42 A.M.   Dear Sir: Dear Ms. O'Connor:

8. Use quotation marks to enclose a direct quotation. When a quotation is interrupted, use two sets of quotation marks. Use single quotation marks for a quotation within a quotation.
   "Are you sure," asked my mother, "that you had your keys when you left home?"
   "Chief Seattle's speech begins, 'My words are like the stars that never change,'" stated the history teacher.

9. Always place commas and periods inside closing quotation marks. Place colons and semicolons outside closing quotation marks. Place question marks and exclamation points inside closing quotation marks only when those marks are part of the quotation.
   "Giraffes," said Ms. Wharton, "spend long hours each day foraging."
   You must read "The Story of an Hour"; it is a wonderful short story.
   He called out, "Is anyone home?"
   Are you sure she said, "Go home without me"?

10. Use quotation marks to indicate titles of short stories, poems, essays, songs, and magazine or newspaper articles.
    "The Thrill of the Grass" (short story)
    "My Country 'Tis of Thee" (song)

11. Italicize (underline) titles of books, plays, films, television series, paintings and sculptures, and names of newspapers and magazines.
    Up from Slavery (book)
    Free Willy (film)
    The Spirit of '76 (painting)
    Chicago Tribune (newspaper)
    Weekend Woodworker (magazine)

12. Add an apostrophe and -*s* to form the possessive of singular indefinite pronouns, singular nouns, and plural nouns not ending in -*s*. Add only an apostrophe to plural nouns ending in -*s* to make them possessive.
    everyone**'s** best friend
    the rabbit**'s** ears
    the children**'s** toys
    the farmer**s'** fields

13. Use an apostrophe in place of omitted letters or numerals. Use an apostrophe and -*s* to form the plural of letters, numerals, and symbols.

    is + not = isn't

    will + not = won't

    1776 is '76

    Cross your *t*'s and dot your *i*'s.

14. Use a hyphen to divide words at the end of a line.

    esti-mate   mone-tary   experi-mentation

15. Use a hyphen in a compound adjective that precedes a noun. Use a hyphen in compound numbers and fractions used as adjectives.

    a blue-green parrot

    a salt-and-pepper beard

    twenty-nine

    one-third cup of flour

16. Use a hyphen after any prefix joined to a proper noun or a proper adjective. Use a hyphen after the prefixes *all-*, *ex-*, and *self-* joined to a noun or adjective, the prefix *anti-* joined to a word beginning with *i-*, and the prefix *vice-* except in the case of *vice president.*

    all-knowing   ex-spouse   self-confidence

    anti-inflammatory   vice-principal

17. Use dashes to signal a break or change in thought.

    I received a letter from Aunt Carla—you have never met her—saying she is coming to visit.

18. Use parentheses to set off supplemental material. Punctuate within the parentheses only if the punctuation is part of the parenthetical expression.

    Place one gallon (3.8 liters) of water in a plastic container.

19. Abbreviate a person's title and professional or academic degrees.

    Ms. K. Soga, **Ph.D.**

    Dr. Quentin

20. Use the abbreviations *A.M.* and *P.M.* and *B.C.* and *A.D.*

    9:45 A.M.   1000 B.C.   A.D. 1455

21. Abbreviate numerical measurements in scientific writing but not in ordinary prose.

    The newborn snakes measured 3.4 **in.** long.

    Pour 45 **ml** warm water into the beaker.

22. Spell out cardinal and ordinal numbers that can be written in one or two words or that appear at the beginning of a sentence.

    Two hundred twenty runners crossed the finish line.

    Observers counted **forty-nine** sandhill cranes.

23. Express all related numbers in a sentence as numerals if any one should be expressed as a numeral.

    There were **127** volunteers, but only **9** showed up because of the bad weather.

24. Spell out ordinal numbers.
    Nina won **third** place in the spelling bee.

25. Use words for decades, for amounts of money that can be written in one or two words, and for the approximate time of day or when A.M. or P.M. is not used.
    the **ninties**   **ten** dollars   **sixty** cents   half past **five**

26. Use numerals for dates; for decimals; for house, apartment, and room numbers; for street or avenue numbers; for telephone numbers; for page numbers; for percentages; for sums of money including both dollars and cents; and to emphasize the exact time of day or when A.M. or P.M. is used.
    June **5, 1971**   Apartment **4G**   **$207.89**
    0.0045   **1520 14**th Street   **8:20** A.M.

VOCABULARY AND SPELLING

1. Clues to the meaning of an unfamiliar word can be found in its context. Context clues include definition, the meaning stated; example, the meaning explained through one familiar case; comparison, similarity to a familiar word; contrast, opposite of a familiar word; and cause and effect, a reason and its results.

2. The meaning of a word can be obtained from its base word, its prefix, or its suffix.
    telegram **tele** = distant   dentate **dent** = tooth
    subartic **sub** = below   marvelous **-ous** = full of

3. The *i* comes before the *e*, except when both letters follow a *c* or when both letters are pronounced together as an $\bar{a}$ sound. However, many exceptions exist to this rule.
    y**ie**ld (*i* before *e*) rec**ei**ve (*ei* after *c*) w**ei**gh ($\bar{a}$ sound) h**ei**ght (exception)

4. An unstressed vowel is a vowel sound that is not emphasized when the word is pronounced. Determine how to spell this sound by comparing it to a known word.
    inform**a**nt (compare to inform**a**tion)   hospit**a**l (compare to hospit**a**lity)

5. When joining a prefix that ends in the same letter as the word, keep both consonants.
    illegible   **diss**ervice

6. When adding a suffix to a word ending in a consonant + *y*, change the *y* to *i* unless the prefix begins with an *i*. If the word ends in a vowel + *y*, keep the *y*.
    tr**ied**   play**ed**   spra**ying**

7. Double the final consonant before adding a suffix that begins with a vowel to a word that ends in a single consonant preceded by a single vowel if the accent is on the root's last syllable.
    pop**ping**   transfer**red**   unforget**table**

8. When adding a suffix that begins with a consonant to a word that ends in silent *e*, generally keep the *e*. If the suffix begins with a vowel or *y*, generally drop the *e*. If the suffix begins with *a* or *o* and the word ends in *ce* or *ge*, keep the *e*. If the suffix begins with a vowel and the word ends in *ee* or *oe*, keep the *e*.
    state**ly**   nois**y**   courage**ous**   agree**able**

9. When adding *-ly* to a word that ends in a single *l*, keep the *l*. If it ends in a double *l*, drop one *l*. If it ends in a consonant + *le*, drop the *le*.

   meal, meal**ly**   full, ful**ly**   incredible, incredib**ly**

10. When forming compound words, maintain the spelling of both words.
    backpack   honeybee

11. Most nouns form their plurals by adding *-s*. However, nouns that end in *-ch*, *-s*, *-sh*, *-x*, or *-z* form plurals by adding *-es*. If the noun ends in a consonant + *y*, change *y* to *i* and add *-es*. If the noun ends in *-lf*, change *f* to *v* and add *-es*. If the noun ends in *-fe*, change *f* to *v* and add *-s*.

    mark**s**   leach**es**   rash**es**   fox**es**
    fl**ies**   el**ves**   l**ives**

12. To form the plural of proper names and one-word compound nouns, follow the general rules for plurals. To form the plural of hyphenated compound nouns or compound nouns of more than one word, make the most important word plural.

    Wilson**s**   Diaz**es**   housekeeper**s**
    sister**s**-in-law   editor**s**-in-chief

13. Some nouns have the same singular and plural forms.
    deer   moose

Composition

Writing Themes and Paragraphs

1. Use **prewriting** to find ideas to write about. One form of prewriting, **freewriting**, starts with a subject or topic and branches off into related ideas. Another way to find a topic is to ask and answer questions about your starting subject, helping you to gain a deeper understanding of your chosen topic. Also part of the prewriting stage is determining who your readers or **audience** will be and deciding your **purpose** for writing. Your purpose—writing to persuade, to explain, to describe, or to narrate—is partially shaped by who your audience will be.

2. To complete your first **draft**, organize your prewriting into an introduction, body, and conclusion. Concentrate on unity and coherence of the overall piece. Experiment with different paragraph orders: **chronological order** places events in the order in which they happened; **spatial order** places objects in the order in which they appear; and **compare/contrast order** shows similarities and differences in objects or events.

3. **Revise** your composition if necessary. Read through your draft, looking for places to improve content and structure. Remember that varying your sentence patterns and lengths will make your writing easier and more enjoyable to read.

4. In the editing stage, check your grammar, spelling, and punctuation. Focus on expressing your ideas clearly and concisely.

5. Finally, prepare your writing for presentation. Sharing your composition, or ideas, with others may take many forms: printed, oral, or graphic.

Outlining

1. The two common forms of outlines are sentence outlines and topic outlines. Choose one type of outline and keep it uniform throughout.

2. A period follows the number or letter of each division. Each point in a sentence outline ends with a period; the points in a topic outline do not.

3. Each point begins with a capital letter.

4. A point may have no fewer than two subpoints.

SENTENCE OUTLINE	TOPIC OUTLINE
I. This is the main point.	I. Main point
A. This is a subpoint of *I.*	A. Subpoint of *I*
1. This is a detail of *A.*	1. Detail of *A*
a. This is a detail of *1.*	a. Detail of *1*
b. This is a detail of *1.*	b. Detail of *1*
2. This is a detail of *A.*	2. Detail of *A*
B. This is a subpoint of *I.*	B. Subpoint of *I*
II. This is another main point.	II. Main point

Writing Letters

1. Personal letters are usually handwritten in indented form (first line of paragraphs, each line of the heading and inside address, and the signature are indented). Business letters are usually typewritten in block or semiblock form. Block form contains no indents; semiblock form indents only the first line of each paragraph.

2. The five parts of a personal letter are the heading (the writer's address and the date), salutation (greeting), body (message), complimentary close (such as "Yours truly,"), and signature (the writer's name). Business letters have the same parts and also include an inside address (the recipient's address).

PERSONAL LETTER

Heading _____
_____
_____

_____ Salutation
_____
_____
_____
_____
Body _____
_____
_____
_____
_____
_____

Complimentary Close _____
Signature ——————

BUSINESS LETTER

Heading _____
_____

_____ Inside Address
_____
_____ Salutation
_____
_____
_____ Body
_____
_____
_____
_____
_____

Complimentary Close _____
Signature ——————

3. Reveal your personality and imagination in colorful personal letters. Keep business letters brief, clear, and courteous.

4. **Personal letters** include letters to friends and family members. **Thank-you notes** and **invitations** are personal letters that may be either formal or informal in style.

5. Use a **letter of request**, a type of business letter, to ask for information or to place an order. Be concise, yet give all the details necessary for your request to be fulfilled. Keep the tone of your letter courteous, and be generous in allotting time for a response.

6. Use an **opinion letter** to take a firm stand on an issue. Make the letter clear, firm, rational, and purposeful. Be aware of your audience, their attitude, how informed they are, and their possible reactions to your opinion. Support your statements of opinion with facts.

*T*roubleshooter

Sentence Fragments

PROBLEM 1

Fragment that lacks a subject

frag	Martha asked about dinner. (Hoped it was lasagna.)
frag	I jogged around the park twice. (Was hot and tired afterward.)
frag	Li Cheng raced to the bus stop. (Arrived just in the nick of time.)

SOLUTION

Martha asked about dinner. She hoped it was lasagna.
I jogged around the park twice. I was hot and tired afterward.
Li Cheng raced to the bus stop. He arrived just in the nick of time.

Make a complete sentence by adding a subject to the fragment.

PROBLEM 2

Fragment that lacks a predicate

frag	The carpenter worked hard all morning. (His assistant after lunch.)
frag	Ant farms are fascinating. (The ants around in constant motion.)
frag	Our class went on a field trip. (Mammoth Cave.)

PROBLEM 3

Fragment that lacks both a subject and a predicate

frag   I heard the laughter of the children. (In the nursery.)

frag   (After the spring rain.) The whole house smelled fresh and clean.

frag   The noisy chatter of the squirrels awakened us early. (In the morning.)

SOLUTION

I heard the laughter of the children in the nursery.

After the spring rain, the whole house smelled fresh and clean.

The noisy chatter of the squirrels awakened us early in the morning.

Combine the fragment with another sentence.

More help in avoiding sentence fragments is available in Lesson 6.

Run-on Sentences

PROBLEM 1

Two main clauses separated only by a comma

run-on (Extra crackers are available, they are next to the salad bar.)

run-on (Hurdles are Sam's specialty, he likes them best.)

SOLUTION A

Extra crackers are available. They are next to the salad bar.

Make two sentences by separating the first clause from the second with end punctuation, such as a period or a question mark, and starting the second sentence with a capital letter.

SOLUTION B

Hurdles are Sam's specialty; he likes them best.

Place a semicolon between the main clauses of the sentence.

PROBLEM 2

Two main clauses with no punctuation between them

run-on (The law student studied hard she passed her exam.)

run-on (Kamil looked for the leash he found it in the closet.)

SOLUTION A

The law student studied hard. She passed her exam.

Make two sentences out of the run-on sentence.

SOLUTION B

Kamil looked for the leash, and he found it in the closet.

Add a comma and a coordinating conjunction between the main clauses.

PROBLEM 3

Two main clauses without a comma before the coordinating conjunction

run-on   You can rollerskate like a pro but you cannot ice skate.

run-on   Julian gazed at the moon and he marveled at its brightness.

SOLUTION

You can rollerskate like a pro, but you cannot ice skate.
Julian gazed at the moon, and he marveled at its brightness.

Add a comma before the coordinating conjunction.

More help in avoiding run-on sentences is available in Lesson 7.

Lack of Subject-Verb Agreement

PROBLEM 1

A subject separated from the verb by an intervening prepositional phrase

agr   The stories in the newspaper (was) well written.

agr   The house in the suburbs (were) just what she wanted.

SOLUTION

The stories in the newspaper were well written.

The house in the suburbs was just what she wanted.

Make sure that the verb agrees with the subject of the sentence, not with the object of a preposition. The object of a preposition is never the subject.

PROBLEM 2

A sentence that begins with here *or* there

agr   Here (go) the duck with her ducklings.

agr   There (is) the pencils you were looking for.

agr   Here (is) the snapshots from our vacation to the Grand Canyon.

> **SOLUTION**
>
> **Here goes the duck with her ducklings.**
> **There are the pencils you were looking for.**
> **Here are the snapshots from our vacation to the Grand Canyon.**
>
> In sentences that begin with *here* or *there,* look for the subject after the verb. Make sure that the verb agrees with the subject.

PROBLEM 3

An indefinite pronoun as the subject

agr	Each of the animals (have) a unique way of walking.
agr	Many of the movies (was) black and white.
agr	None of the leaves (is) turning colors yet.

> **SOLUTION**
>
> **Each of the animals has a unique way of walking.**
> **Many of the movies were black and white.**
> **None of the leaves are turning colors yet.**
>
> Some indefinite pronouns are singular, some are plural, and some can be either singular or plural. Determine whether the indefinite pronoun is singular or plural, and make the verb agree.

PROBLEM 4

A compound subject that is joined by **and**

agr	The students and the teacher (adores) the classroom hamster.
agr	The expert and best source of information (are) Dr. Marlin.

SOLUTION A

The students and the teacher adore the classroom hamster.

Use a plural verb if the parts of the compound subject do not belong to one unit or if they refer to different people or things.

SOLUTION B

The expert and best source of information is Dr. Marlin.

Use a singular verb if the parts of the compound subject belong to one unit or if they refer to the same person or thing.

PROBLEM 5

A compound subject that is joined by **or** *or* **nor**

agr	Either Hester or Sue (are) supposed to pick us up.
agr	Neither pepper nor spices (improves) the flavor of this sauce.
agr	Either Caroline or Robin (volunteer) at the local food pantry.
agr	Neither the coach nor the screaming fans (agrees) with the referee's call.

> ### SOLUTION
>
> **Either Hester or Sue is supposed to pick us up.**
>
> **Neither pepper nor spices improve the flavor of this sauce.**
>
> **Either Caroline or Robin volunteers at the local food pantry.**
>
> **Neither the coach nor the screaming fans agree with the referee's call.**
>
> Make the verb agree with the subject that is closer to it.

 More help with subject-verb agreement is available in Lessons 48–51.

Incorrect Verb Tense or Form

PROBLEM 1

An incorrect or missing verb ending

tense	We (talk) yesterday for more than an hour.
tense	They (sail) last month for Barbados.
tense	Sally and James (land) at the airport yesterday.

SOLUTION

We talked yesterday for more than an hour.
They sailed last month for Barbados.
Sally and James landed at the airport yesterday.

To form the past tense and the past participle, add *-ed* to a regular verb.

PROBLEM 2

An improperly formed irregular verb

tense	Our hair (clinged) to us in the humid weather.
tense	Trent (drinked) all the orange juice.
tense	The evening breeze (blowed) the clouds away.

SOLUTION

Our hair clung to us in the humid weather.

Trent drank all the orange juice.

The evening breeze blew the clouds away.

Irregular verbs vary in their past and past participle forms. Look up the ones you are not sure of. Consider memorizing them if you feel it is necessary.

PROBLEM 3

Confusion between a verb's past form and its past participle

tense   Helen has took first place in the marathon.

SOLUTION

Helen has taken first place in the marathon.

Use the past participle form of an irregular verb, and not its past form, when you use the auxiliary verb *have*.

More help with correct verb forms is available in Lessons 19–24.

Incorrect Use of Pronouns

PROBLEM 1

A pronoun that refers to more than one antecedent

pro	The wind and the rain came suddenly, but (it) did not last.
pro	Henry ran with Philip, but (he) was faster.
pro	When Sarah visits Corinne, (she) is glad for the company.

SOLUTION

The wind and the rain came suddenly, but the rain did not last.
Henry ran with Philip, but Philip was faster.
When Sarah visits Corinne, Corinne is glad for the company.

Substitute a noun for the pronoun to make your sentence clearer.

PROBLEM 2

Personal pronouns as subjects

pro	(Him) and Mary unfurled the tall, white sail.
pro	Nina and (them) bought theater tickets yesterday.
pro	Karen and (me) heard the good news on the television.

SOLUTION

He and Mary unfurled the tall, white sail.

Nina and they bought theater tickets yesterday.

Karen and I heard the good news on the television.

Use a subject pronoun as the subject part of a sentence.

PROBLEM 3

Personal pronouns as objects

pro	The horse galloped across the field to Anne and I.
pro	The new signs confused Clark and they.
pro	Grant wrote she a letter of apology.

SOLUTION

The horse galloped across the field to Anne and me.

The new signs confused Clark and them.

Grant wrote her a letter of apology.

An object pronoun is the object of a verb or preposition.

 More help with correct use of pronouns is available in Lessons 25–29.

Incorrect Use of Adjectives

PROBLEM 1

Incorrect use of **good, better, best**

adj	Is a horse (more good) than a pony?
adj	Literature is my (most good) subject.

SOLUTION

Is a horse better than a pony?
Literature is my best subject.

The words *better* and *best* are the comparative and superlative forms of the word *good*. Do not use the words *more* or *most* before the irregular forms of comparative and superlative adjectives.

PROBLEM 2

Incorrect use of **bad, worse, worst**

adj	That game was the (baddest) game our team ever played.

SOLUTION

That game was the worst game our team ever played.

Do not use the suffixes *-er* or *-est* after the irregular forms of comparative and superlative adjectives. Do not use the words *more* or *most* before the irregular forms of comparative and superlative adjectives.

PROBLEM 3

Incorrect use of comparative adjectives

> adj   This bike is (more faster) than my old bike.

> **SOLUTION**
>
> **This bike is faster than my old bike.**
>
> Do not use *-er* and *more* together.

PROBLEM 4

Incorrect use of superlative adjectives

> adj   Kara said it was the (most biggest) lawn she ever had to mow.

> **SOLUTION**
>
> **Kara said it was the biggest lawn she ever had to mow.**
>
> Do not use *-est* and *most* together.

 More help with the correct use of adjectives is available in Lessons 30–33.

Incorrect Use of Commas

Troubleshooter

PROBLEM 1

Missing commas in a series of three or more items

com	We saw ducks geese and seagulls at the park.
com	Jake ate dinner watched a movie and visited friends.

SOLUTION

We saw ducks, geese, and seagulls at the park.

Jake ate dinner, watched a movie, and visited friends.

If there are three or more items in a series, use a comma after each item except the last one.

PROBLEM 2

Missing commas with direct quotations

com	"The party" said José "starts at seven o'clock."
com	"My new book" Roger exclaimed "is still on the bus!"

PROBLEM 3

Missing commas with nonessential appositives

com	Maria our new friend is from Chicago.
com	The old lane a tree-lined gravel path is a great place to walk on a hot afternoon.

SOLUTION

Maria, our new friend, is from Chicago.
The old lane, a tree-lined gravel path, is a great place to walk on a hot afternoon.

Decide whether the appositive is truly essential to the meaning of the sentence. If it is not essential, set it off with commas.

PROBLEM 4

Missing commas with nonessential adjective clauses

com   Karen who started early finished her work before noon.

SOLUTION

Karen, who started early, finished her work before noon.

Decide whether the clause is truly essential to the meaning of the sentence. If it is not essential, then set it off with commas.

PROBLEM 5

Missing commas with introductory adverb clauses

com   When the wind rises too high the boats lower their sails.

SOLUTION

When the wind rises too high, the boats lower their sails.

Place a comma after an introductory adverbial clause.

 More help with commas is available in Lessons 72–76.

Incorrect Use of Apostrophes

PROBLEM 1

Singular possessive nouns

apos	(Pablos) new bicycle is in (Charles) yard.
apos	(Bills) video collection is really great.
apos	That (horses) saddle has real silver on it.

SOLUTION

Pablo's new bicycle is in Charles's yard.

Bill's video collection is really great.

That horse's saddle has real silver on it.

Place an apostrophe before a final -*s* to form the possessive of a singular noun, even one that ends in -*s*.

PROBLEM 2

Plural possessive nouns that end in -s

apos	The (girls) team won the tournament.
apos	The (boats) sails are very colorful against the blue sky.
apos	The model (cars) boxes are in my room.

> ### SOLUTION
>
> **The girls' team won the tournament.**
> **The boats' sails are very colorful against the blue sky.**
> **The model cars' boxes are in my room.**
>
> Use an apostrophe by itself to form the possessive of a plural noun that ends in -*s*.

PROBLEM 3

Plural possessive nouns that do not end in -s

apos	The (deers) best habitat is a deep, unpopulated woodland.
apos	The (childrens) clothes are on the third floor.

> ### SOLUTION
>
> **The deer's best habitat is a deep, unpopulated woodland.**
> **The children's clothes are on the third floor.**
>
> When a plural noun does not end in -*s*, use an apostrophe and an -*s* to form the possessive of the noun.

PROBLEM 4

Possessive personal pronouns

apos	The poster is (her's,) but the magazine is (their's.)

> **SOLUTION**
>
> **The poster is hers, but the magazine is theirs.**
>
> Do not use apostrophes with possessive personal pronouns.

PROBLEM 5

Confusion between its *and* it's

> apos   The old tree was the last to lose (it's) leaves.
>
> apos   (Its) the best CD I have ever heard them put out.

> **SOLUTION**
>
> **The old tree was the last to lose its leaves.**
> **It's the best CD I have ever heard them put out.**
>
> Use an apostrophe to form the contraction of *it is.* The possessive of the personal pronoun *it* does not take an apostrophe.

More help with apostrophes and possessives is available in Lessons 11 and 80.

Incorrect Capitalization

PROBLEM 1

Words that refer to ethnic groups, nationalities, and languages

cap   Many (irish) citizens speak both (english) and (gaelic.)

SOLUTION

Many Irish citizens speak both English and Gaelic.

Capitalize proper nouns and adjectives referring to ethnic groups, nationalities, and languages.

PROBLEM 2

The first word of a direct quotation

cap   Yuri said, ("the) rain off the bay always blows this way."

SOLUTION

Yuri said, "The rain off the bay always blows this way."

Capitalize the first word of a direct quotation if it is a complete sentence. A direct quotation is the speaker's exact words.

More help with capitalization is available in Lessons 63–70.

Grammar

THREE

Unit 1: Subjects, Predicates, and Sentences

Lesson 1
Kinds of Sentences: Declarative and Interrogative

A sentence is a group of words that expresses a complete thought. All sentences begin with a capital letter and end with a punctuation mark. Different kinds of sentences have different purposes.

A declarative sentence makes a statement. It ends with a period.

Last summer I went on a long trip.

An interrogative sentence asks a question. It ends with a question mark.

Where did you go on your vacation?

▶ **Exercise 1** **Insert a period if the sentence is declarative. Insert a question mark if it is interrogative.**

My family and I went to Alaska .

1. Have you ever been that far north ?

2. Alaska is a wonderful and wild state .

3. Isn't it the largest state in the union ?

4. Was the weather hotter than you expected ?

5. Some days were so warm that I wore shorts .

6. In some parts of Alaska, the sun never sets in summer .

7. Summers in Alaska don't last very long .

8. Are Alaskan winters as cold as they say ?

9. The ground under much of Alaska is permanently frozen .

10. How can animals live in such a cold climate ?

11. All the animals in Alaska are equipped for the cold .

12. Did you see any bears in Alaska ?

13. We saw a lot of brown bears at Katmai National Monument .

14. Male brown bears can be as tall as ten feet .

15. Can an animal that big move very fast ?

16. A brown bear can run as fast as twenty-five miles per hour .

17. Do you think you'd be afraid of a brown bear ?

18. Did you know that the highest mountain in North America is in Alaska ?

19. The mountain is called Denali .

20. What does *Denali* mean ?

21. *Denali* is a Native American word that means "the great one" .

22. At one time only Native Americans lived in Alaska .

23. Who were the first white settlers in Alaska ?

24. Russians built a settlement on Kodiak Island in 1784 .

25. Why did the Russians want to settle in Alaska ?

26. They went there to look for furs .

27. Russia sold Alaska to the United States in 1867 .

28. How much did the United States pay for Alaska ?

29. Alaska cost the United States $7.2 million .

30. Does that seem like a lot of money to you ?

31. When did Americans begin going to Alaska ?

32. Americans began going to Alaska during the 1890s and 1900s .

33. They went there to look for gold .

34. Large amounts of "black gold" were discovered in Alaska in 1968 .

35. What is "black gold" ?

36. "Black gold" is another name for oil .

37. Alaska also has coal, platinum, copper, and uranium .

38. Did you take many pictures during your trip ?

39. I took a great shot of an eagle catching a salmon .

40. Do you want to see some other pictures I took ?

Lesson 2
Kinds of Sentences: Exclamatory and Imperative

In addition to declarative and interrogative sentences, there are two other types of sentences. An **exclamatory sentence** shows strong feeling. It ends with an exclamation point.

I never saw so much traffic!

An **imperative sentence** commands someone to do something. The subject *you* is understood. An imperative sentence can end with either a period or an exclamation point.

(You) Look both ways before crossing the street. (You) Look out!

Grammar

▶ **Exercise 1** Write *exc.* in the blank before each exclamatory sentence and *imp.* before each imperative sentence.

__exc.__   That alarm clock is too loud!

__imp.__   **1.** Give the orange juice to Cecilia.

__exc.__   **2.** How sleepy I am!

__exc.__   **3.** What a funny dream I had last night!

__exc.__   **4.** I can hardly wait for the dance!

__imp.__   **5.** Please don't talk so loudly.

__imp.__   **6.** Tell Kwasi that it's time to get up.

__imp.__   **7.** Put the timer where you'll be sure to see it.

__exc.__   **8.** I love peanut butter sandwiches!

__exc.__   **9.** The toast is burning!

__imp.__ **10.** Give this bottle to the baby.

__exc.__ **11.** Becky spilled all her cereal!

__imp.__ **12.** Mop it up with a paper towel.

__imp.__ **13.** Help me set the table.

__exc.__ **14.** I'm in trouble if I'm late for school!

__exc.__ **15.** Jan forgot to do her math homework!

imp. **16.** Please take these books back to the library.

imp. **17.** Pour some more milk for Ricardo.

exc. **18.** How I would love to be a rock star!

imp. **19.** Get that cat off the table!

exc. **20.** The puppy chewed a hole in my sock!

imp. **21.** Pull up the anchor so we can be on our way.

exc. **22.** Gordo is such a cute puppy!

imp. **23.** Take these old magazines to your art teacher.

imp. **24.** Be careful not to drop the plates.

exc. **25.** My new sneakers are covered with mud!

imp. **26.** Comb Tina's hair and put a ribbon in it.

exc. **27.** I wish Dad would drive us to school!

exc. **28.** I can't believe you ate all of that!

exc. **29.** Oh, no, the car won't start!

imp. **30.** Make sure you have enough air in your bike tires.

imp. **31.** Put your dishes in the sink before you leave.

imp. **32.** Don't forget to call me when you get home.

exc. **33.** I dropped my ring into the sink!

exc. **34.** You spilled juice on the floor!

imp. **35.** Make sure you tie your shoes before jogging.

imp. **36.** Put this apple in your pocket.

▶ **Writing Link** **Write a paragraph explaining how to play a game. Use exclamatory and imperative sentences.**

_____

_____

_____

_____

_____

Lesson 3
Subjects and Predicates: Simple and Complete

Every sentence has two parts: a subject and a predicate. The subject part of a sentence names whom or what the sentence is about. The predicate part of a sentence tells what the subject does or has. It can also describe what the subject is or is like.

SUBJECT PART	PREDICATE PART
The mountain climbers	reached the peak.

The complete subject is all of the words in the subject part of a sentence. The complete predicate is all of the words in the predicate part of a sentence.

COMPLETE SUBJECT	COMPLETE PREDICATE
The horse's black mane	was blowing in the wind.

The simple subject is the main person or thing in the subject part of a sentence. The simple predicate is the main word or group of words in the predicate part of a sentence.

SIMPLE SUBJECT	SIMPLE PREDICATE
The horse's black **mane**	**was blowing** in the wind.

▶ **Exercise 1 Draw one line under each complete subject and two lines under each complete predicate.**

The bottle of milk is in the refrigerator.

1. That little dog is following us to school.

2. Brian forgot his flute.

3. The yellow canary fell in love with the shiny mirror.

4. Those plaid slacks are much too long for me.

5. Kisha hated the movie.

6. The big, shaggy animals in the pen are yaks.

7. The girl's long red hair shone in the sun.

8. The Yellow Hornets won the softball game.

9. My cousin Diana hit the ball right over the fence.

10. A sudden rainstorm ended the game.

Grammar

11. He spilled the popcorn on the person in front of him.

12. Franco walked home alone.

13. The fire engine raced by on the way to a fire.

14. Dad's tie was ruined by the gooey mess.

15. The red construction paper is in the cabinet.

16. Captain Kidd was a fearsome pirate.

17. The band played for two hours.

18. The small boat sank in the big waves.

19. The brave soldier was rescued.

20. Alison's stepmother teaches English at the high school.

▶ **Exercise 2** Draw one line under each simple subject and two lines under each simple predicate.

I am twelve years old today.

1. Marco was born in Venice, Italy.

2. Chanel's father traded his used car for a new one.

3. He traveled all the way to China by himself.

4. Those two were the first to cross the finish line.

5. In March, I returned all of my library books.

6. At least one hundred people waited in line.

7. He told his little sister a bedtime story.

8. Scott's cousin lost his favorite jacket.

9. The diagram showed three secret passageways.

10. Chen's nickname was "Louisville Slugger."

11. Marina never told people her secret.

12. The musician strummed the guitar quietly.

13. Christopher read every book by his favorite author.

14. The red skirt cost more than the blue skirt.

15. The Buckeroos made Gary an honorary member of the team.

Lesson 4
Subjects and Predicates: Compound

Some sentences have more than one simple subject or simple predicate. A compound subject is two or more simple subjects that have the same predicate. The simple subjects are joined by *and, or,* or *but*.

Mummies and **art objects** are found in Egyptian tombs.

A compound predicate is two or more simple predicates that have the same subject. The simple predicates are connected by *and, or,* or *but*.

The archaeologists **excavated** the tomb and **discovered** the treasure.

Some sentences have both a compound subject and a compound predicate.

The **pharaoh** and his **wife loved** the people and **did** many good works.

▶ **Exercise 1** Draw one line under the compound subject and two lines under the simple predicate that they share.

Volcanoes and earthquakes cause great destruction.

1. Rome and Florence are two cities in Italy.

2. Both Sara and Caroline were chosen for the team.

3. Cinders and ashes rose from the fire.

4. People and animals mingle at the zoo.

5. Historians, archaeologists, and tourists love to explore ancient ruins.

6. Paintings and other objects were on display at the museum.

7. Smoke and car exhaust pollute the air.

8. Hot dogs and hamburgers sizzled on the grill.

9. In Egypt mummies and pyramids are favorite subjects of study.

10. My uncle and brother visited me in the hospital.

11. In the summer Shama and I swim every day.

12. Gold and silver cost more than copper.

13. Food and dishes filled the table.

14. The doctor and her nurse waited for the next patient.

15. <u>Teeth</u> and <u>bones</u> <u>need</u> calcium for strength.

16. <u>Emily</u> and <u>Bill</u> <u>met</u> Ron at the movies.

17. The <u>lion</u> and <u>cheetah</u> <u>are</u> predators.

18. The <u>Ohio River</u> and the <u>Missouri River</u> <u>flow</u> into the Mississippi River.

19. The <u>librarian</u> and their <u>teacher</u> <u>helped</u> them.

20. Most <u>men</u> and <u>women</u> <u>exercise</u> to stay in shape.

▶ **Exercise 2 Draw one line under each simple or compound subject and two lines under each compound predicate.**

<u>LaToya</u> <u>opened</u> her book and <u>raised</u> her hand.

1. <u>Farmers</u> <u>raise</u> crops and <u>sell</u> them to food companies.

2. <u>Mom</u> and <u>Juan</u> <u>made</u> a casserole and <u>put</u> it in the oven.

3. <u>They</u> <u>left</u> the party and <u>headed</u> home.

4. <u>We</u> <u>changed</u> our clothes and <u>went</u> out for dinner.

5. Both <u>Ahmed</u> and <u>Tanika</u> <u>study</u> hard and <u>get</u> good grades.

6. The <u>cat</u> <u>opened</u> its mouth and <u>yawned</u>.

7. <u>Shawn</u> <u>ignored</u> the television and <u>did</u> his homework.

8. <u>Mom</u> and <u>Dad</u> <u>built</u> a doghouse and <u>painted</u> it.

9. My <u>stepbrother</u> <u>opened</u> the door and <u>ran</u> into the yard.

10. The <u>dog</u> <u>followed</u> him and <u>barked</u>.

11. At night <u>we</u> <u>sit</u> on the front porch and <u>tell</u> stories.

12. Our <u>team</u> <u>scored</u> a run and <u>won</u> the game.

13. <u>Sarah</u> <u>will turn</u> on the light and <u>close</u> the curtain.

14. <u>Alicia</u> and <u>Consuelo</u> <u>went</u> to the store and <u>bought</u> milk.

15. The <u>thunder</u> and <u>lightning</u> <u>scared</u> the campers and <u>kept</u> them awake.

16. <u>Kevin</u> <u>likes</u> hamsters and <u>keeps</u> them as pets.

17. <u>I</u> <u>will wash</u> the dishes and <u>put</u> them away.

18. The <u>4-H Club</u> <u>raises</u> animals and <u>shows</u> them at fairs.

Lesson 5
Simple and Compound Sentences

A simple sentence has one subject and one predicate.

SUBJECT	PREDICATE
Natalie	**won** the marbles tournament.
Bill and **Edward**	**signed** up for the paper drive.
The **runners**	**lined** up and **waited** for the starting signal.

A compound sentence contains two or more simple sentences joined by a comma and *and*, *but*, or *or*. They can also be joined by a semicolon (;).

Jessica's cake won first prize, **and** Katherine won the sack race.
Jessica's cake won first prize; Katherine won the sack race.

▶ **Exercise 1** **Write *S* in the blank before each simple sentence and *C* before each compound sentence.**

___S___   You and I should go to the fair and see the sights.

___S___   **1.** Both adults and kids love to go to the fair.

___C___   **2.** You buy the tickets, and I'll get the popcorn.

___C___   **3.** The animals are over there, and the crafts are down this way.

___S___   **4.** Julieta won a blue ribbon for her painting.

___S___   **5.** The games and contests are along the crowded fairway.

___S___   **6.** The bubble gum contest and the juggling contest are almost over.

___C___   **7.** Al blew a huge bubble, but Fernanda's bubble was bigger.

___C___   **8.** Jack's pig is groomed well; it's friendly, too.

___S___   **9.** The pig got away and escaped into the crowd.

___C___ **10.** I want a hot dog, but Mom says to wait.

___C___ **11.** Mrs. Collins bakes wonderful pies, and her children eat them.

___C___ **12.** I want to ride the Ferris wheel, but Ted is afraid.

___S___ **13.** The roller coaster and the spaceship are the most popular rides.

___C___ **14.** Give the calf's rope to me, or tie it to the post.

___C___ **15.** Anita won first prize; Franco came in second.

____S____ **16.** My frog, Big Nell, had the longest legs and jumped farthest.

____C____ **17.** You can put the trophy on the mantel, or you can put it on the shelf.

____C____ **18.** The cats slept in their cages, and their owners waited nervously.

____C____ **19.** Puff was the prettiest cat, but she didn't win.

____C____ **20.** I'd like to take a kitten home, but we already have too many cats.

____S____ **21.** The goat ate its blue ribbon and took a nap.

____C____ **22.** Anita raised the champion cow; her brother showed it at the fair.

____S____ **23.** The chicken and the rooster stood side by side.

____C____ **24.** Randi raises rabbits, and Shelly shears sheep.

____S____ **25.** The biggest pumpkin and the biggest tomato are on that table.

____C____ **26.** Dad picked the lettuce; I made a prizewinning salad.

____C____ **27.** Jenny feeds the rabbits, and Andy brushes them.

____S____ **28.** My sister and her friends made that quilt.

____C____ **29.** She made the squares for the quilt, and Mandy sewed them together.

____S____ **30.** At the dog show, two terriers got into a fight.

____S____ **31.** The grape jelly and the orange marmalade taste wonderful on toast.

____C____ **32.** Give the chickens some corn, and fill their water dish.

____S____ **33.** The ponies and the horses are in the barn.

____C____ **34.** My sister found a wallet, and I took it to the lost-and-found.

____C____ **35.** Throw a table tennis ball into the goldfish bowl, and win a prize.

____C____ **36.** Herbie won a stuffed gorilla; Alma won a stuffed tiger.

▶ **Writing Link** **Write a paragraph that explains how to prepare your favorite food. Use at least two compound sentences.**

_____

_____

_____

_____

_____

Lesson 6
Sentence Fragments

A sentence must have both a subject and a predicate to express a complete thought. A group of words that lacks a subject, a predicate, or both is a **sentence fragment**. A fragment does not express a complete thought and should be avoided in writing.

Almost stopped them. (lacks a subject)
The three explorers. (lacks a predicate)
Almost to the top. (lacks a subject and a predicate)

► **Exercise 1** Draw one line under the complete subject and two lines under the complete predicate of each complete sentence. If a sentence is not complete, write *F* (fragment) in the blank.

___F___   Of brave explorers.

_____   **1.** History tells tales of brave explorers.

___F___   **2.** Christopher Columbus.

___F___   **3.** Sailed in three ships.

_____   **4.** Christopher Columbus and his men sailed in three ships.

_____   **5.** Their long voyage brought them to the New World.

___F·___   **6.** The explorer Amerigo Vespucci.

_____   **7.** America was named for the Italian explorer Amerigo Vespucci.

_____   **8.** Sir Edmund Hillary was the first to climb Mt. Everest.

___F___   **9.** A very high mountain.

_____   **10.** Everest is a high mountain in Nepal.

_____   **11.** Hillary and his group almost died in the cold.

___F___   **12.** Hard to breathe.

_____   **13.** It is hard to breathe on extremely high mountains.

_____   **14.** Oxygen is very thin that high up.

_____   **15.** Peary reached the North Pole first.

_____   **16.** His dogs pulled him on a sled.

_____F_____ **17.** Arrived there before him.

_____ **18.** Captain Cook, <u>might have arrived there before him</u>.

_____ **19.** Other explorers <u>found the Northwest Passage</u>.

_____F_____ **20.** Atlantic and Pacific oceans.

_____ **21.** This watery passage <u>joins the Atlantic and Pacific oceans</u>.

_____F_____ **22.** Many of today's explorers.

_____ **23.** Many of today's explorers <u>look to the skies</u>.

_____ **24.** Others <u>explore the deep oceans</u>.

_____ **25.** You <u>can also explore without leaving your room</u>.

_____ **26.** You <u>can explore with your mind</u>.

_____ **27.** Some scientific discoveries <u>are based on theories</u>.

_____ **28.** Johannes Kepler <u>discovered the cause of tides</u>.

_____ **29.** Few people <u>believed him</u>.

_____ **30.** Isaac Newton <u>made many important scientific discoveries</u>.

_____F_____ **31.** Without these people.

_____ **32.** These people <u>made a difference in our world</u>.

_____ **33.** Modern astronauts <u>depend on their discoveries</u>.

_____ **34.** Today's scientists <u>are still exploring new ideas</u>.

_____F_____ **35.** Much different from today's.

_____ **36.** Tomorrow's world <u>will be much different</u>.

_____ **37.** Space travel <u>may be common</u>.

_____F_____ **38.** The world tomorrow.

▶ **Writing Link** **Write two complete sentences about a process you would like to learn more about.**

_____

_____

_____

_____

Lesson 7
Run-On Sentences

A **run-on sentence** is two or more sentences incorrectly written as one sentence. Correct a run-on sentence by writing separate sentences or by combining the sentences with a semicolon (;) or with a comma and *and, or,* or *but.*

RUN-ON SENTENCE
Bill won the race, the crowd cheered.

CORRECTED SENTENCE
Bill won the race. The crowd cheered.
Bill won the race; the crowd cheered.
Bill won the race, and the crowd cheered.

▶ **Exercise 1** **Write *R* next to each run-on sentence.**

___R___ You took a chance you lost the game.

___R___ **1.** Architects design buildings, their buildings can take years to complete.

_____ **2.** Lionel took the subway and then transferred to a bus.

_____ **3.** The colors in his painting are quite striking.

_____ **4.** I ordered a small sweatshirt, but I received a large one.

___R___ **5.** Preheat the oven, bake for one hour.

_____ **6.** The tower cleared the runway, but the plane still could not take off.

___R___ **7.** Yori took an aspirin, there was only one left.

___R___ **8.** The bill comes to almost twenty dollars, are you going to pay it?

_____ **9.** Of all the birds at the pet store, we liked the parrots best.

_____ **10.** Subtract ten from twelve for the answer.

_____ **11.** Here is your present, but don't open it until your birthday.

___R___ **12.** Clean your room first and then we can go to the movie.

___R___ **13.** Daryl's first test was too easy, his second test was much more difficult.

_____ **14.** Go to the first street; then turn left.

_____ **15.** The first store had the best selection, but the second store had the album I

wanted.

___R___ **16.** Look at all the people at the parade I wonder where we can sit.

_____ **17.** Susie is planning a surprise party; Karen doesn't suspect a thing.

___R___ **18.** The night sky was clear many stars could be seen.

___R___ **19.** George and Hernando are walking to the park, I am riding my bicycle.

_____ **20.** Saturday's softball game will have to be postponed if it rains.

___R___ **21.** Tonight we are going to see a skating competition I hope it is like the Olympics.

_____ **22.** Cynthia wrote a letter to Cousin Jane, and Dad mailed it for her.

_____ **23.** Mike is reading *The Adventures of Tom Sawyer,* but Jamie is reading *The Prince and the Pauper.*

___R___ **24.** The actors are sewing their own costumes it is quite a challenge.

_____ **25.** Scott's jacket is colorful; it is also very warm.

___R___ **26.** The new bridge has several special features one of them is a carving of a ship.

_____ **27.** We can eat first, or we can start the tour.

_____ **28.** Buy the seeds this week, and plant them next week.

▶ **Exercise 2** **Underline each run-on sentence in the paragraph.**

If you're looking for something to do with your free time, you might think about starting a collection. There are millions of collectors in the world. Some people collect baseball cards, some people collect the autographs of famous people, did you know there are even some people who collect colorful shopping bags from different stores? If you have a special interest in sports or music, you might decide to collect baseball caps or photos of musicians. If you like nature, you could collect seashells, fossils, or wooden carvings of ducks. Collecting is fun, collecting can be profitable. The items you collect can double or even triple in value over the years, stamps and coins are good examples of this. Most people enjoy collecting because they like looking for new items to add to their collection. Finding a rare shell or discovering a one-of-a-kind baseball card in your grandmother's attic is a real thrill for most collectors.

Unit 1 **Review**

Grammar

▶ **Exercise 1** Write *dec.* in the blank before each declarative sentence, *int.* before each interrogative sentence, *exc.* before each exclamatory sentence, and *imp.* before each imperative sentence.

__exc.__	What a great skateboard this is!
__int.__	**1.** Should I bring an umbrella?
__dec.__	**2.** It's been raining for three days.
__imp.__	**3.** Come with me to the store.
__int.__	**4.** Are your shoes too tight?
__exc.__	**5.** My library card is ruined!

▶ **Exercise 2** Write *S* before each simple sentence, *C* before each compound sentence, and *F* before each sentence fragment.

__S__	The oldest zoo in the United States is in Philadelphia.
__S__	**1.** Washington and Jefferson liked to fish.
__C__	**2.** I want to get a cat, but my sister wants a dog.
__F__	**3.** In the doghouse behind the garage.
__C__	**4.** The horses are in the barn; the cows are in the field.
__S__	**5.** Bring it here, please.

▶ **Exercise 3** Draw one line under each simple subject. Draw two lines under each simple predicate. Separate the complete subject and complete predicate with a vertical line (|).

Many children | love animals.

1. Big dogs | need lots of space.

2. Kendall | made a valentine for his stepmother and gave it to her.

3. The postcard from Eliza | is on the table.

4. The dog and cat | chased the squirrel up the tree.

5. The red book | belongs to Eliza and Ted.

Cumulative Review: Unit 1

▶ **Exercise 1** Write *dec.* if the sentence is declarative, *int.* if it is interrogative, *exc.* if it is exclamatory, or *imp.* if it is imperative.

___int.___ Is Bobby home?

___dec.___ 1. The lightbulb is burned out.

___int.___ 2. Will you help me shovel the driveway?

___exc.___ 3. Wow, that was a fantastic movie!

___imp.___ 4. Please give Miss Kitty some milk.

___dec.___ 5. Your red shirt is in the dryer.

___exc.___ 6. What a cold day it is!

___int.___ 7. Did you wear your boots today?

___dec.___ 8. The cat is chasing the dog.

___imp.___ 9. Don't drop these eggs.

___int.___ 10. Is it my turn now?

▶ **Exercise 2** Draw one line under each simple subject. Draw two lines under each simple predicate. Separate the complete subject from the complete predicate with a vertical line (|).

The pirates | sailed down the coast.

1. Alma and Phil | swam laps together.

2. My mom | found the money.

3. My friend's dog and my neighbor's cat | growl at each other.

4. The third pig's house | was made of brick.

5. The straw basket | was full of apples and nuts.

6. The small boy | led the way to the castle and opened the door.

7. The tired soldiers | charged up the hill.

8. The pizza and drinks | were eight dollars.

9. Cara and Tim | closed their eyes during the scary movie.

10. Cora's aunt | knitted her a sweater and a hat.

Unit 2: Nouns

Lesson 8
Nouns: Proper and Common

A **noun** is a word that names a person, place, thing, or idea.

There are two basic kinds of nouns: common nouns and proper nouns.

A **common noun** names any person, place, thing, or idea.

A **proper noun** names a particular person, place, thing, or idea. It may consist of one or more words. Always begin a proper noun with a capital letter. If a proper noun has more than one word, capitalize the first word and all the important words.

	COMMON NOUN	PROPER NOUN
People:	student	Jan Lopez
	police officer	Captain Michael Millay
Places:	school	Dewey Middle School
	park	Central Park
Things:	poem	"Jabberwocky"
	painting	*Mona Lisa*

▶ **Exercise 1** Write *com.* above each common noun and *prop.* above each proper noun.

      com.   com.   com.

My stepfather bought me blue slacks and a red jacket.

     prop.   prop.   com.

1. Uncle Lloyd, Aunt June, and I went to a movie.

     prop.   com.   com.

2. The Cubs won the first game of the season.

     prop.   com.   com.   prop.

3. Felicia scored ten points in the game against Davis School.

        prop.   prop.   prop.

4. The Americans fought the British in the Battle of New Orleans.

     prop.   com.   com.

5. Brenda is a new student in our class.

     prop.   com.   com.   prop.

6. Jaime got a good grade on his paper about Albert Einstein.

           com.   com.   prop.

7. We left our bags at the station in Pittsburgh.

     prop.   com.

8. In Philadelphia we visited many historical places.

       com.   prop.   prop.

9. Does this book on Egypt belong to Maria?

          com.   prop.   com.

10. May we have a picnic at Lincoln Park this weekend?

         com.   com.   com.
11. I could see the fear in the eyes of the little dog.

         com.   com.   com.
12. My mother is a supervisor at the factory.

         com.   com.   prop.
13. The water in the pool at Shelby Park is nice and warm.

         com.   prop.
14. Many boats sail on the Charles River.

        prop.   com.
15. Superman is my hero.

                    com.   prop.
16. The pink and green skateboard belongs to Akimi.

        com.   com.   com.   com.
17. The rain and snow kept the children inside for the day.

              prop.   prop.
18. Have you read *Alice in Wonderland* by Lewis Carroll?

  prop.   com.
19. Jack says this book is the funniest he has ever read.

    prop.   com.   com.
20. Gordo, my puppy, ate all the meat.

           com.   com.   com.   com.
21. Put your guitar on the chair and your coat in the closet.

    prop.   com.   prop.
22. Broadway is a famous street in New York City.

            prop.   prop.   com.
23. We're going to Texas and Louisiana to visit my cousins.

    prop.   com.   prop.
24. Uncle Antoine keeps his boat on Lake Pontchartrain.

    prop.   com.
25. Ask Mr. Capozza if he knows where my mitt is.

    com.   prop.
26. Last winter we skated on Walden Pond.

  prop.   com.   prop.   prop.
27. Jo is a character in *Little Women* by Louisa May Alcott.

    com.   prop.   prop.
28. My father was born in Dublin, Ireland.

        com.   com.   com.
29. Put more sauce on this plate of spaghetti.

    com.   com.   prop.
30. The car got all dirty on the long drive from Omaha.

    com.   com.   com.
31. The apples for the pie came from our own trees.

  prop.   com.   prop.
32. Nance left the house before Louisa did.

    com.   com.   prop.
33. That building across the street is the Empire State Building.

           prop.   prop.
34. I've seen the Atlantic, but I haven't seen the Pacific.

        com.   com.   prop.
35. There are many schools and colleges in and around Boston.

    com.   prop.
36. This bus will take you to Park Street.

Lesson 9
Nouns: Singular and Plural

A **singular noun** names one person, place, thing, or idea. A **plural noun** names more than one. Most plural nouns are formed by adding -*s* or -*es* to the singular form of the noun. To write the plural forms of some nouns, however, you need to know special rules.

FORMING PLURAL NOUNS

NOUNS ENDING WITH	TO FORM PLURAL	EXAMPLE
s, z, -zz, ch, sh, x	Add -*es*.	church, church**es**
o preceded by a vowel	Add -*s*.	patio, patio**s**
o preceded by a consonant	Usually add -*es*. Sometimes add -*s*.	echo, echo**es** piano, piano**s**
y preceded by a vowel	Add -*s*.	monkey, monke**ys**
y preceded by a consonant	Usually change *y* to *i* and add -*es*.	fly, fl**ies**
f or *fe*	Usually change *f* to *v* and add -*es*.	knife, kni**ves**
	Sometimes add -*s*.	earmuff, earmu**ffs**

▶ **Exercise 1** Write *S* above each singular noun. Write *P* above each plural noun.

     P   P   P
My parents want us children to do the dishes.

       P   S   S
1. The paintings were in the old wing of the museum.

       P   P
2. The donkeys ran through the fields.

       P   S   P
3. All the books in the library have special numbers.

            S   S
4. Did you see the cat run down the alley?

      S   S
5. The game Josh is playing is the hardest.

      S   P
6. That sailor has several medals.

      P   P
7. The calves stood calmly beside their mothers.

    P   P
8. Scientists work on many serious problems.

      S   P
9. This store sells supplies for school.

             P   P
10. Do you have any autographs of famous singers?

      P   S   S
11. The cliffs of Dover in England are white.

S   S
12. I wonder if the astronaut was afraid as he floated in space.
           S   S
13. We shouted into the cave and heard an echo.
                     P
14. There are not enough forks to go around.
         S   S   S
15. Jupiter is the largest planet in the solar system.
           S   S   P
16. The baby has outgrown his coat and mittens.
                                        P   S
17. I have to go to two birthday parties this weekend.
         P   S   P   S
18. Lions live on the plain, and tigers live in the jungle.
             S   P
19. The car has four flat tires.
           S   P   P
20. Jamie has read several books of historical fiction.

▶ Exercise 2 Complete each sentence by writing the correct form of the noun in parentheses. Use a dictionary if necessary.

Mom says that all the soldiers are ___heroes___. (hero)

1. The little boy was carrying three ___bunches___ of flowers. (bunch)

2. The squirrel is sitting on the ___roof___ of the house. (roof)

3. The torn screen allowed ___flies___ to come in. (fly)

4. Is it very sunny on the ___patio___? (patio)

5. Ami and Cyndi played a duet on two ___pianos___. (piano)

6. Three ___ladies___ were ahead of us in line. (lady)

7. The submarine was sunk by the enemy's ___torpedo___. (torpedo)

8. The yodeler's cry rang through the ___valley___. (valley)

9. Yvonne has lived in several large ___cities___. (city)

10. I just finished raking up that huge pile of ___leaves___. (leaf)

11. The campers dug ___trenches___ to keep water out of their tents. (trench)

12. I never saw so many ___photos___ of one cat. (photo)

13. Did you boil enough ___potatoes___ for the salad? (potato)

14. The ___bus___ going downtown is usually crowded. (bus)

15. Maddie found three ___pennies___ on the sidewalk. (penny)

Lesson 10
Nouns: Collective

Words that name a group of people or things, such as *crowd* and *team,* are called
collective nouns. A collective noun can take either a singular or a plural verb.
Make the verb singular when the group acts as a unit. Make it plural when each
member of the group acts separately.

The **crowd was** excited by the close game.
The **crowd were** pushing each other to get through the gate.

▶ **Exercise 1 Underline each collective noun. Above it write *S* if it is singular and *P* if it
is plural.**

      S
The class is putting on a musical this year.

      P
1. The audience were shifting restlessly in their seats.

            S
2. All of a sudden the crowd rose to its feet.

          S
3. The construction crew works at night.

    S
4. The herd of cattle is grazing peacefully on the hillside.

    S
5. The jury is glad to take a break.

      S
6. Carla's family is going to visit relatives in Mexico.

    P
7. The jury are carefully discussing the evidence.

        S
8. A scientific team is searching for a cure.

    S
9. The public is unhappy with the politicians.

     P
10. The group of students were talking and laughing.

    P
11. My family disagree with each other about the movie.

    S
12. The club I belong to does fund-raising for charity.

       P
13. The baseball team take their positions on the field.

    S
14. The committee has finally reached a decision.

S
15. The <u>swarm</u> of bees was following the queen bee.

P
16. My <u>class</u> are taking turns watering the plants.

S
17. The <u>band</u> is playing at the dance.

S
18. The <u>class</u> is about equally divided between girls and boys.

S
19. The <u>flock</u> of pigeons flew to the top of the building.

S
20. The <u>orchestra</u> plays in the park on Sundays.

▶ **Exercise 2** **Draw a line under the verb in parentheses that best completes the sentence.**

The committee (<u>is</u>, are) unanimous in its decision.

1. My family (<u>is</u>, are) spending the weekend at Grandma's house.

2. The class (has, <u>have</u>) different ideas on how to decorate the gym.

3. The big crowd (<u>was</u>, were) surprisingly quiet.

4. Jessica's family (is, <u>are</u>) taking vacations in different places.

5. The Spanish club (<u>is</u>, are) raising money for a trip to Mexico.

6. The group (<u>has</u>, have) followers from all over the world.

7. The team (is, <u>are</u>) running in all directions.

8. The audience (was, <u>were</u>) reading or chatting before the show started.

9. A flock of geese (<u>is</u>, are) flying overhead.

10. The public (<u>is</u>, are) very happy with the new mayor.

11. The office staff (<u>is</u>, are) having a picnic on Saturday.

12. Our team (<u>is</u>, are) ahead by one point.

13. The band of cowhands (<u>is</u>, are) herding the horses across the river.

14. The orchestra (was, <u>were</u>) all playing the wrong notes.

15. The staff (is, <u>are</u>) all members of different health clubs.

16. Only the best team (<u>is</u>, are) going to the playoffs.

17. Do you know if the senate (<u>is</u>, are) meeting today?

18. The crowd (<u>is</u>, are) on its feet.

Lesson 11
Nouns: Possessives

A noun that shows ownership of things or qualities is a **possessive noun**.

The **lion's** mane is shaggy.
All of the **clowns'** costumes are bright and colorful.
The **children's** tickets to the circus are in my pocket.

FORMING POSSESSIVE NOUNS

NOUNS	TO FORM POSSESSIVE	EXAMPLES
Most singular nouns	Add an apostrophe and -s ('s).	The seal's ball is red.
Singular nouns ending in -s	Add an apostrophe and -s ('s).	Chris's ticket got lost.
Plural nouns ending in -s	Add an apostrophe (').	The tigers' trainer is brave.
Plural nouns not ending in -s	Add an apostrophe and -s ('s).	The people's faces are happy.

Remember that possessive nouns always contain apostrophes. Plural nouns do not.

The **acrobats** have capes.   Where are the **acrobats'** capes?

▶ **Exercise 1 Underline each possessive noun. Above it write _S_ if it is singular and _P_ if it is plural.**

      P
The clowns' red noses look like cherries.

               S
1. Do you think the human cannonball's trick is dangerous?

      S
2. The ringmaster's voice has to be very loud.

    P
3. The lions' roars don't seem to scare the trainer.

                 P
4. Someone must carefully check the trapeze artists' ropes.

          S
5. Please don't eat all of your sister's popcorn.

            S
6. The trainer is putting his head in the lion's mouth!

      P
7. I dare you to count the zebras' stripes.

     S
8. The rider stood on the horse's back.

Grammar

9. The audience's applause rang through the arena.
        S

10. The trainer's belief is that lions can be trained but not tamed.
      S

11. The big cats' tempers can be very fierce.
        P

12. The baby elephants grabbed their mothers' tails.
                  P

13. The circus's winter home is in Florida.
      S

14. The woman's costume is the same color as her poodles' fur.
      S   P

15. The acrobats' legs must be very strong.
      P

▶ **Exercise 2 Complete each sentence by writing the possessive form of the word in parentheses.**

The worker braided the _____ horse's _____ mane. (*horse*)

1. The _____ Ringling Brothers' _____ circus was one of the most famous. (*Ringling Brothers*)

2. The human _____ cannonball's _____ act is next. (*cannonball*)

3. The _____ cannon's _____ fuse is about to be lit. (*cannon*)

4. The lion _____ trainer's _____ bravery is amazing. (*trainer*)

5. The _____ clowns' _____ antics delight everyone. (*clowns*)

6. The _____ explosion's _____ noise is frightful. (*explosion*)

7. Are most _____ performers' _____ acts dangerous? (*performers*)

8. The _____ children's _____ smiles lit up the arena. (*children*)

9. The circus _____ animals' _____ coats are sleek and shiny. (*animals*)

10. Look! That _____ dog's _____ toenails are painted red. (*dog*)

11. The circus _____ band's _____ conductor raised her baton. (*band*)

12. The _____ tiger's _____ fangs are long and sharp. (*tiger*)

13. This is supposed to be the _____ world's _____ biggest circus. (*world*)

14. The toddler pulled the _____ monkey's _____ tail. (*monkey*)

15. The _____ performers' _____ capes are made of silk. (*performers*)

Unit 2 Review

► **Exercise 1** Write *prop.* above each proper noun, *com.* above each common noun, and *col.* above each collective noun.

    prop.   prop.   com.
Jamie and Pat live in the same neighborhood.

             com.   prop.
1. Have you seen my copy of *Jem's Island*?

   prop.   prop.   col.
2. Sharon and Akira belong to the club.

    com.   com.   prop.
3. The balloons sailed through the sky above Walker Stadium.

           col.   com.
4. Watch out for that swarm of bees.

    com.   prop.
5. The clothing at Frederico's Department Store is very expensive.

          com.   prop.   com.
6. All the middle schools in Newton have large libraries.

    col.   com.
7. Our family is trying to spend more time together.

      prop.   com.
8. The red Ford belongs to my sister.

    col.   com.   com.
9. The crowd of runners is almost at the line.

        col.   com.
10. Do you think the audience liked the play?

► **Exercise 2** Write *S* above each singular noun and *P* above each plural noun. Draw a line under each singular or plural noun that is also a possessive noun.

       S   S
That is <u>Steve's</u> black truck.

    P   S
1. Your shirts are in this drawer.

   S   P   S
2. <u>Alma's</u> shoes are under the bed.

          P   S
3. Look at the books in this library!

    S   P
4. This town has two newspapers.

        S   S   P
5. Is this the <u>librarian's</u> list of books?

   S   P   P
6. The team needs new bats and gloves.

Cumulative Review: Units 1–2

▶ **Exercise 1** Write *dec.* beside each declarative sentence, *int.* beside each interrogative sentence, *exc.* beside each exclamatory sentence, and *imp.* beside each imperative sentence.

__exc.__		That was a spectacular hit!
__imp.__	**1.**	Bring us our check, please.
__int.__	**2.**	Are you nervous about giving your speech?
__dec.__	**3.**	The live butterfly exhibit at the park is worth seeing.
__dec.__	**4.**	Fifteen skiers are competing in the downhill race.
__exc.__	**5.**	Help! I think I'm going to fall!
__int.__	**6.**	Will you give me a hand with my science project?
__imp.__	**7.**	Take the Main Street bus to Mulberry.
__dec.__	**8.**	I wanted the blue hat, but the green one will have to do.
__int.__	**9.**	May I borrow your tape player for the party?
__exc.__	**10.**	Congratulations, you take first place!

▶ **Exercise 2** Write *S* beside each simple sentence, *C* beside each compound sentence, and *F* beside each sentence fragment.

__F__		The road through the orchards and valleys.
__C__	**1.**	Mom will bake a cake, and Bill will frost it.
__S__	**2.**	The teacher and the principal are laughing.
__C__	**3.**	You can take a nap, or you can read a book.
__F__	**4.**	All that work.
__C__	**5.**	Fish have scales, and birds have feathers.
__C__	**6.**	Maizie will turn on the light, and you can unlock the door.
__S__	**7.**	The dog and the cat are sleeping on the porch.
__C__	**8.**	Alicia wrote the paper, and Jaime drew the pictures.
__S__	**9.**	I'm glad you are here.
__F__	**10.**	Mountains and mountains of ice cream.

▶ **Exercise 3** Write *prop.* above each proper noun and *com.* above each common noun. Draw a line under each possessive noun.

    prop.   com.   prop.   prop.
Neil plays soccer with David and Justin.

    prop.   prop.   prop.
1. Allen and Margaret live on Kenmore Street.

             com.   com.
2. The butterflies' wings are orange.

            com.   com.   com.
3. The hospital is on the other side of town.

    prop.   com.
4. Mom wants to use the telephone.

                com.   com.
5. I'll meet you at the doctor's office.

       prop.   com.   com.
6. Officer D'Amico is giving a talk on safety today.

                      com.   com.
7. It was too noisy to hear the singers' voices.

     com.   com.   com.
8. The driver's jacket is on the chair.

          com.   com.
9. Can you see the cars' headlights?

   prop. com.   com.   com.
10. Kerry's aunt sent her a box of chocolates.

▶ **Exercise 4** Complete each sentence by writing the plural form of the noun in parentheses.

The ___girls___ took medicine for their allergies. (girl)

1. I like everything in my salad except ___tomatoes___. (tomato)

2. Oil ___paints___ dry more slowly than other paints. (paint)

3. Please get a book from the library about the ___lives___ of people in early Rome. (life)

4. The music department has three grand ___pianos___. (piano)

5. Their tool ___benches___ were covered with wood shavings. (bench)

6. Jason and his sister rode ___donkeys___ into the Grand Canyon. (donkey)

7. She applied for a few ___jobs___ last week. (job)

8. How many ___classes___ are on your schedule? (class)

9. Part of her salary will go toward state ___taxes___. (tax)

10. There aren't enough ___dictionaries___ to go around. (dictionary)

▶ **Exercise 5** **Draw a line under the verb in parentheses that best completes the sentence.**

A school of fish (swims, swim) past the shark.

1. The class (begins, <u>begin</u>) their book reports tomorrow.

2. The committee (argues, <u>argue</u>) among themselves.

3. Raphael's family (<u>lives</u>, live) next to the school on Mound Street.

4. The audience (<u>applauds</u>, applaud) when the performance is over.

5. Our team (has, <u>have</u>) different ideas on how to win the volleyball tournament.

6. The jazz band (<u>plays</u>, play) in the park on Sundays.

7. The senate (<u>reads</u>, read) each bill out loud.

8. The stage crew (<u>moves</u>, move) the scenery off the stage.

9. The crowd (<u>cheers</u>, cheer) the team.

10. A gaggle of geese (<u>visits</u>, visit) our pond every winter.

▶ **Exercise 6** **Complete each sentence by writing the possessive form of the word in parentheses.**

The _____cars'_____ engines were fast enough to win the race. (cars)

1. The crowd cheered the _____referee's_____ call. (referee)

2. He groaned when he realized he had backed into his _____boss's_____ car. (boss)

3. I found my dad's tie in the _____men's_____ department. (men)

4. Zachary delivers papers to all the _____neighbors'_____ homes. (neighbors)

5. My _____sister's_____ team is in fourth place this year. (sister)

6. Mystery _____writers'_____ books usually keep the reader in suspense. (writers)

7. Which _____child's_____ toy is best for this age group? (child)

8. Mr. _____Jones's_____ watch has an alarm that wakes him for work. (Jones)

9. The _____cowhands'_____ horses were trained to herd cattle. (cowhands)

10. Who is the president of the _____women's_____ club this year? (women)

Unit 3: Verbs

Lesson 12

Action Verbs and Direct Objects

An **action verb** is a word that describes what someone or something does. An action verb names an action, although not always a physical action. Some action verbs describe mental action.

Tyler swam faster than anyone else at camp. (The action verb *swam* describes a physical action.)

Alicia **calculated** the score in her head. (The verb *calculated* describes a mental action.)

Sometimes an action verb is followed by a **direct object**. A direct object receives the action of the verb. It answers the question *what* or *whom*? after an action verb.

Kelsey's soccer team won yesterday's game. (The action verb, *won*, is followed by the direct object, *game,* which answers the question *what?*)

▶ **Exercise 1 Draw two lines under the action verb in each sentence.**

Yellowstone National Park <u>attracts</u> many visitors.

1. Yellowstone <u>covers</u> more than two million acres of land.

2. Its boundaries <u>reach</u> into three states.

3. The park <u>features</u> thousands of hot springs.

4. Some hot springs <u>shoot</u> columns of water and steam into the air.

5. We <u>call</u> them geysers.

6. Yellowstone's geysers <u>attract</u> visitors from all over the world.

7. Nearly two hundred geysers <u>dot</u> the park's landscape.

8. Old Faithful, the largest, <u>erupts</u> almost hourly.

9. It <u>shoots</u> water more than one hundred feet into the air.

10. Enormous crowds <u>gather</u> beside it.

11. Yellowstone National Park <u>contains</u> many other attractions.

12. The Yellowstone River <u>divides</u> the park north to south.

13. It carves a canyon through the mountains.

14. In several places, the river falls from steep cliffs.

15. Visitors to Yellowstone observe a variety of wildlife.

16. Many species of wildflowers grow in the Rocky Mountains.

17. Moose roam the area.

18. Herds of bison graze in the park.

19. Both grizzlies and black bears live in the park.

20. Yellowstone's famous bears sometimes frighten campers.

▶ **Exercise 2 Draw two lines under the action verb in each sentence. If the action verb has a direct object, circle the direct object.**

The Grand Canyon attracts millions of visitors each year.

1. Millions more catch glimpses of the canyon though airplane windows.

2. Grand Canyon National Park contains the most spectacular sections of the gorge.

3. The park encompasses more than one million acres.

4. At visitor centers, people study maps of the park.

5. They learn interesting facts about the area's geology.

6. An enormous sea once covered this part of North America.

7. The Colorado River carved the canyon over many years.

8. Many visitors hike the park's trails.

9. Trails lead hikers down from the canyon's rim and back up.

10. Some people ride mules instead of hiking.

11. Visitors notice fossils in the canyon walls.

12. Sandstone, limestone, and shale form multicolored layers.

13. Weather constantly changes the rock formations.

14. Wind and rain erode the soft rock.

15. Sometimes big chunks of rock fall.

16. Changing light constantly alters the canyon's appearance.

Lesson 13
Action Verbs and Indirect Objects

An **indirect object** can appear only in a sentence that has a direct object. Just as a direct object answers the question *whom?* or *what?* after an action verb, an indirect object answers the question *to whom?* or *for whom?* An indirect object always comes before the direct object.

James bought **Corey** a cold drink. (The indirect object *Corey* answers the question, *James bought a cold drink for whom?*)

Naomi gives the **class** red pencils. (The indirect object *class* answers the question *Naomi gives red pencils to whom?*)

▶ **Exercise 1** Write *DO* in the blank if the italicized word is a direct object or *IO* if it is an indirect object.

IO   The doctor gave *Maya* a vision test.

IO   **1.** My cousin Rita brought *us* fresh-picked vegetables.

DO   **2.** Loud music gives my mother *headaches*.

DO   **3.** Janelle baked her family double-chocolate *brownies*.

IO   **4.** Louie's sister made the *team* a pitcher of lemonade.

IO   **5.** Ezra read *us* the newspaper from Mexico City.

DO   **6.** Colleen showed her father her new gymnastics *routine*.

IO   **7.** Camille loaned *us* her tent.

DO   **8.** He offered my mother a *ride* to her office.

IO   **9.** My sister gave the *dog* a dish of water.

DO   **10.** The president gave me his *autograph*.

IO   **11.** Carmen sewed her new *niece* a crib quilt.

IO   **12.** My father prepared *us* a feast.

IO   **13.** The middle school sent the *shelter* more than five hundred cans of food.

DO   **14.** Oma gave Carl three *dollars*.

DO   **15.** Mr. Alvarez told me the new teacher's *name*.

_____IO____ **16.** Carlos showed *me* his baseball card collection.

_____DO____ **17.** Peter played us three new *songs*.

_____IO____ **18.** Kristi made *everyone* a handcrafted gift.

_____DO____ **19.** My Uncle Randall gave me his old *computer*.

_____DO____ **20.** I will give Tyler some *gum*.

▶ **Exercise 2 Circle each direct object. Underline each indirect object.**

The Wildcats baked their coach a birthday cake

1. The tour guide gives each visitor a map

2. My sister lent me her new magazine

3. Oleg's father bought him a leather jacket

4. Ms. Kumin read the class the last chapter.

5. My grandmother mailed me seventeen postcards

6. We cooked Carol dinner.

7. Clayton built his sisters a playhouse

8. The class gave Officer Wallace its full attention

9. Someone sent Kim a dozen roses

10. The hotel offered its guests free breakfast.

11. I ordered my mother a silver necklace

12. Julia told the children a funny story.

13. My mother ordered Uncle Rob a cup of coffee.

14. Chris paid his brother five dollars

15. Louisa sings the baby a song.

16. I bought my friend some basketball cards

17. She read Raul the directions

18. Aaron left Gabriel a doughnut.

19. Charlie made his family lasagna

20. Amy gave her sister three old books

Grammar

Lesson 14
Transitive and Intransitive Verbs

An action verb that is followed by a direct object is called a transitive verb. An action verb that is not followed by a direct object is called an intransitive verb. Some verbs can be either transitive or intransitive, depending on the words that follow them. Remember that a direct object answers the question *what?* or *whom?*

The polar bears **eat** slowly.

The word *slowly* tells how the bears eat. It does not answer the question *what?* or *whom?* In this sentence, the action verb *eat* is intransitive because it is not followed by a direct object.

The polar bears **eat** fish.

The word *fish* answers the question *what?* In this sentence, the action verb *eat* is transitive because it is followed by the direct object *fish*.

▶ **Exercise 1 Draw two lines under the action verb in each sentence. Write *T* in the blank if the verb is transitive. Write *I* if the verb is intransitive.**

T   Mitchell repaired the computer.

I   **1.** The baby cried loudly.

I   **2.** Marta finished early.

T   **3.** We climbed three flights of stairs.

I   **4.** Carly sings better than I do.

T   **5.** My brother pedaled his bike down the sidewalk.

I   **6.** The peanut butter cookies burned.

T   **7.** My aunt called me yesterday.

I   **8.** The pet store opened late.

I   **9.** Peter's goldfish eats in the morning.

T   **10.** Jen sank the ball through the hoop.

T   **11.** After school, Zach ate two apples.

T   **12.** The alarm woke Ethan at seven.

I   **13.** The bathtub overflowed.

_____I_____ **14.** Aisha practiced every day.

_____T_____ **15.** The city closed our street during the construction.

_____I_____ **16.** My neighbor's dog barked all night.

_____T_____ **17.** Tamara washed her mother's car on Saturday.

_____T_____ **18.** William found the doctor's phone number.

_____I_____ **19.** The upstairs phone rang.

_____T_____ **20.** Ingrid packed her sister's lunch.

_____I_____ **21.** Heavy snow fell during the night.

_____T_____ **22.** Ruby starts piano lessons tomorrow.

_____T_____ **23.** We watched a video in class.

_____I_____ **24.** Our elaborate plans failed.

_____T_____ **25.** Jamie's father grows prize-winning pumpkins.

_____I_____ **26.** My grandfather snores loudly.

_____I_____ **27.** Maureen and Sarah skated for two hours.

_____T_____ **28.** I dropped my key.

_____T_____ **29.** Gordon borrowed nine books from the library.

_____T_____ **30.** The track team broke three records.

_____I_____ **31.** Kaitlin scored in the second inning.

_____T_____ **32.** Gilberto asked the librarian.

_____I_____ **33.** She painted more carefully than ever.

_____T_____ **34.** A kitten followed me home.

_____I_____ **35.** The hall door slammed.

_____I_____ **36.** The doctor's office closes at five.

_____T_____ **37.** A wave knocked Cameron off his feet.

_____I_____ **38.** Andy and Jorge's boat sailed swiftly across the pond.

_____T_____ **39.** The band played only jazz.

_____I_____ **40.** The class decorated for the fall festival.

Lesson 15
Linking Verbs and Predicate Words

A linking verb connects a sentence's subject with a noun or an adjective in the predicate. The predicate word tells what a sentence's subject *is* or *is like.*

An avocado **is a fruit.** (The linking verb *is* connects the subject *avocado* with *fruit.*)

In the sentence above, *fruit* is a predicate noun. It tells what the subject, *avocado,* is. Some sentences have a predicate adjective, an adjective that follows a linking verb and tells what the subject is like.

This avocado is **ripe.** (*Ripe* is a predicate adjective. It tells what the subject *avocado* is like.)

COMMON LINKING VERBS

appear	become	grow	seem
am, is, are, was, were	feel	look	taste

▶ **Exercise 1** Draw two lines under the verb in each sentence. Write *AV* in the blank if the verb is an action verb. Write *LV* if it is a linking verb.

__LV__   Dogs are popular pets.

__AV__ **1.** Many dogs use their tails for communication.

__AV__ **2.** A dog's tail expresses playfulness or fear.

__LV__ **3.** Some dogs' tails are long and thin.

__AV__ **4.** Other dogs have fluffy or curly tails.

__LV__ **5.** Dogs are very good smellers.

__LV__ **6.** Their noses are extremely sensitive.

__LV__ **7.** Certain dogs actually become detectives.

__AV__ **8.** They search with their noses.

__LV__ **9.** A dog's hearing is also very strong.

__AV__ **10.** Dogs hear many things.

__AV__ **11.** Dogs' ears move in different directions.

__LV__ **12.** Dogs seem sensitive to sounds.

Grammar

___AV___ 13. Most dogs have forty-two teeth.

___AV___ 14. Different types of teeth serve different purposes.

___LV___ 15. Some dogs are web-footed.

___AV___ 16. Webbed feet make dogs good swimmers.

___LV___ 17. Canine eyesight is different from human eyesight.

___LV___ 18. Small details look fuzzy to dogs.

___LV___ 19. Most colors appear gray to them.

___AV___ 20. In the dark, dogs see better than humans.

▶ **Exercise 2** **Draw two lines under the linking verb in each sentence. Write *PA* in the blank if the verb is followed by a predicate adjective. Write *PN* if it is followed by a predicate noun.**

___PN___ Snakes are very interesting animals.

___PA___ 1. Not all of them are poisonous.

___PN___ 2. Earth is home to more than two thousand species of snakes.

___PA___ 3. About a dozen snake species are rare.

___PN___ 4. One endangered snake is the indigo.

___PA___ 5. Indigos seem very friendly.

___PA___ 6. They are native to Florida and Georgia.

___PA___ 7. Some snakes grow extremely long.

___PA___ 8. A few become longer than thirty feet.

___PN___ 9. The South American anaconda is a large snake.

___PA___ 10. Some anacondas are thick.

___PN___ 11. Thread snakes are the smallest snakes.

___PA___ 12. Some of them appear tiny.

___PA___ 13. A snake's scaly skin looks slippery.

___PA___ 14. Its skin is only temporary.

___PA___ 15. Some snakes are poisonous.

___PN___ 16. All snakes are carnivores.

Lesson 16
Verb Tenses: Present, Past, and Future

A verb's **tense** tells when an action takes place. The **present tense** describes an action that happens regularly.

We **visit** my grandmother on Sundays.

It can also express a general truth.

We **visit** many relatives.

The **past tense** describes an action that has already taken place. The past tense is most often formed by adding *-ed* to the verb.

We **visited** my aunt last weekend.

The **future tense** describes an action that will take place in the future. The future tense is formed by adding the helping verb *will* (or *shall*) to the verb.

We **will visit** my grandmother next Sunday.

▶ **Exercise 1** Draw two lines under the verb in each sentence. Write the tense in the blank: *past, present,* or *future.*

present	Jimmy loves to fish.
past	1. We traveled to Ontario last summer.
present	2. My father makes the best whole wheat rolls.
future	3. I will be there by six o'clock.
present	4. Mr. Glazer's class recycles the most paper.
past	5. India shared her ideas for after-school activities.
future	6. The karate class will begin promptly at three.
future	7. My brother will paint the mural.
past	8. No one unlocked the storage room.
present	9. We always plant pumpkins behind the garage.
future	10. The club will sell cookbooks.
past	11. George returned his library books on time.
future	12. Each student will contribute one poem to the book.

Grammar

<u>past</u>   **13.** The band <u>practiced</u> for weeks.

<u>present</u>   **14.** Amy <u>watches</u> her younger brother on weekends.

<u>past</u>   **15.** We <u>discussed</u> the Brazilian rain forest.

<u>past</u>   **16.** Carol <u>walked</u> ten blocks in the rain.

<u>present</u>   **17.** André <u>lives</u> next door to Mr. Batten.

<u>future</u>   **18.** Sharla's mother <u>will pick</u> her up after practice.

<u>future</u>   **19.** Indira <u>will call</u> for a taxi.

<u>present</u>   **20.** Stephen <u>waits</u> for a ride.

<u>past</u>   **21.** I <u>locked</u> my bike to the fence.

<u>present</u>   **22.** Louis <u>helps</u> me with my algebra.

<u>future</u>   **23.** The newspaper <u>will list</u> the score from last night's game.

<u>past</u>   **24.** Three girls <u>studied</u> together for the geography test.

<u>past</u>   **25.** We <u>hiked</u> to the top of the ridge.

<u>future</u>   **26.** Clarence <u>will audition</u> for the spring play.

<u>present</u>   **27.** I usually <u>wear</u> jeans on Saturday.

<u>future</u>   **28.** We <u>will order</u> pizza for everyone in the group.

<u>present</u>   **29.** Ms. Tapp <u>teaches</u> social studies and history.

<u>future</u>   **30.** Our new yard <u>will be</u> smaller than our old one.

<u>present</u>   **31.** Barry <u>listens</u> to classical music.

<u>past</u>   **32.** Pat <u>skated</u> around the sink.

<u>future</u>   **33.** I <u>will keep</u> the key in my backpack.

<u>present</u>   **34.** Ezra <u>washes</u> the dishes on Wednesday.

<u>future</u>   **35.** They <u>will hold</u> the first meeting in the library.

<u>past</u>   **36.** I <u>watched</u> *The Yearling* last year.

<u>present</u>   **37.** The museum <u>closes</u> early on Sunday.

<u>past</u>   **38.** Rami <u>called</u> each person on the list.

<u>future</u>   **39.** Perry <u>will use</u> his sister's computer.

<u>past</u>   **40.** Together we <u>cleaned</u> the whole apartment in two hours.

Lesson 17
Main Verbs: Principal Parts

Verbs have four principal parts: the base form, the present participle, the past form, and the past participle. These principal parts are often combined with helping verbs to form verb phrases. The main verb is always the last verb in a verb phrase.

Base Form: I **learn** at least one new song every week.
Present Participle: I **am learning** how to play guitar. (The main verb, *learning*, is the last verb in the verb phrase.)
Past Form: I **learned** two songs last week.
Past Participle: I **have learned** fourteen songs so far. (The main verb, *learned,* is the last verb in the verb phrase.)

▶ **Exercise 1** Draw one line under the entire verb phrase. Draw two lines under the main verb.

Her uncle <u>was <u>bringing</u></u> the soft drinks.

1. Darnel <u>is <u>selling</u></u> me his skateboard.

2. Kelsa <u>has <u>donated</u></u> her old soccer ball.

3. Travis <u>is <u>playing</u></u> a tape for the class.

4. I <u>have <u>written</u></u> my grandmother several poems.

5. The jeweler <u>is <u>repairing</u></u> Allyson's necklace.

6. People <u>have <u>walked</u></u> in the flower bed.

7. Carin <u>was <u>learning</u></u> the history of ballet.

8. NASA <u>is <u>postponing</u></u> the shuttle mission.

9. Throughout history, people <u>have <u>valued</u></u> gold.

10. Troy <u>has <u>flown</u></u> in a 747.

11. We <u>were <u>hoping</u></u> for a first-place trophy.

12. Craig's grandmother <u>is <u>coming</u></u> to the game tonight.

13. The dictionary <u>is <u>sitting</u></u> on the windowsill.

14. Ms. Chang <u>had <u>opened</u></u> the door for the children.

15. The bus driver <u>was <u>waiting</u></u> for Kerwin.

▶ **Exercise 2** **Draw two lines under the main verb. Write** *past* **in the blank if it is a past participle. Write** *pres.* **if it is a present participle.**

**pres.** Mira's family is <u>camping</u> this summer.

**past** **1.** They have <u>planned</u> their trip carefully.

**past** **2.** Mira's mother has <u>selected</u> the destination.

**past** **3.** She has <u>decided</u> on an isolated island.

**pres.** **4.** Now everyone is <u>preparing</u> for the trip.

**past** **5.** Mira's brother has <u>formed</u> a list of supplies.

**pres.** **6.** He is <u>borrowing</u> as many items as he can.

**pres.** **7.** Mira is <u>reading</u> books and magazines about wilderness camping.

**past** **8.** She had <u>hoped</u> for a different sort of vacation.

**pres.** **9.** She was <u>dreaming</u> of a swimming pool and a new bathing suit.

**past** **10.** She had <u>imagined</u> air-conditioned restaurants and hotel rooms.

**pres.** **11.** Now she is <u>learning</u> about fishing bait and camp stoves.

**past** **12.** Mira had <u>wanted</u> to send postcards to her friends.

**past** **13.** Her mother has <u>reminded</u> her that there is no post office.

**pres.** **14.** Mira is <u>trying</u> hard to be positive.

**past** **15.** She has <u>decided</u> to make the best of this trip.

▶ **Writing Link** **Write a short paragraph about a trip you have taken. Use at least one present participle and one past participle. Circle the main verbs.**

_____

_____

_____

_____

_____

_____

_____

_____

Lesson 18
Helping Verbs

A **helping verb** is a verb that helps the main verb express an action or make a statement. Forms of the helping verb *be* are used with the present participle.

SINGULAR	**PLURAL**
I **am** memorizing my lines.	We **are** memorizing our lines.
You **are** memorizing your lines.	You **are** memorizing your lines.
She **is** memorizing her lines.	They **are** memorizing their lines.
I **was** memorizing my lines.	We **were** memorizing our lines.
You **were** memorizing your lines.	You **were** memorizing your lines.
He **was** memorizing his lines.	They **were** memorizing their lines.

Forms of the helping verb *have* are used with the past participle of a main verb.

SINGULAR	**PLURAL**
I **have** visited Florida.	We **have** visited Florida.
You **have** visited Florida.	You **have** visited Florida.
He **has** visited Florida.	They **have** visited Florida.
I **had** visited Florida.	We **had** visited Florida.
You **had** visited Florida.	You **had** visited Florida.
She **had** visited Florida.	They **had** visited Florida.

▶ **Exercise 1** **Underline the helping verb in each sentence.**

Lenore and her father <u>are</u> watching the basketball game.

1. Carol <u>has</u> helped her brother with his homework.

2. The three friends <u>were</u> pedaling uphill slowly.

3. Steven <u>had</u> started a new project.

4. Lee <u>is</u> steering the orange canoe.

5. Both girls <u>are</u> riding red bicycles.

6. Lisa <u>had</u> removed her helmet.

7. Andrew <u>was</u> sliding into home plate.

8. No one <u>had</u> practiced.

9. She <u>is</u> hoping to set a new record.

10. Carlos <u>was</u> wearing a blue jacket.

Grammar

11. Loren <u>had</u> tried to call three times.

12. He <u>has</u> waited all week for this moment.

13. Tova's father <u>is</u> watching from the car.

14. The three of them <u>were</u> meeting for pizza.

15. Nadim <u>has</u> trained the puppy to sit.

16. Each player <u>had</u> hit the tennis ball twice.

17. My mother <u>is</u> helping us with the new song.

18. Tom <u>had</u> cleaned all the windows before lunch.

19. We <u>have</u> seen this movie twice.

20. Anna <u>has</u> kept her opinion a secret.

▶ **Exercise 2** **Draw one line under the helping verb and two lines under the main verb in each sentence.**

My great-aunt Marta <u>is</u> <u>learning</u> about herbs.

1. She <u>has</u> <u>loved</u> cooking for many years.

2. She <u>has</u> <u>used</u> herbs in her recipes.

3. She <u>has</u> <u>grown</u> parsley and chives on windowsills.

4. Now she <u>is</u> <u>starting</u> an herb garden.

5. Her garden <u>is</u> <u>expanding</u> slowly.

6. Every spring, she <u>has</u> <u>added</u> two or three plants.

7. Marta's neighbor, Irene, <u>was</u> <u>teaching</u> her what to plant where.

8. Irene <u>has</u> <u>shared</u> many plants from her own garden.

9. Now Marta <u>has</u> <u>planted</u> a dozen or so different herbs.

10. Mint <u>has</u> <u>appeared</u> near the water faucet.

11. Garlic <u>is</u> <u>growing</u> by the fence.

12. Marta <u>had</u> <u>arranged</u> her garden by color.

13. Violet flowers <u>are</u> <u>blooming</u> right now.

14. Bees <u>are</u> <u>hovering</u> over the chives.

15. Lavender <u>is</u> <u>filling</u> the air with a sweet scent.

Grammar

Lesson 19
Verb Forms: Present Progressive and Past Progressive

Verbs in the progressive form describe action that continues. The **present progressive** form of a verb describes an action that is continuing at the present time. The present progressive form consists of a helping verb (*am*, *are*, or *is*) plus the present participle of the main verb.

SINGULAR	PLURAL
I **am laughing**.	We **are laughing**.
You **are laughing**.	You **are laughing**.
She, he, or it **is laughing**.	They **are laughing**.

The **past progressive** form of a verb describes an action that was continuing at an earlier time. The past progressive form consists of a helping verb (*was* or *were*) plus the present participle of the main verb.

SINGULAR	PLURAL
I **was laughing**.	We **were laughing**.
You **were laughing**.	You **were laughing**.
She, he, or it **was laughing**.	They **were laughing**.

Notice that verbs in the progressive form always end in *-ing*.

▶ **Exercise 1** **Fill in the blank with the progressive form of the verb in parentheses. Change present tense verbs to the present progressive form and past tense verbs to the past progressive form.**

Mr. Ling's class ___is studying___ mammals. (studies)

1. The students ___were watching___ a video about opossums. (watched)

2. Now they ___are looking___ up facts about other animals. (look)

3. Jacob ___is listening___ to a recording of whale sounds. (listens)

4. Mr. Ling ___is requiring___ everyone to give a report. (requires)

5. Tamara ___is planning___ to talk about horses. (plans)

6. She ___is visiting___ a stable to do research. (visits)

7. The entire class ___was working___ at the library today. (worked)

8. The librarian ___is helping___ Charlie find information. (helps)

9. Ved ___is showing___ Molly where the books about mammals are. (shows)

10. Molly _____was hoping_____ to read about Labrador retrievers. (hoped)

11. Jacob's parents _____are studying_____ veterinary medicine. (study)

12. They _____are coming_____ to talk to the class on Thursday. (come)

13. Mr. Ling _____was planning_____ to bring his rabbit on Friday. (planned)

14. Thursday night, he _____was changing_____ his plans, however. (changed)

15. The rabbit _____was having_____ babies. (had)

16. Mr. Ling _____is postponing_____ the visit until next week. (postpones)

17. The class _____is adopting_____ a guinea pig named Greta. (adopts)

18. Molly's cousin Derek _____was donating_____ it. (donated)

19. Derek _____is moving_____ to England next month. (moves)

20. Everyone _____is helping_____ to prepare Greta's new home. (helps)

▶ **Exercise 2** Draw two lines under the verb phrase. Write *pres. prog.* in the blank if the verb is in the present progressive form. Write *past prog.* if the verb is in the past progressive form.

_____pres. prog._____ Peter's swimming skills are improving.

_____pres. prog._____ **1.** Raul is listening to the game on the radio.

_____past prog._____ **2.** My mother was driving home in the storm.

_____past prog._____ **3.** The boys were waiting forty-five minutes.

_____pres. prog._____ **4.** I am reading a book about Houdini.

_____past prog._____ **5.** Tim was watching a cardinal.

_____past prog._____ **6.** The dishwasher was leaking all over the kitchen floor.

_____pres. prog._____ **7.** The Ecology Club is meeting on Tuesday.

_____pres. prog._____ **8.** She is eating dinner with us.

_____past prog._____ **9.** My bike tire was losing air.

_____pres. prog._____ **10.** You are looking at an aerial view.

_____past prog._____ **11.** The newspaper was blowing away.

_____past prog._____ **12.** The teachers were planning a field trip.

Lesson 20
Perfect Tenses: Present and Past

The **present perfect tense** of a verb is used to describe an action that happened at an indefinite time in the past. It is also used to describe something that happened in the past and is still going on. The present perfect tense is formed by combining the helping verb *have* or *has* with the past participle of the main verb.

Ms. Taylor **has recycled** glass jars for years.

The **past perfect tense** of a verb describes an action that happened before another action or event in the past. The past perfect tense is formed by combining the helping verb *had* with the past participle of the main verb.

Until she started collecting cans, Marella **had recycled** only newspapers.

▶ **Exercise 1 Complete each sentence by changing the verb in parentheses to the tense indicated.**

Darrell's family _____traveled_____ to Washington, D.C., last summer. (past/*travel*)

1. They _____stayed_____ with his aunt in nearby Virginia. (past/*stay*)

2. Darrell and his father _____had visited_____ some attractions on previous trips. (past perfect/*visit*)

3. His stepsister Emily _____had wanted_____ to see the Air and Space Museum. (past perfect/*want*)

4. Darrell _____has visited_____ the Air and Space Museum twice. (present perfect/*visit*)

5. Space travel _____fascinates_____ Darrell's father. (present/*fascinate*)

6. He _____agreed_____ to visit the museum with Emily. (past/*agree*)

7. Darrell and his stepmother _____had decided_____ earlier to visit monuments. (past perfect/*decide*)

8. They _____had planned_____ to see the Washington Monument first. (past perfect/*plan*)

9. Both of them _____have wanted_____ to ride the elevator to the top. (present perfect/*want*)

10. Before they even reached the monument, rain _____had started_____ to fall. (past perfect/*start*)

11. The rain _____lasted_____ for only a few minutes, however. (past/*last*)

12. The sun reappeared before the two _____had purchased_____ their tickets. (past perfect/*purchase*)

13. They _____had believed_____ they would be able to see a great distance from the top, but the fog was too dense. (past perfect/*believe*)

14. By the time they _____had walked_____ down all 898 steps, both of them needed a rest. (past perfect/*walk*)

15. When Darrell is sightseeing, he always _____carries_____ a bottle of drinking water in his backpack. (present/*carry*)

16. That day, his stepmother _____had packed_____ a drink too. (past perfect/*pack*)

17. They _____looked_____ for a shady spot. (past/*look*)

18. After their rest, Darrell's stepmother _____had wanted_____ to visit the Vietnam Veterans Memorial. (past perfect/*want*)

19. He _____looked_____ at his watch. (past/*look*)

20. Darrell _____prefers_____ walking if there is enough time. (present/*prefer*)

21. They _____had planned_____ to meet the others for lunch. (past perfect/*plan*)

22. Darrell _____believed_____ they had plenty of time. (past/*believe*)

23. That morning, he _____had asked_____ his father for directions. (past perfect/*ask*)

24. They _____had determined_____ that the Vietnam Veterans Memorial was not far from the Washington Monument. (past perfect/*determine*)

25. Darrell _____has studied_____ the Vietnam War in school. (present perfect/*study*)

26. Families of veterans _____wanted_____ a monument to honor Americans lost in the war. (past/*want*)

27. Darrell _____has read_____ a book about the sculptor who designed the memorial. (present perfect/*read*)

28. Maya Lin _____had entered_____ her design in a national competition. (past perfect/*enter*)

Grammar

Lesson 21
Irregular Verbs I

Verbs that do not form their past and past participle by adding the ending -ed are called irregular verbs. With some irregular verbs, one vowel changes in the past form and past participle.

BASE FORM	PAST FORM	PAST PARTICIPLE
begin	began	begun
drink	drank	drunk
sing	sang	sung
swim	swam	swum

With other irregular verbs, the past form and the past participle are the same.

BASE FORM	PAST FORM	PAST PARTICIPLE
bring	brought	brought
buy	bought	bought
catch	caught	caught
feel	felt	felt
lay	laid	laid
leave	left	left
make	made	made
sit	sat	sat
sleep	slept	slept
teach	taught	taught
think	thought	thought

▶ **Exercise 1 Write in the blank the past form of the verb in parentheses.**

After school, Lisa ___left___ her books in the library. (leave)

1. Jack ___slept___ in the green tent. (sleep)

2. Martin ___won___ the essay contest. (win)

3. She ___taught___ me how to do a cartwheel. (teach)

4. Each cast member ___made___ a costume. (make)

5. We ___swam___ the length of the pool twice. (swim)

6. The telephone ___rang___ while I was in the shower. (ring)

7. Thomas ___sold___ his old skateboard. (sell)

8. After ten minutes, we ___caught___ up. (catch)

Grammar

9. Paul _____ lost _____ his watch somewhere at school. (lose)

10. Carla _____ felt _____ ready for the math test. (feel)

11. José _____ paid _____ for two tickets. (pay)

12. My mother _____ lent _____ me two dollars. (lend)

13. She _____ kept _____ her rock collection on the top shelf. (keep)

14. Carl _____ brought _____ the yellow poster board. (bring)

15. Tara _____ bought _____ one book for each child. (buy)

16. The demonstration _____ began _____ at precisely two o'clock. (begin)

▶ **Exercise 2** **Write in the blank the past participle of the verb in parentheses.**

Enzo's team has _____ won _____ three games. (win)

1. My mother has _____ swum _____ across the lake several times. (swim)

2. I have _____ shrunk _____ my favorite sweater. (shrink)

3. Carmela has _____ taught _____ me a new song. (teach)

4. This phone hasn't _____ rung _____ at all today. (ring)

5. I had _____ thought _____ it would be sunny on Saturday. (think)

6. Andrew has _____ lost _____ three umbrellas this year. (lose)

7. She had _____ felt _____ it was the best choice. (feel)

8. Kim's father has _____ caught _____ a bigger trout. (catch)

9. Gina had _____ laid _____ her clean clothes in the suitcase. (lay)

10. Zoe has _____ made _____ sure that someone will be home. (make)

11. She believed the dog had _____ slept _____ all day. (sleep)

12. A new baseball season has _____ begun _____. (begin)

13. Nathan has _____ sat _____ in the back seat all day. (sit)

14. Courtney's grandmother had _____ kept _____ all of her artwork. (keep)

15. The screen door has _____ swung _____ open three times today. (swing)

16. Jan has _____ brought _____ us some delicious oatmeal raisin cookies. (bring)

Grammar

Lesson 22
Irregular Verbs II

With some irregular verbs, the past form ends in *-ew,* and the past participle ends in *-wn.*

BASE FORM	PAST FORM	PAST PARTICIPLE
blow	blew	blown
draw	drew	drawn
fly	flew	flown
grow	grew	grown
know	knew	known

With other irregular verbs, the base form, past form, and past participle are all the same.

BASE FORM	PAST FORM	PAST PARTICIPLE
cut	cut	cut
let	let	let

With others, the past form and the past participle do not follow any pattern.

BASE FORM	PAST FORM	PAST PARTICIPLE
be	was, were	been
do	did	done
go	went	gone
wear	wore	worn

▶ **Exercise 1 Write in the blank the past form of the irregular verb in parentheses.**

Ms. Chandra's class _____grew_____ tomatoes. (grow)

1. Aunt Karin _____cut_____ my hair last night. (cut)

2. The wind _____blew_____ down four trees. (blow)

3. She _____wore_____ her hair in a braid. (wear)

4. My mother _____let_____ me spend the night at Sandra's house. (let)

5. Miriam _____knew_____ all the answers. (know)

6. Tom _____tore_____ up lettuce for the salad. (tear)

7. Damon _____was_____ the first to eat all the berries he picked. (be)

8. My brother _____grew_____ five inches last year. (grow)

9. I _____cut_____ out only recent photos. (cut)

Grammar

10. She _____let_____ me borrow her necklace. (let)

11. All three of us _____went_____ to the same doctor. (go)

12. Kareem's mother _____flew_____ to Los Angeles on business. (fly)

13. His baby sister _____tore_____ a page out of the book. (tear)

14. Melinda _____wore_____ my green dress to the wedding. (wear)

15. I _____knew_____ the name of the main character. (know)

16. Ms. Pritchard _____blew_____ up a balloon for the experiment. (blow)

17. Keith _____went_____ swimming on Saturday. (go)

18. He _____did_____ the same problem twice. (do)

19. Mikki _____wore_____ a wool sweater over her blouse. (wear)

20. He _____cut_____ his finger making lunch. (cut)

▶ **Exercise 2** **Underline the word in parentheses that best completes each sentence.**

Charlie has (drew, <u>drawn</u>) a line down the middle of the driveway.

1. We have (blew, <u>blown</u>) out the candles.

2. I wish I had (did, <u>done</u>) that last year.

3. We (<u>knew</u>, known) most of the answers.

4. She has (drew, <u>drawn</u>) a name out of the hat.

5. David (<u>wore</u>, worn) his favorite sweatshirt twice this week.

6. Jim has (wore, <u>worn</u>) his new boots before.

7. Kelly has (tore, <u>torn</u>) open all her presents.

8. Katie had (drew, <u>drawn</u>) two other pictures.

9. She (<u>did</u>, done) a spectacular job.

10. Our class has (went, <u>gone</u>) to the art museum before.

11. She has (knew, <u>known</u>) my parents for a long time.

12. He had (threw, <u>thrown</u>) the boomerang across the park.

13. My father had (went, <u>gone</u>) grocery shopping on Thursday.

14. This plant has (grew, <u>grown</u>) an inch since yesterday.

Lesson 23
Irregular Verbs III

With some irregular verbs, the base form and the past participle are the same.

BASE FORM	PAST FORM	PAST PARTICIPLE
become	became	become
come	came	come
run	ran	run

With other irregular verbs, the past participle ends in *-en*.

BASE FORM	PAST FORM	PAST PARTICIPLE
bite	bit	bitten or bit
break	broke	broken
choose	chose	chosen
drive	drove	driven
eat	ate	eaten
fall	fell	fallen
give	gave	given
ride	rode	ridden
rise	rose	risen
see	saw	seen
speak	spoke	spoken
steal	stole	stolen
take	took	taken
write	wrote	written

▶ **Exercise 1 Write in the blank the past participle of the irregular verb in parentheses.**

With the snow melting, mud has ___**become**___ a problem. (become)

1. Wayne had ___**spoken**___ loud enough for everyone to hear. (speak)

2. We had ___**run**___ around the track twice. (run)

3. Ted had ___**come**___ home on the late bus. (come)

4. My uncle has ___**become**___ a vegetarian. (become)

5. My mother had ___**driven**___ most of the way. (drive)

6. Keisha has ___**seen**___ a deer in her yard. (see)

7. The temperature has ___**risen**___ this afternoon. (rise)

8. At camp, Diana had ___**ridden**___ a horse for the first time. (ride)

9. Someone has ____broken____ the popcorn popper. (break)

10. Michelle has ____spoken____ to Mr. Dietz about the science fair. (speak)

11. We have ____eaten____ all the potato salad. (eat)

12. Tom has ____chosen____ the music for the program. (choose)

13. Most of the leaves have ____fallen____ off my poinsettia. (fall)

14. Hannah has ____written____ a letter to her great-grandmother. (write)

15. Marc's new puppy has ____bit *or* bitten____ him twice. (bite)

16. We had ____given____ the server our order half an hour before the food arrived. (give)

▶ **Exercise 2 Complete each sentence by changing the verb in parentheses to the form indicated.**

Smoke ____rose____ from the chimney. (past/*rise*)

1. The kitten ____grew____ faster than I expected. (past/*grow*)

2. Three inches of rain have ____fallen____. (past participle/*fall*)

3. The whistle ____blew____ at noon and six o'clock. (past/*blow*)

4. We have ____chosen____ our classes for next semester. (past participle/*choose*)

5. Maria ____did____ more work than anyone else. (past/*do*)

6. She has ____done____ that every week. (past participle/*do*)

7. The geese ____flew____ away. (past/*fly*)

8. The Lightfoots have ____eaten____ dinner. (past participle/*eat*)

9. I ____came____ ten minutes early. (past/*come*)

10. Abraham has ____grown____ pumpkins to sell. (past participle/*grow*)

11. We have ____chosen____ a class president. (past participle/*choose*)

12. Phil ____saw____ a moon rock at the museum. (past/*see*)

13. The president ____threw____ out the first ball. (past/*throw*)

14. We have ____driven____ through two states today. (past participle/*drive*)

15. In art class, we ____drew____ pictures of dragons. (past/*draw*)

16. Perry and Daniel have ____become____ excellent athletes. (past participle/*become*)

Lesson 24
More Practice with Verb Forms

▶ **Exercise 1** Write *AV* in the blank if the verb is an action verb or *LV* if it is a linking verb. Above each italicized word write *DO* for direct object, *IO* for indirect object, *PN* for predicate noun, or *PA* for predicate adjective.

                                PN
__LV__   Balto was a sled *dog* in Alaska.

                    IO
__AV__   **1.** He brought *miners* food and tools.

                                DO
__AV__   **2.** In February 1925, he saved the *town* of Nome.

                         PN
__LV__   **3.** Nome was a remote frontier *town.*

                             PA
__LV__   **4.** Some people in Nome became very *sick.*

                     DO
__AV__   **5.** They caught a *disease* called diphtheria.

                    DO
__AV__   **6.** Nome had only one *doctor.*

                       DO
__AV__   **7.** The doctor needed special *medicine.*

                  PA
__LV__   **8.** The medicine was *scarce.*

                         IO
__AV__   **9.** A hospital 800 miles away sent the *doctor* some medicine by train.

                   PA
__LV__ **10.** The train soon became *stuck* in deep snow.

                   DO
__AV__ **11.** Dog sleds carried the *medicine* the rest of the way.

                DO
__AV__ **12.** Balto led *one* of those teams.

                   PA
__LV__ **13.** The February weather was *brutal.*

                 DO
__AV__ **14.** A blizzard blew *snow* in the sled dogs' eyes.

                   DO
__AV__ **15.** Deep snowdrifts blocked the *trail.*

                 DO
__AV__ **16.** The dogs crossed frozen *rivers.*

             PA   PA
__LV__ **17.** They grew very *tired* and *weak.*

                 DO
__AV__ **18.** Balto led his *team* for twenty continuous hours.

                 DO
__AV__ **19.** The sick people received the *medicine.*

              PN
__LV__ **20.** Balto was a *hero.*

Grammar

Name _____ Class _____ Date _____

▶ **Exercise 2** **Complete each sentence by changing the verb in parentheses to the form indicated.**

Newspapers everywhere _____printed_____ stories about Balto. (past/*print*)

1. People _____paid_____ tribute to Balto with parades. (past/*pay*)

2. Balto had _____caught_____ the attention of people around the world. (past participle/*catch*)

3. A statue of Balto still _____stands_____ in New York City's Central Park. (present/*stand*)

4. By 1927, however, many people had _____forgotten_____ about Balto. (past participle/*forget*)

5. A greedy man had _____put_____ Balto in a traveling show. (past participle/*put*)

6. Balto had _____grown_____ very thin and frail. (past participle/*grow*)

7. Some concerned people _____became_____ alarmed. (past/*become*)

8. The man _____sold_____ Balto to them for two thousand dollars. (past/*sell*)

9. Schoolchildren had _____collected_____ much of the money to save Balto. (past participle/*collect*)

10. Balto _____went_____ to Cleveland, Ohio. (past/*go*)

11. The people there _____gave_____ him another parade. (past/*give*)

12. The parade _____drew_____ fifteen thousand people. (past/*draw*)

13. Then the people _____took_____ Balto to a zoo. (past/*take*)

14. They had _____found_____ him a safe place to live. (past participle/*find*)

15. Balto _____lived_____ out his days at the zoo. (past/*live*)

16. Thousands of people _____saw_____ him there. (past/*see*)

17. The people _____took_____ good care of him. (past/*take*)

18. Balto _____grew_____ to be eleven years old. (past/*grow*)

19. Today Balto _____stands_____ in a museum. (present/*stand*)

20. Balto's story has _____taught_____ many people about bravery. (past participle/*teach*)

Unit 3 Review

▶ **Exercise 1** Draw two lines under each action verb. Circle each direct object. Write each indirect object in the blank. If there is no indirect object, write *none*.

___student___   Mr. Rosenblum gave each student a poetry (notebook).

___us___   1. Mareka read us an (article) about pesticides.

___none___   2. My mother marked the (appointment) on her calendar.

___Tory___   3. Mr. Kalish paid Tory three (dollars) for washing his car.

___sister___   4. Pat showed her sister the old silver (necklace).

___father___   5. Cora painted her father a (picture) of his dog.

___none___   6. The students wrote a weekly (newsletter).

___me___   7. My grandfather brought me an autographed (baseball).

___friends___   8. Carlos sent his friends two (postcards) each.

___family___   9. Elizabeth baked her family a special (dessert).

___none___   10. We measure the (plants) every morning.

___none___   11. Tannie's family visited two (museums) on Saturday.

___friend___   12. I made my friend a (bracelet) with turquoise beads.

___Mrs. Domingo___   13. We bring Mrs. Domingo library (books) every week.

___stranger___   14. I gave the stranger a suspicious (look).

___van___   15. My brother gave the van a (coat) of wax.

___grandmother___   16. Clyde brought his grandmother some (daffodils).

___none___   17. We always eat (pizza) on Saturday night.

___puppy___   18. I threw the puppy a tennis (ball).

Cumulative Review: Units 1–3

▶ **Exercise 1** Draw one line under each simple subject and two lines under each simple predicate.

Aunt Margie is cooking chicken parmigiana for dinner.

1. The cottage lies just beyond the river.

2. My necklace is made of gold and silver.

3. A new adventure movie opens at the local theater tonight.

4. Carlos and Tyler are learning the game of rugby.

5. The Fishers will vacation in Arizona this year.

6. Myra located Tanzania on a world map.

7. Some lemonade would taste wonderful right now.

8. Greta and her parents saw a production of *Sunday in the Park with George.*

9. Mark received a telescope for his birthday.

10. The wind blew Simone's kite into a tree.

11. Manuella wanted a view of the Caribbean Sea.

12. The farmer sold his best milk cow to a friend.

13. One coat in the store window was purple.

14. Cheryl is making a guest list for the party.

15. Everyone held his or her breath during the aerialist's daring jump.

16. The telephone company prints new directories every year.

17. Airplanes from Cleveland land three times each day.

18. These library shelves hold many books.

19. A pagoda is a type of tower with many levels.

20. Lenny is fishing for trout and bass.

21. Lydia plays silly songs on the piano.

22. Colorful leaves fall from every tree on the street.

▶ **Exercise 2** Write *prop.* above each proper noun (except possessives), *col.* above each collective noun, and *poss.* above each possessive noun.

   poss.   prop.
Abbey's jacket came from China.

        prop.   poss.
1. The Goldenrod Restaurant is featuring Sally's pot roast.

    col.   prop.
2. Our team voted to give Coach Howard a plaque.

   prop.   poss.
3. Mrs. Clark sent Tina's homework to her so that she wouldn't fall behind.

                   col.
4. The famous singer thrilled the crowd with her soulful singing.

  poss.   col.
5. Gillian's favorite game is chess, but our class prefers checkers.

  poss.   prop.
6. Damian's father has been appointed ambassador to Haiti.

     prop.   prop.
7. The Lincoln Memorial is located in Washington, D.C.

     col.   prop.
8. My church group took a tour of Jerusalem last spring.

   prop.   col.
9. Judge Lucas waited for the jury to reach a verdict.

      prop.   prop.
10. Turn left at Taylor Avenue and look for Monroe Middle School on the right.

   col.
11. The choir performed three selections at the festival.

   poss.
12. Dr. Callahan's first patient was early, so I did not have to wait long.

    col.
13. My entire family enjoys the game of croquet.

 prop.   prop.   prop.
14. Lorna and Meg have tickets to *Cats*.

   poss.
15. The airplane's seats were unusually comfortable.

    col.
16. The student body elected to have a holiday party.

                  poss.
17. We knew we were in trouble when the car's engine sputtered and stopped.

     prop.   prop.
18. The capital of California is Sacramento.

 poss.   prop.
19. Ivan's grandparents, who are from Russia, are coming for a visit.

      col.
20. The finance committee submitted its report to the president.

▶ **Exercise 3** Write the tense of each italicized verb in the blank: *pres.* (present), *past, pres. prog.* (present progressive), *past prog.* (past progressive), *pres. perf.* (present perfect), or *past perf.* (past perfect).

_____past_____ The story *involved* an opera singer and her ambition to become a star.

_____past_____ 1. My little sister *climbed* a tree and scraped her arm.

   past perf.   **2.** The teachers *had hoped* for perfect attendance.

   pres. prog.   **3.** Two women *are loading* the moving van.

   pres.   **4.** Dylan *wants* to name the kittens after planets.

   pres. prog.   **5.** Her uncle *is going* to drive us home from the game.

   pres. perf.   **6.** The preschoolers *have gone* on a field trip to the fire station.

   past prog.   **7.** Because the temperature was dropping, the rain *was freezing* on the sidewalks.

   pres. prog.   **8.** Jim's father *is attending* classes at the university.

   past perf.   **9.** Our pets *had waited* long enough to be fed.

   past prog.   **10.** Aunt Joan *was painting* her kitchen peach.

   past   **11.** Roberto *made* a birdfeeder for his mother's yard.

   past perf.   **12.** The movie *had begun* five minutes late.

   pres. perf.   **13.** Both girls *have sung* solos in previous concerts.

   pres. prog.   **14.** Kylee *is drinking* an entire bottle of juice.

   pres.   **15.** Not everyone who enters the contest *wins* a prize.

   pres. perf.   **16.** Josh *has paid* for his uniform already.

   past perf.   **17.** The phone *had rung* four times before I could get to it.

   past   **18.** Marta's directions *led* us to a dead-end street.

   pres. prog.   **19.** Aaron *is making* plans for the weekend.

   pres.   **20.** We *keep* the seedlings warm with lights.

   past   **21.** Kelly *caught* three fly balls in the first inning.

   past prog.   **22.** Mary *was sleeping* when the storm began.

Grammar

Unit 4: Pronouns

Lesson 25
Personal Pronouns

Grammar

A **pronoun** takes the place of a noun, a group of words acting as a noun, or another pronoun. A **personal pronoun** refers to a person or thing. A personal pronoun that is the subject of a sentence is a **subject pronoun**. Subject pronouns are *I, you, he, she, it, we, you,* and *they.* A personal pronoun that is the direct or indirect object of a verb is an **object pronoun**. Object pronouns are *me, you, him, her, it, us, you,* and *them.*

He has a paper route. (The subject pronoun *he* is the subject of the sentence.)

Paula asked **him** for help. (The object pronoun *him* is the object of the verb *asked.*)

▶ **Exercise 1 Circle each personal pronoun.**

(I) walk one mile to school every day.

1. Helen gave (him) a schedule of the club's meetings.

2. After swimming for hours, (he) was very tired.

3. Have (you) seen (them) lately?

4. Gary is not sure if (he) wants to go to the museum with (us.)

5. (We) taught (them) the new computer game.

6. (I) will happily call (you) tomorrow morning.

7. (They) waited excitedly for the parade to reach (them.)

8. When the power went out, (we) lit candles and played charades.

9. (He) watched the sun as (it) sank in a blaze of orange and red.

10. (We) nervously watched the big, brown dog approach (us.)

11. (She) enjoyed reading *The Secret Garden.*

12. (I) watched a show about the great grizzly bear.

13. The trained dog calmly guided (him) to the bus stop.

14. The eagle soared higher and higher until (it) disappeared behind a cloud.

15. After eating the cake, (I) told Mom that (I) really enjoyed (it).

▶ **Exercise 2** **Replace each italicized word or group of words with a personal pronoun. Write the pronoun above the words. Write *subj.* in the blank if the pronoun is a subject and *obj.* if it is an object.**

us
obj.   Mrs. Yoshida drove *Kay, Don, and me* to the movie.

She
subj.   **1.** *Consuela* fishes almost every weekend.

her
obj.   **2.** Dad asked *Mindy* to the game.

it
obj.   **3.** Give *the eraser* to Meagan so she can erase the chalkboard.

They
subj.   **4.** *Hiroshi and Ray* had been playing chess for hours.

It
subj.   **5.** *The sun* always rises in the east.

it
obj.   **6.** Did you taste *the kiwifruit*?

him
obj.   **7.** Kenji told *Jack* a funny joke.

She
subj.   **8.** *Cheryl* proudly opened a bank account with money earned from baby-sitting.

them
obj.   **9.** Mom took *Tom and Mitch* with her.

We
subj. **10.** *Sumi and I* sang the duet in perfect harmony.

she
subj. **11.** With great care, *Pam* chose a gift for her best friend.

He
subj. **12.** *The little boy* pushed the shopping cart for his grandmother.

They
subj. **13.** *The powerful horses* thundered across the prairie.

us
obj. **14.** Mrs. Cuevas quietly told *Janie and me* the sad news.

them
obj. **15.** Have you seen *Terry and Rachel*?

▶ **Writing Link** **Write a few sentences about a make-believe awards program you would give for your friends or family. Use at least four pronouns besides the pronoun *I*.**

_____

_____

_____

_____

_____

Grammar

Lesson 26
Using Pronouns Correctly

Use a subject pronoun as the subject of a sentence. Use an object pronoun as the object of a verb. Be sure to use a subject pronoun in a compound subject and an object pronoun in a compound object.

Jamal and I fly model planes. (compound subject)
Debra met **Jamal and me** in the park. (compound object)

In formal writing and speaking, always use a subject pronoun after a linking verb.

The last one in line was **he**.   Yes, this is **she**.

▶ **Exercise 1** **Underline the pronoun in parentheses that best completes each sentence.**

The baby-sitter and (I, me) watched the squirrels play in the yard.

1. Mom called (we, us) in for supper.

2. (He, Him) and Derek will get to school early.

3. Byron lent (I, me) this video.

4. Are (they, them) ever going to arrive?

5. Who is (he, him)?

6. Aunt Cara brought (she, her) for a visit.

7. Roger and (I, me) rode our new bikes.

8. (We, Us) were late for our appointment.

9. Please tell (I, me) the answer?

10. Uncle Clyde told my sisters and (I, me) a story.

11. We took out the eggs and boiled (they, them) in water.

12. My mom drove Eloise and (she, her) to the concert.

13. The rain really soaked (he, him).

14. No one asked (I, me) about it.

15. (They, Them) mow lawns during summer vacation.

16. Todd bought (they, them) sodas.

Grammar

17. Evelyn and (<u>she</u>, her) never run out of things to talk about.

18. Julie, Jennifer, and (<u>I</u>, me) made toys for the kindergarten class.

19. Scott and Carl helped (we, <u>us</u>).

20. (<u>They</u>, them) took Emily to the zoo last Saturday.

▶ **Exercise 2 Write _C_ in the blank if the pronoun in italics is correct. If it is incorrect, write the correct pronoun in the blank.**

__he__	Susan and *him* love that new album by the Trees.
__C__	**1.** Karen and *she* took the bus.
__I__	**2.** Bill and *me* saw the movie.
__C__	**3.** Ahmed called Carol and *me*.
__he__	**4.** Mom and *him* are in the room.
__she__	**5.** The best artist is *her*.
__I__	**6.** Marla and *me* saw the Renoir painting.
__C__	**7.** Sally wrote Ted and *me* letters from camp.
__I__	**8.** Wendy and *me* read about Chief Joseph.
__me__	**9.** Mom gave Akira and *I* a job for the afternoon.
__him__	**10.** Sharks interest Patti and *he*.
__C__	**11.** The tallest student is *he*.
__I__	**12.** Jim and *me* think that natural resources are important.
__C__	**13.** Darla and *we* agreed about the picnic.
__we__	**14.** Carl and *us* saw the ballet *Swan Lake*.
__them__	**15.** The coach showed Nat and *they* a few tricks.
__us__	**16.** Wayne invited *we* to the golf tournament.
__C__	**17.** Charlotte and *I* sang a duet at the festival.
__me__	**18.** Barbara bought Vicki and *I* souvenirs.
__him__	**19.** Linda gave *he* a pumpkin from her garden.
__he__	**20.** She and *him* fish in the pond behind their house.

Grammar

Lesson 27
Pronouns and Antecedents

The word or group of words that a pronoun refers to is its **antecedent**. The pronoun must agree with its antecedent in number and gender.

The **girl** in the blue dress is my sister. **She** is my sister. (*Girl* is the antecedent of the pronoun *she*).

The **students** wear gym clothes on Friday. **They** have gym for one hour. (*Students* is the antecedent of the pronoun *they*.)

▶ **Exercise 1** **Fill in the blank with the correct pronoun. Then circle the antecedent of the pronoun.**

The word (Renaissance) is a French word. ____It____ means *rebirth*.

1. The (Middle Ages) came before the Renaissance. ____They____ lasted from about A.D. 500 to A.D. 1500.

2. The (Renaissance) took place in Europe. ____It____ lasted from the fourteenth century to the sixteenth century.

3. (Achievements) in art and literature shaped the Renaissance. ____They____ made it a special time in history.

4. Modern (science) also began during the Renaissance. ____It____ traces its beginnings to this time period.

5. The (Renaissance) started in Europe. ____It____ began with the study of the ancient history of Italy.

6. Many great (thinkers) shaped the Renaissance. ____They____ held different opinions about many different things.

7. (Petrarch) headed the study of Italy's history. ____He____ was an Italian.

8. Gifted (artists) lived during this time. ____They____ were Raphael, Titian, Michelangelo, and Leonardo da Vinci.

9. People called "patrons" supported these (artists). They gave ____them____ money and other things to pay for their work.

10. The (Sistine Chapel) is in Rome. Michelangelo painted ____it____ .

11. Michelangelo painted the (ceiling) of the Sistine Chapel. He began painting ____it____

in 1508.

12. Pope Julius II gave (Michelangelo) the job of painting the chapel. Julius II supported

____him____ while he worked.

13. (Music) also flourished during the Renaissance. ____It____ developed a specific style.

14. Renaissance (buildings) were also unusual. Architects of today often imitate ____them____ .

▶ **Exercise 2** Write *C* in the blank if the italicized pronoun in the second sentence agrees
with its antecedent in the first sentence. Circle the antecedent. If it does not agree with its
antecedent, write the correct pronoun in the blank.

____C____ The (Mona Lisa) hangs in the Louvre in Paris. *It* is one of the best-known

paintings in the world.

____C____ **1.** (Leonardo da Vinci) painted the *Mona Lisa*. *He* is famous for achievements in

both art and science.

____he____ **2.** Born in 1452, (da Vinci) lived during a period of great artistic expression. Early

in his career *it* was an art apprentice.

____It____ **3.** Da Vinci met Michelangelo in (Florence), Italy. *He* was a city where many artists

lived.

____him____ **4.** Da Vinci and (Michelangelo) worked together. Da Vinci taught *her* how to show

movement in art.

____They____ **5.** Da Vinci painted the (Mona Lisa) and (The Last Supper). *It* are two of his most

famous paintings.

____C____ **6.** Da Vinci's (paintings) hang in many museums. People come from faraway

places to see *them*.

____C____ **7.** (Da Vinci) created breathtaking paintings, and *he* also crafted great sculptures.

____They____ **8.** Two (notebooks) written by da Vinci were found in 1965. *Them* revealed many

of da Vinci's plans and ideas.

Lesson 28
Possessive Pronouns

Possessive pronouns are another kind of personal pronoun. A possessive pronoun takes the place of a person or thing that owns or possesses something. It can come before the noun that is possessed or it can stand alone in a sentence.

Dan's father is a doctor. **His** father is a doctor. (*His* comes before the noun *father*.)

The lunch bag on the table belongs to Donna. The lunch bag on the table is **hers**. (*Hers* stands alone.)

USED BEFORE NOUNS
Singular: my, your, her, his, its
Plural: our, your, their

USED ALONE
mine, yours, hers, his, its
ours, yours, theirs

▶ **Exercise 1** **Circle each possessive pronoun. Write in the blank *SA* for "stands alone" or *BN* for "before a noun."**

_SA_   The yellow skateboard is (his)

_BN_   **1.** Mia left (her) notebook on the bus.

_SA_   **2.** Is this house key (mine)?

_SA_   **3.** The colorful picture of the flowers is (mine.)

_BN_   **4.** The proud parents brought home (their) new baby girl.

_BN_   **5.** Will strummed (his) guitar and invited everyone to sing.

_SA_   **6.** The red house on the corner is (ours.)

_BN_   **7.** The computer quickly stores information in (its) huge memory.

_BN_   **8.** These warm chocolate chip cookies melt in (your) mouth.

_BN_   **9.** The cheetah lay in the tall grass, planning (its) attack.

_BN_   **10.** (Her) hand shot up when the teacher asked for volunteers.

_SA_   **11.** I didn't get a cheeseburger, so I tasted (hers.)

_BN_   **12.** Is (your) seat belt always fastened?

_SA_   **13.** The fluffy, brown puppy is (theirs.)

_SA_   **14.** (Yours) is the third seat in the first row.

Grammar

_____**BN**_____ 15. (My) cousin from Nebraska is staying with us.

▶ **Exercise 2** Write the correct possessive pronoun above each italicized word or words.

 Her
 Karen's friend showed us her new game.

 its
1. The hungry dog pushed *the dog's* dish with its nose across the kitchen floor.
 its
2. The bird flapped *the bird's* long wings and flew away.
 her
3. Dave gladly carried *Shari's* backpack for her.
 her
4. Tonya grabbed my notebook by mistake, and I took *Tonya's* notebook.
 theirs
5. The clever idea was *Jim's and Akira's*.
 His
6. *Greg's* sister is graceful and smart.
 mine
7. Robert's style of skating is different from *my style of skating*.
 Her
8. *My aunt's* smile is full of love and warmth.
 its
9. The young chimpanzee spends many happy hours playing with *the young chimpanzee's*

 brothers and sisters.
 his
10. John dreams of flying high in the clouds in *John's* own plane one day.
 hers
11. Chloe claimed that the purse was *Chloe's*.
 theirs
12. The telescope is not mine. It is *Billy's, Tim's, and Jane's*.
 our
13. My family looked everywhere for *my family's* dog.
 his
14. The biggest fish caught that day was *Juan's*.
 mine
15. This yellow parka looks similar to *my parka*.

▶ **Writing Link** Write a few sentences describing your classroom and the things in it. Use as many possessive pronouns as possible.

_____

_____

_____

_____

_____

_____

Lesson 29
Indefinite Pronouns

An **indefinite pronoun** refers to a person, place, or thing in a more general way than a personal pronoun does. If the indefinite pronoun is singular, it takes a singular verb. If it is plural, it takes a plural verb. Some indefinite pronouns—*all, any, most, none,* and *some*—may take either a singular or a plural verb, depending on the context of the sentence.

Everybody knows the answer. **Many know** the answer.
Some of the pie **is** gone. **Some** of the neighbors **are** gone.

Singular Indefinite Pronouns: *another, anybody, anyone, anything, each, either, everybody, everyone, everything, much, neither, nobody, no one, nothing, one, somebody, someone, something*
Plural Indefinite Pronouns: *both, few, many, others, several*

▶ **Exercise 1** Underline the word in parentheses that best completes each sentence.

Everybody (<u>has</u>, have) a chance to win the contest.

1. Everyone (<u>likes</u>, like) the pizza in the cafeteria.

2. One of the answers (<u>is</u>, are) correct.

3. Everybody (<u>crowds</u>, crowd) around the stage.

4. (<u>Is</u>, Are) anyone allowed to borrow books from the library?

5. No one (<u>lives</u>, live) in the middle of the desert.

6. All of the frightened sheep (tries, <u>try</u>) to run away from the snarling wolf.

7. Most of the neighbors (was, <u>were</u>) enjoying the cool summer breeze.

8. Either of the songs (<u>seems</u>, seem) perfect for the party.

9. Both of the girls (plays, <u>play</u>) soccer well.

10. Several of the club members (meets, <u>meet</u>) in the library each week.

11. Both of the movies (was, <u>were</u>) good.

12. Neither of the boys (<u>is</u>, are) able to ski.

13. Nothing (<u>smells</u>, smell) as good as Aunt Velda's roast beef.

14. Much of the work (<u>was</u>, were) done by the time we joined the group.

Grammar

15. Each (<u>has</u>, have) its own water dish.

16. Few of the puppies (knows, <u>know</u>) how to fetch a ball.

17. (<u>Is</u>, Are) anything as good as a chocolate ice-cream cone on a hot day?

18. Everything (<u>was</u>, were) calm and quiet after the rainstorm.

19. No one (<u>calls</u>, call) after 11:00 P.M.

20. Anybody (<u>is</u>, are) welcome to write a poem for the contest.

21. Both (takes, <u>take</u>) dancing lessons.

22. The others (flies, <u>fly</u>) behind the lead goose.

23. (<u>Has</u>, Have) someone checked the answering machine for messages?

24. Each (<u>chirps</u>, chirp) happily when the mother returns to the nest.

25. Nobody (<u>has</u>, have) a better sense of humor than Jen.

26. Many (visits, <u>visit</u>) Mrs. Cruz in the hospital.

27. (Does, <u>Do</u>) any of the printers in the computer lab work?

28. (<u>Is</u>, Are) everyone allowed to go on the field trip tomorrow?

29. No one (<u>lives</u>, live) in the house next to ours.

30. All of us (tries, <u>try</u>) our best to get good grades.

31. Everyone (<u>watches</u>, watch) in awe as the space shuttle lifts off.

32. Many of the firefighters (is, <u>are</u>) willing to go into the burning building.

33. Much of the movie (<u>remains</u>, remain) to be watched.

34. Some of the stars (shines, <u>shine</u>) more brightly than others.

35. Several (has, <u>have</u>) tried to beat Amad at checkers, but few (has, <u>have</u>) succeeded.

36. Few (hits, <u>hit</u>) the ball over the ballpark fence.

37. Some of the popsicles (has, <u>have</u>) melted.

38. Most of the turkey (<u>was</u>, were) eaten.

39. Everybody in this choir (<u>sings</u>, sing) off-key.

40. Several of those teenagers (visits, <u>visit</u>) this nursing home.

Name _____ Class _____ Date _____

▶ **Exercise 1** **Fill in the blank with the pronoun that best completes each sentence.**

John F. Kennedy was the thirty-fifth president of the United States. _____**He**_____ was the youngest president ever elected.

1. Anthropology is the study of humans and _____**their**_____ beginnings, development, and cultures.

2. Mother told Ahmed to put away each toy in the place were _____**it**_____ belongs.

3. When the birds fluttered around the birdhouse, Jessie ran to feed _____**them**_____.

4. After Hannah and Roberto finished their homework, _____**they**_____ went to the movie.

5. Valerie ordered three books, but _____**she**_____ hasn't received them yet.

6. At the beach, I picked up a seashell that reminded _____**me**_____ of home.

7. Carla waved to her mother in the crowd as _____**she**_____ joined _____**her**_____ teammates on the court.

8. When my pencil broke, I asked the teacher if I could sharpen _____**it**_____.

9. When Kristen and I dug the garden, my mother gave _____**us**_____ seeds to plant.

10. The test questions were not as difficult as _____**they**_____ looked.

11. Sam was running late this morning, and _____**he**_____ missed his bus.

12. After searching for his wallet for an hour, Brian found _____**it**_____.

13. Ever since Kari had a bike accident, _____**she**_____ has worn a helmet.

14. I finished my math homework quickly because my sister helped _____**me**_____ figure out the hard problems.

15. Victor and I told mother that _____**we**_____ could clean the garage ourselves.

16. Our school uniforms are much more comfortable than _____**they**_____ used to be.

17. Miss Darnell asked the students if _____**they**_____ would mind helping Mr. Lenox.

18. Ariel and _____**I**_____ sometimes do our homework together.

19. As I was leaving, Mrs. Dillman gave _____**me**_____ a big hug.

20. "Is this Marsha?" asked the voice on the phone. "Yes," said Marsha, "this is _____**she**_____."

Grammar

Cumulative Review: Units 1–4

▶ **Exercise 1** Draw one line under each direct object and two lines under each verb. Write in the blank *tr.* if the verb is transitive or *int.* if it is intransitive.

__int.__ The schools closed because of the snowstorm.

__tr.__ 1. Renee bought a CD with her baby-sitting money.

__int.__ 2. My mother's plane arrived late.

__tr.__ 3. Fish have gills instead of lungs.

__tr.__ 4. Crowds of people attended the concert.

__int.__ 5. My grandfather's health improved slowly.

__int.__ 6. We sat on my porch for at least an hour.

__tr.__ 7. The Stevensons keep horses on their small farm.

__int.__ 8. Nigan and I walk to the practice field together.

__int.__ 9. The fireworks went off with a bang and a burst of color.

__tr.__ 10. Our neighbor rescued an injured bird.

__tr.__ 11. My sister and I play tennis with our dad.

__int.__ 12. Ariel writes to her pen pal every Saturday.

__tr.__ 13. The choir sang the song in perfect unison.

__tr.__ 14. Miguel corrected his mistakes before handing in his paper.

__int.__ 15. We jogged to school and back for our morning exercise.

▶ **Exercise 2** Write *pers.* for personal pronoun (subject or object), *poss.* for possessive, or *ind.* for indefinite above each pronoun.

   ind.
Someone spilled juice on the table.

  pers.   poss.
1. Tell them about your favorite book.

        pers.   poss.
2. When the travelers arrived, they were weary from their journey.

pers.   poss.
3. She will present her report to the class.

      poss.
4. Is this flute yours?

  ind.
5. No one thinks the quiz will be today.

                                                    poss.
6. The spelling bee participants carefully studied their long word lists.
        ind.
7. Somebody forgot to turn off the light.
                                    pers.
8. Although the girl is often sick, she is always cheerful.
                                        poss.
9. Allison said the idea for the project was hers.
        ind.
10. Is anyone responsible for taking attendance today?
                poss.
11. Rayna pulled her desk closer to Judy's.
    ind.   poss.
12. Few knew of her change in plans.
        poss.   poss.
13. For their birthday, Sabra gave her twin daughters matching sweaters.
    pers.   pers.   ind.   poss.   poss.
14. We will tell you several of our objections to their program.
        ind.   pers.   pers.
15. Neither of us had heard of him before.

▶ **Exercise 3 Draw a line under the simple subject of the sentence. Draw two lines under the simple predicate.**

She called me at six o'clock this morning.

1. In three giant leaps, the cat crossed the busy highway.

2. I read that story, too!

3. Emily sang in the chorus.

4. The bicycle chain rattled against the wheel.

5. The buses chugged noisily through the school parking lot.

6. Sally and he told us that silly joke again.

7. Henry painted a watercolor portrait of Camilla.

8. They laughed through the entire play.

9. This old movie makes my sister cry.

10. Have Ali and you written the postcards yet?

11. We laughed at the clowns.

12. The homework is still not done.

13. Will it never rain?

14. Kevin and the varsity team played really hard.

15. <u>Can</u> <u>you</u> <u>find</u> Lake Erie on the map?

▶ **Exercise 4** **Write the correct possessive pronouns above the words in italics.**

His

Dad's car is new.

Her
1. *Mary's* foul shot won the game.

Its
2. *The tree's* color is a beautiful red-gold.

His
3. *Ted's* book is missing.

Our
4. *Bill's and my* bikes both need new tires.

Their
5. *Monica and Alina's* project is finished.

your
6. Renee, is this *Renee's* notebook?

her
7. This ring looks like *Cathy's* ring.

His
8. *George Washington's* military skill and daring helped win America's independence from Britain.

our
9. Priscilla, where are *your and my* new jackets?

yours
10. Trina, is this magazine *Trina's*?

Her
11. *Queen Victoria's* long reign is known as the Victorian Age.

theirs
12. Are these concert tickets *Patti's and Carla's*?

ours
13. Those tennis rackets are *Terri's and mine*!

yours
14. Ricardo and Larry, I'm pretty sure these baseball cards are *Ricardo's and Larry's*.

His
15. *Baron Karl Friedrich Hieronymus von Münchhausen's* wild stories are unbelievable but very funny.

their
16. Unfortunately, *the books'* covers were torn during the move.

Her
17. *Tricia's* new home is in a lovely small town.

its
18. *The drama club's* members were excited about the spring play.

theirs
19. This telescope is *Pedro's and Jeff's*.

his
20. I love this spaghetti; may I eat *my brother's*?

Unit 5: Adjectives

Lesson 30
Adjectives and Proper Adjectives

A word that describes persons, places, or things is an adjective. An adjective usually answers one of three questions about the noun or pronoun it modifies.

What kind?	Please use the **drawing** paper.
How many?	Wanda had **three** sisters.
Which one?	**That** seat is taken.

Usually the adjective comes just before the noun it modifies. However, when the noun is the subject followed by a linking verb, its adjective follows the linking verb as part of the predicate. These adjectives are called predicate adjectives.

The puppy became **frisky.**

A proper adjective is an adjective formed from a proper noun. Sometimes the proper adjective is the same word as the noun that forms it. At other times it has a special ending. All proper adjectives begin with a capital letter.

the **Wyoming** foothills   **Chinese** checkers

▶ **Exercise 1 Draw an arrow from each adjective in italics to the noun or pronoun it modifies.**

The *first* robots were built in the Middle Ages.

1. Some *early* robots can still be seen today.

2. In Venice, Italy, two *human-sized* robots dressed in *medieval* clothing strike the clock tower bell every hour.

3. In Germany, figures dance and play *musical* instruments under a *church* clock.

4. Although their movements are *simple,* they are entertaining.

5. These robots get their power from *clock* parts.

6. Today robots work on land, in *outer* space, or on the *ocean* floor.

7. *Japanese* scientists are creating a *crablike* robot to work underwater.

8. This robot can take a *great* deal of *underwater* pressure.

9. The abilities of this robot are *awesome.*

10. Robots are *important* to *space* exploration.

11. *American* spacecraft landed robots on Mars in 1977.

12. These robots tested *Martian* soil and atmosphere.

13. The Soviet Union used robots in 1978 to take the *first* pictures of the surface of Venus.

14. The pictures showed *rust-colored* rocks and an *orange* sky.

15. The pictures were truly *breathtaking.*

▶ **Exercise 2 Underline each adjective.**

Robots with <u>human</u> shape are called "androids" or "humanoids."

1. <u>Many</u> androids or humanoids are run by <u>remote</u> control.

2. <u>True</u> robots run on <u>computer</u> power.

3. <u>Some</u> robots perform <u>household</u> chores.

4. However, <u>household</u> robots are <u>rare.</u>

5. <u>Household</u> robots are also <u>expensive.</u>

6. <u>Household</u> robots could easily cost as much as <u>new</u> houses.

7. <u>Future</u> robots will answer doorbells, clear the <u>dinner</u> table, and keep the <u>kitchen</u> cupboard full.

8. <u>Industrial</u> robots are already quite <u>common.</u>

9. In <u>automobile</u> factories, robots paint cars.

10. On <u>assembly</u> lines, robots are run by computers.

11. <u>Large</u> companies often use <u>these</u> robots to deliver mail.

12. <u>Industrial</u> robots are usually <u>strong.</u>

13. They can use <u>various</u> tools.

14. In <u>one</u> Japanese factory, robots are building <u>other</u> robots.

15. <u>One</u> advantage of robots is that they never become <u>tired.</u>

Lesson 31
Articles and Demonstratives

An **article** is a special kind of adjective. There are three articles, the words *a, an,* and *the. The* describes one specific item or items.

The program was canceled because of **the** snowstorm.

A and *an* refer to any one item of a group. Use *a* before words that begin with a consonant sound. Use *an* before words that begin with a vowel sound.

A giraffe is **an** elegant animal.

Demonstrative adjectives are used to point out something. The words *this, that, these,* and *those* are demonstrative adjectives. *This* and *that* are singular. *These* and *those* are plural. *This* and *these* refer to things that are close. *That* and *those* refer to things that are at a distance.

Read **this** book.   He washed **these** apples. (close to the speaker)
Take **that** train.   **Those** boys are on the other team. (at a distance from the speaker)

Demonstratives often appear before the nouns they modify, but they can stand alone. When a demonstrative is used by itself, it is a **demonstrative pronoun**.

Give **this** to your sister. I like **those** the best.

▶ **Exercise 1** Write in the blank the article that best completes each sentence.

Do you have _____ a _____ ticket for _____ the _____ class play?

1. _____ The _____ moon is really bright tonight.

2. It is helpful to have _____ a _____ calculator.

3. My dad keeps maps in _____ the _____ car glove compartment.

4. _____ The _____ field hockey team has a match after school.

5. Sara hopes to get _____ a _____ bicycle for her birthday.

6. My father thinks ordering pizza is _____ an _____ excellent idea.

7. I read my little sister a story about _____ a _____ unicorn.

8. _____ An _____ index of street names appears on most maps.

9. I will be attending _____ a *or* the _____ school on Maple Street.

10. My mom wants to buy _____a_____ sports car.

11. Please put your backpack on _____the_____ kitchen table.

12. The Metropolitan Museum of Art is _____a_____ huge museum.

13. _____The_____ closest parks are across town.

14. Jeff went shopping for _____a_____ baseball mitt.

15. Many of my friends have _____an_____ interest in astronomy.

▶ **Exercise 2 Draw a line under the demonstrative in parentheses that best completes each sentence. Write *P* in the blank if it is a pronoun or *A* if it is an adjective.**

___P___ (That, These) is the biggest pumpkin I've ever seen!

___A___ **1.** (This, Those) baby's skin is as smooth as silk.

___A___ **2.** Miriam told (those, that) same joke yesterday.

___A___ **3.** (Those, That) elephants are sleeping in the shade of the tree.

___P___ **4.** (This, These) takes two solid hours to complete.

___P___ **5.** Is (those, this) your favorite song?

___A___ **6.** (That, Those) icicles look like long, jagged teeth.

___P___ **7.** (This, Those) is the worst I have seen!

___A___ **8.** (This, These) ants are busy at work.

___P___ **9.** (That, These) are the best days of our lives.

___A___ **10.** I have climbed (those, that) tree a hundred times.

___A___ **11.** The pilot calmly steered us through (that, these) big cloud.

___P___ **12.** (This, Those) makes a high, piercing noise.

___A___ **13.** Her eyes shining, the little girl pointed to (those, that) piece of candy.

___P___ **14.** May I buy five of (that, those), please?

___A___ **15.** (Those, That) students want to transfer to our school.

___P___ **16.** (Those, That) sounds like an interesting movie.

___P___ **17.** (This, These) is what we bought for Dad.

___P___ **18.** Liam, take (this, these) and put it over there.

Grammar

Lesson 32
Adjectives That Compare

Some kinds of adjectives compare two or more nouns or pronouns.

The comparative form of an adjective compares two things or people. It is usually formed by adding -er to an adjective that has only one syllable. If an adjective has more than one syllable, the comparative is usually formed by adding the word *more* before the adjective.

Pedro is **older** than his brother Carlos.
The long coat is **more expensive** than the short one.

The superlative form of an adjective compares more than two people or things. It is usually formed by adding -est to an adjective that has only one syllable. If the adjective has more than one syllable, the superlative is usually formed by adding *most* before the adjective.

Pedro is the **oldest** of the three Castino children.
The long coat is the **most expensive** of all the coats.

▶ **Exercise 1** **Underline the adjective in parentheses that best completes each sentence.**

Brian is (taller, tallest) than his brother.

1. The park by the ocean is the (peacefulest, most peaceful) place I have ever been.

2. Jimmy Carter is a (more recent, recentest) president than John F. Kennedy.

3. Granite is the (most hard, hardest) rock nature makes.

4. Mt. Shasta is the (higher, highest) mountain I have ever seen.

5. An airplane moves at (greater, more great) speed than a car.

6. The (most big, biggest) problem we have is reading the German book.

7. My brother thinks New York is the (most exciting, excitingest) city in the world.

8. Joseph was (later, more late) than Juan.

9. The English test was (more difficult, difficultest) than the math test.

10. Yellow is the (most light, lightest) color on Brenda's painting.

11. We had the (thrillingest, most thrilling) time at the amusement park!

12. Apples have (most smooth, smoother) skin than cantaloupes.

13. The bananas were the (more ripe, <u>ripest</u>) fruit in the store.

14. The (most short, <u>shortest</u>) path is the one through the parking lot.

15. The newspaper is (<u>more current</u>, currenter) than the magazine.

▶ **Exercise 2** **Write in the blank the correct form of the adjective in parentheses.**

A sweater was the _____warmest_____ thing she had to wear. (warm)

1. I think this is the _____nicest_____ shirt I own. (nice)

2. Of all the ideas, Emily's was the _____most likely_____ to happen. (likely)

3. Gasoline is _____more explosive_____ than water. (explosive)

4. Mount Everest is the _____highest_____ mountain in the world. (high)

5. The salad bar lettuce seems _____fresher_____ today than yesterday. (fresh)

6. This is the _____greenest_____ forest I have ever seen! (green)

7. The flowers outside are much _____more fragrant_____ than the ones in the vase. (fragrant)

8. We walked barefoot through the _____thickest_____ grass imaginable. (thick)

9. The kitten was _____more adorable_____ than I remember. (adorable)

10. The shortstop has the _____strongest_____ arm on the team. (strong)

11. This song is far _____more popular_____ than the one they just played. (popular)

12. The cushion was _____older_____ than the chair. (old)

13. I think the lamb is the _____gentlest_____ of our farm animals. (gentle)

14. Spider webs are among the _____most delicate_____ things in nature. (delicate)

15. This grammar test is the _____hardest_____ one so far. (hard)

▶ **Writing Link** **Write three sentences about your favorite story. Use adjectives to compare it with others you have read.**

_____

_____

_____

_____

Lesson 33
Special Adjectives That Compare

The comparative and superlative forms of some adjectives are not formed in the regular way. Never add *more* or *most* before these adjectives.

ADJECTIVE	COMPARATIVE	SUPERLATIVE
good	better	best
bad	worse	worst
much, many	more	most
little (amount)	less	least

▶ **Exercise 1 Write in the blank the correct form of the adjective in parentheses.**

There is _____less_____ corn than spinach in the pantry. (little)

1. My cold is _____worse_____ today than it was yesterday. (bad)

2. Many old books are very _____good_____. (good)

3. Felicia had _____less_____ money in her pocket than she thought. (little)

4. Nelson did the _____least_____ amount of work possible. (little)

5. A computer costs far _____more_____ money than a typewriter. (much)

6. Baking bread has the _____best_____ smell in the world. (good)

7. That movie was the _____better_____ one of the two. (good)

8. That was the _____worst_____ team we played all year. (bad)

9. The score was far _____worse_____ than the last time we lost. (bad)

10. There is _____little_____ help we can give her. (little)

11. The creamy chocolate pie is _____better_____ than the apple pie. (good)

12. All the apples in that bag were _____bad_____. (bad)

13. _____More_____ glazed doughnuts were left than plain doughnuts. (many)

14. While _____most_____ students preferred spring, a few preferred summer. (many)

15. Is it _____better_____ to coach softball than to play it? (good)

16. Our team has _____better_____ players than theirs. (good)

17. Not ____much____ paint is left. (much)

18. Shana likes ____most____ movies she sees. (much)

19. We have had ____less____ snow than usual. (little)

20. The museum had ____more____ paintings by French artists than by German artists. (many)

21. The potato soup is very ____good____. (good)

22. I am ____better____ at skiing than at football. (good)

23. Our team had the ____least____ number of players of any team in the tournament. (little)

24. Today's weather was ____worse____ than yesterday's. (bad)

25. The magician's act was ____better____ than the comedian's. (good)

26. There are ____more____ trees in Blendon Woods than in Houston Woods. (much)

27. We waited a ____little____ while and then went home. (little)

28. Which of the three plans will cause the ____least____ trouble? (little)

29. After the bike was painted, it looked ____better____ than ever. (good)

30. That was the ____worst____ movie I had ever seen. (bad)

▶ **Writing Link** **Write a short paragraph that describes your neighborhood or a favorite place. Include comparative and superlative forms of the adjectives *good*, *bad*, *much*, and *little*.**

_____

_____

_____

_____

_____

_____

_____

_____

_____

✓ Unit 5 **Review**

▶ **Exercise 1** **Draw one line under each article and two lines under each comparative or superlative adjective. Circle all other adjectives.**

(That) mouse scooted across the most slippery part of the floor.

1. The (Victorian) house is closer than the (modern) house.

2. The Constitution guarantees (free) speech.

3. There was a (dark) spot on the carpet.

4. The (little) dog barked at the (letter) carrier.

5. More people attended the concert (this) year than (last) year.

6. Here is the ripest pear I could find.

7. The slowest way to get there is by boat.

8. Thanksgiving is the busiest time of year for airports.

9. In the spring, (red) roses grow in the park.

10. In 1994 we had the worst winter in (five) years.

11. The (heavy) box held a (new) (sewing) machine.

12. Please pass (those) (delicious) chocolates.

13. Aleta was the earliest arrival.

14. The (old) (oak) tree was taller than the house.

15. Rashad thinks (Chinese) food is better than (Mexican) food.

16. (This) bucket is (full) of (soapy) water.

Grammar

Cumulative Review: Units 1–5

▶ **Exercise 1** **Draw one line under each simple subject. Draw two lines under each simple predicate.**

The <u>clown</u> <u><u>brought</u></u> a pony to the birthday party.

1. <u>Mother</u> <u><u>rented</u></u> a good movie for us.

2. The <u>book</u> <u><u>is called</u></u> *The Lion King.*

3. <u>Cody</u> and <u>Brian</u> <u><u>have</u></u> a new game.

4. <u>They</u> <u><u>ran</u></u> to the park.

5. Over and over <u>they</u> <u><u>threw</u></u> and <u><u>caught</u></u> the ball.

6. <u>Maria</u> and <u>Juan</u> <u><u>baked</u></u> chocolate cookies this afternoon.

7. <u>Harve</u> <u><u>built</u></u> a small robot, and <u>Kelly</u> <u><u>painted</u></u> it for him.

8. His older <u>sister</u> <u><u>took</u></u> him to the store.

9. The <u>Morgans</u> and the <u>Morenos</u> <u><u>are</u></u> our new neighbors.

10. <u>Jamie</u> <u><u>wants</u></u> hot dogs, but <u>Simon</u> <u><u>prefers</u></u> hamburgers.

▶ **Exercise 2** **Write in the blank the past tense for each verb.**

sit <u>sat</u>

1. run <u>ran</u>
2. go <u>went</u>
3. smile <u>smiled</u>
4. eat <u>ate</u>
5. call <u>called</u>
6. do <u>did</u>
7. leave <u>left</u>
8. ask <u>asked</u>
9. buy <u>brought</u>
10. watch <u>watched</u>

11. squawk <u>squawked</u>
12. take <u>took</u>
13. let <u>let</u>
14. write <u>wrote</u>
15. speak <u>spoke</u>
16. croak <u>croaked</u>
17. smell <u>smelled</u>
18. fall <u>fell</u>
19. squeak <u>squeaked</u>
20. laugh <u>laughed</u>

Name _____ Class _____ Date _____

▶ **Exercise 3** Draw two lines under each verb or verb phrase. Write its tense
in the blank: *present, past, future, pres. prog.* (present progressive), *past prog.*
(past progressive), *pres. perf.* (present perfect), or *past perf.* (past perfect.)

past prog.	The principal <u><u>was speaking</u></u> to the student.
future	1. My dad and I <u><u>will bake</u></u> brownies tonight.
past perf.	2. I <u><u>had</u></u> already <u><u>heard</u></u> the rumor.
present prog.	3. The snow <u><u>is falling</u></u> in big flakes.
past	4. The editor of the school paper <u><u>wrote</u></u> an editorial.
present perf.	5. You <u><u>have made</u></u> my day!
present	6. Fiona <u><u>enjoys</u></u> computer games.
past prog.	7. My sister <u><u>was riding</u></u> the exercise bike.
past	8. Charles Schulz <u><u>created</u></u> the "Peanuts" comic strip.
future	9. Our dog <u><u>will stay</u></u> in a kennel during our vacation.
present prog.	10. Our class <u><u>is studying</u></u> endangered species.
past perf.	11. Rebecca <u><u>had hurried</u></u> to the mall.
past prog.	12. Everyone <u><u>was cheering</u></u> for the home team.
present perf.	13. Mrs. Santos <u><u>has discovered</u></u> the missing workbooks.
past	14. General Sherman <u><u>commanded</u></u> the Union army in the Civil War.
past perf.	15. The light <u><u>had burned</u></u> out in the kitchen.

▶ **Exercise 4** Replace the word or words in parentheses with an appropriate pronoun.

She (Glenda) practiced playing the piano every night.

They 1. (The squirrels) scampered up the tree.

_it_ 2. I have seen (the movie) five times.

_He_ 3. (Samuel) gets up every morning at 6:00.

_We_ 4. (Mark and I) played catch in the summer sun.

his 5. My sister borrowed (Kyle's) bike yesterday.

you 6. Mrs. Simpson wants to call (you and your sister) about raking her leaves.

Grammar

them **7.** We can't find (Betty, Kai, and Marillu) anywhere.

Our **8.** (Levi's and my) model airplane is red.

her **9.** We saw (your aunt) at the shopping mall.

Its **10.** (The fish's) gills moved quickly in and out.

they **11.** Do you know if (the Gonzaleses) are coming?

her **12.** We all applauded Carlos and (Maria).

she **13.** Does (Julie) know her sweater is on backwards?

_it_ **14.** My dad carried (the luggage) upstairs.

_us_ **15.** Tricia lent (Jules and me) her library card.

▶ **Exercise 5 Draw one line under each regular adjective and two lines under each predicate adjective. Circle all proper adjectives.**

The Pennsylvania mountains seem large and rugged.

1. The big barn appears spacious and roomy.

2. The heavy sea thundered against the black basalt rock of the cliffs.

3. A cousin of mine owns a Belgian horse.

4. This new flavor of strawberry sherbet tastes delicious.

5. The outdated steamship became a popular attraction for tourists.

6. Did you see that Italian sports car in front of the old house?

7. I saw the science book on the antique table and the French grammar book on the

   kitchen counter.

8. Are those beach houses in greater danger from hurricanes than these tall hotels?

9. The English mystery movie interests me more than this Japanese cartoon.

10. June was the driest month on record.

11. The scarlet cardinal sounds happy on this sunny day.

12. The mighty battleship sits quietly at anchor these days, and many people visit it.

13. Glorious sunlight reflects warmly off the brick walls.

14. I like Irish setters; what dog breed do you like?

Unit 6: Adverbs

Lesson 34
Adverbs Modifying Verbs

Grammar

An **adverb** modifies, or describes, a verb, an adjective, or another adverb. An adverb tells *how, when,* or *where* about the word it modifies. An adverb that modifies a verb may appear in different positions in a sentence.

Chan **happily** plays ball. (The adverb *happily* tells *how* Chan plays ball.)
Often the team travels on a bus. (The adverb *often* tells *when* the team travels.)
My sister ran **downstairs.** (The adverb *downstairs* tells *where* my sister ran.)

Most, but not all, words that end in *-ly* are adverbs. This type of adverb is usually formed by adding *-ly* to an adjective.

Adjective: graceful   Adverb: graceful**ly**

Some adverbs that do not end in *-ly* are *soon, after, now, later, hard, not, fast, often, today, always, very,* and *here.*

▶ **Exercise 1 Underline each adverb. Draw an arrow to the verb it modifies.**

The custom of wearing wigs has varied greatly over the centuries.

1. For many centuries both men and women frequently wore wigs.

2. As time passed, wigs gradually became the mark of high fashion.

3. In many countries people grandly dressed their wigs with gold and jewels.

4. Queen Elizabeth I of England dearly loved clothes and jewelry.

5. She soon revived the style of wearing fancy wigs.

6. In France, Queen Marie Antoinette gracefully hid her hair loss with a wig.

7. All of her subjects eagerly followed her style.

8. In the New World many ministers preached energetically against wigs, while other

ministers wore them proudly.

9. Just before the American Revolution, colonists <u>heavily</u> powdered their high, puffy wigs.

10. In those days George Washington <u>surely</u> considered his wig high fashion.

11. People <u>later</u> stopped wearing wigs.

12. Wigs were <u>obviously</u> part of the old world.

13. The new Americans <u>certainly</u> wanted freedom in style as well as in government.

14. Even so, they powdered their hair and tied it <u>tightly</u> at the back of the neck.

15. They soaked their hair <u>heavily</u> in oil to hold the powder.

▶ **Exercise 2 Complete each sentence by writing an appropriate adverb in the blank.**
Answers will vary.

In many ancient lands people _____proudly_____ grew long hair as a mark of honor.

1. People were _____often_____ punished by having their hair cut.

2. When Julius Caesar conquered a new country, he _____usually_____ forced the people to cut their hair.

3. Many people _____firmly_____ believed that long hair increased strength.

4. The story of Samson and Delilah _____clearly_____ illustrates how many people felt about hair.

5. On the other hand, the Greeks shaved their heads and _____respectfully_____ offered the hair to the gods.

6. In return, they _____politely_____ asked for great strength in battle.

7. Peoples like the Anglo-Saxons _____happily_____ dyed their hair in bright colors.

8. They _____greatly_____ admired hair dyed in bright green, blue, or orange.

9. Ancient Germans, on the other hand, _____often_____ preferred hair dyed in bright red.

10. Instead of hair spray, they _____commonly_____ used goat's grease to make their hair stay in place.

Lesson 35
Adverbs Modifying Adjectives and Adverbs

An adverb can also modify an adjective or another adverb. An adverb that modifies an adjective or another adverb tells *how, when,* or *where* about the word it modifies. An adverb that modifies an adjective or another adverb almost always appears immediately before the word it modifies.

Kai is an **unusually** good skater. (The adverb *unusually* tells *how* about the adjective *good.*)
Marta **almost** always sings. (The adverb *almost* tells *when* about the adverb *always.*)

ADVERBS OFTEN USED TO MODIFY ADJECTIVES AND OTHER ADVERBS

very	too	almost	quite
so	extremely	really	partly
rather	nearly	barely	unusually
just	somewhat	totally	hardly

▶ **Exercise 1** Circle each adverb that modifies an adjective or an adverb. In the blank, write *adj.* if the adverb modifies an adjective. Write *adv.* if the adverb modifies another adverb.

__adj.__   I was (barely) awake when the phone rang.

__adj.__   **1.** A (very) nice bowl of flowers arrived in the mail.

__adj.__   **2.** We call my grandmother (nearly) every day.

__adj.__   **3.** Pierre is the (most) popular player on the team.

__adv.__   **4.** He (almost) always turns off the light.

__adj.__   **5.** The floor was marked with (totally) black lines.

__adv.__   **6.** We set the eggs on the counter (very) carefully.

__adj.__   **7.** The circus clown had an (unusually) big, false nose.

__adv.__   **8.** The elderly man walked (rather) slowly.

__adj.__   **9.** My shirt is old and (somewhat) gray.

__adv.__   **10.** My best friend, Tanya, sings (quite) sweetly.

__adj.__   **11.** Bill spends (so) much time working that he has little time for other things.

adj. **12.** Suela's idea was (just) right.

adj. **13.** We had a (really) good pizza last night.

adj. **14.** Mother is (especially) successful in her work.

adv. **15.** They were surprised when the car stopped (so) suddenly.

adj. **16.** Jody was (really) happy to see her cousins.

adv. **17.** We (quite) happily fed the ducks.

adj. **18.** We rode our (nearly) new bicycles to the park.

adj. **19.** Bill is (extremely) eager to race Joel on Saturday.

adv. **20.** Joel is smaller and faster and can (very) easily win the race.

adj. **21.** We all followed the ice cream truck, but Nora was (barely) able to keep up.

adv. **22.** Even though she is slow, she (hardly) ever falls.

adj. **23.** The unexpected visit from my aunt was (too) good to be true.

adj **24.** Balance is (extremely) important when riding a bicycle.

adv. **25.** Pedro (almost) never eats popcorn in the evening.

▶ **Writing Link** **Write about one of your favorite things to do. Use adverbs to modify adjectives and other adverbs.**

_____

_____

_____

_____

_____

_____

_____

_____

_____

_____

Lesson 36
Adverbs That Compare

The **comparative** form of an adverb compares two actions. The **superlative** form of an adverb compares more than two actions. Adverbs that have only one syllable form the comparative by adding *-er* and form the superlative by adding *-est*. Adverbs that have more than one syllable or that end in *-ly* use the word *more* to form the comparative and the word *most* to form the superlative.

Comparative: The little clown ran **faster** than the big one. The little clown ran **more quickly** than the big one.

Superlative: The little clown ran the **fastest** of all of them. The little clown ran the **most quickly** of all of them.

Grammar

▶ **Exercise 1** Write in the blank the missing form of the adverb.

ADVERB	COMPARATIVE	SUPERLATIVE
easily	more easily	most easily
1. fast	faster	fastest
2. firmly	more firmly	most firmly
3. rarely	more rarely	most rarely
4. simply	more simply	most simply
5. hard	harder	hardest
6. regularly	more regularly	most regularly
7. actively	more actively	most actively
8. long	longer	longest
9. soon	sooner	soonest
10. high	higher	highest
11. clearly	more clearly	most clearly
12. close	closer	closest
13. frequently	more frequently	most frequently
14. plainly	more plainly	most plainly
15. truly	more truly	most truly

▶ **Exercise 2 Underline the correct form of the adverb in parentheses.**

It took us (longer, longest) to get to the museum than to the park.

1. Mark ran the (faster, fastest) of all the boys.

2. Mika worked (more hard, harder) than Roger.

3. Maria speaks the (intelligentliest, most intelligently) of all the candidates.

4. He wins (more frequently, most frequently) than his brother.

5. Sarah is studying (more long, longer) than usual because she has a test tomorrow.

6. We arrived (more soon, sooner) than we thought we would.

7. We play tennis (more often, oftener) now that the weather is warmer.

8. An eagle can fly (more high, higher) than a sparrow.

9. Some animals act (more mean, meaner) than they actually are.

10. Cole plays (more noisier, more noisily) on his electric guitar now that he has a new amplifier.

11. Fred sat (closer, closest) to the door than Shelly did.

12. Mary always eats (faster, fastest) than her brother does.

13. The owl can screech (louder, loudest) than any other bird I know.

14. Tad wrote his report (neatlier, more neatly) the second time.

15. She answered (sooner, soonest) of the ten people asked.

16. In sports, Ruth always tries (more hard, harder) than Susan.

17. The cheetah runs (more swiftly, most swiftly) than any other animal.

18. The gold medal winner skated the (more skillfully, most skillfully) of the ten contestants.

19. Mrs. Roth explained the problem (more clearly, most clearly) than Mrs. Groves did.

20. The prize will go to the ballplayer who attends practice (more regularly, most regularly).

Grammar

Lesson 37
Irregular Comparative Forms

Some adverbs have irregular forms of the comparative and the superlative.

IRREGULAR COMPARATIVE FORMS

ADVERB	COMPARATIVE	SUPERLATIVE
well	better	best
badly	worse	worst
little (amount)	less	least
far (distance)	farther	farthest
far (degree)	further	furthest

▶ **Exercise 1** Underline the correct form of the irregular adverb in parentheses.

Robby fixed his stereo (better, best) the second time.

1. I was worried that I did (more badly, worse) on the test.

2. Emilio ate (less, least) quickly than Tom did.

3. Mario could see much (more far, farther) with his new glasses.

4. I don't want to listen any (further, farther).

5. Ariel does (bestest, best) in school after a good night's sleep.

6. I hope they repair the bridge (better, best) this time than last time.

7. The metal fence is (badly, worst) rusted from all the rain.

8. I would like to contribute to my community (better, best) than I have in the past.

9. Pearl is (less, least) clever than her sister.

10. Raoul enjoys baby-sitting (better, best) than he enjoys mowing lawns.

11. Friday I played the (worse, worst) of anyone on the team.

12. Humming is the (less, least) annoying of all your habits.

13. Monarch butterflies migrate the (farther, farthest) of all the butterflies.

14. Always do your (better, best), and you will succeed in life.

15. Julius did (worse, worst) in the 500-meter dash than in the 100-meter dash.

▶ **Exercise 2** **Complete the sentence by writing in the blank the correct form of the irregular adverb in parentheses.**

Vivian traveled _____**less**_____ this year than last year. (little)

1. Last year on vacation we drove as _____**far**_____ as Mexico. (far)

2. Kayla's sister drew animals _____**better**_____ than she drew people. (well)

3. I will think about it _____**further**_____ before next week. (far)

4. Of all the performances, our school play went _____**worst**_____ on opening night. (badly)

5. My dad can throw a football _____**farther**_____ than I can. (far)

6. In our pet contest, the frog jumped _____**farther**_____ than the grasshopper. (far)

7. Lisa performed _____**better**_____ in today's volleyball game than in yesterday's. (well)

8. This video game was the _____**least**_____ enjoyable of the three. (little)

9. Can you explain the problem _____**further**_____ ? (far)

10. The teacher and the students will _____**further**_____ refine the class goals. (far)

11. When choosing pretzels, popcorn, or potato chips, remember that potato chips are the _____**least**_____ healthful of the three. (little)

12. Atlanta is the _____**farthest**_____ south I have ever been. (far)

13. I like the country _____**better**_____ than the city. (well)

14. I like the ocean _____**best**_____ of all. (well)

15. Micah performed his violin solo the _____**best**_____ he ever had. (well)

16. Martin enjoys swimming _____**less**_____ than I do. (little)

17. Juan does _____**worse**_____ in science than in English. (badly)

18. Do you think my big brother dances _____**worse**_____ than I do? (badly)

19. The little girl can speak much _____**better**_____ than she could six months ago. (well)

20. Of any time of day, Jenny sings _____**worst**_____ in the morning. (badly)

Grammar

Lesson 38
Telling Adjectives and Adverbs Apart I

Some adjectives and adverbs are easy to identify within sentences. An adjective modifies a noun or pronoun. An adverb modifies a verb, adjective, or another adverb. When they follow a verb, however, they can be confusing. A predicate adjective follows a linking verb and an adverb follows an action verb.

A leopard is **fast**. (*Fast* is a predicate adjective.)
A leopard runs **fast**. (*Fast* is an adverb.)

► **Exercise 1 Draw one line under each italicized word that is an adjective. Draw two lines under each italicized word that is an adverb.**

Which of the two movies did you like *better*?

1. The king was a *just* ruler.

2. I have *just* started this assignment.

3. Everyone worked *hard* on the projects for the science fair.

4. The toast had become *hard* and cold.

5. We have *less* homework than usual tonight.

6. I enjoyed the stage play *less* than the movie.

7. Jess skates *better* than Tony.

8. This book seems *better* than that one.

9. Peggy can swim *faster* than Carol.

10. The jockey wanted a *faster* horse.

11. The explorers climbed a *high* mountain.

12. The plane flew *high* overhead.

13. Linda took a *long* drink of water.

14. How *long* have you waited here?

15. Come *close,* and I'll tell you a secret.

16. The referee made a *close* call.

17. Only one person arrived *late*.

18. The Changs ate a *late* dinner.

19. This is the *most* popular restaurant in town.

20. *Most* people look forward to weekends.

▶ **Exercise 2** **Underline the adjective or adverb in parentheses that best completes each sentence.**

Mr. Denton (usual, <u>usually</u>) arrives before seven o'clock.

1. Juanita is a (<u>great</u>, greatly) chess player and a good sport.

2. Mom and Dad appeared (great, <u>greatly</u>) pleased with their anniversary gift.

3. Mitzi (near, <u>nearly</u>) collided with Tim in the doorway.

4. A (<u>near</u>, nearly) miss does not count in basketball.

5. Myra looked (sad, <u>sadly</u>) at her friend's broken glasses.

6. The little puppy looked (<u>sad</u>, sadly) and lonely.

7. The rain came down (sudden, <u>suddenly</u>).

8. There was a (<u>sudden</u>, suddenly) shower this afternoon.

9. What is the (<u>probable</u>, probably) cause of the disease?

10. We have (probable, <u>probably</u>) waited too long.

11. It is (unusual, <u>unusually</u>) cold today.

12. A temperature of seventy seems (<u>unusual</u>, unusually) for February in Iowa.

13. It was an absolutely (<u>perfect</u>, perfectly) summer day.

14. Mr. Murphy told us a (perfect, <u>perfectly</u>) ridiculous joke!

15. Could you (possible, <u>possibly</u>) help me with this math problem?

16. Well, that is one (<u>possible</u>, possibly) solution to the problem.

17. The long white envelope looked quite (<u>ordinary</u>, ordinarily).

18. I would not (ordinary, <u>ordinarily</u>) read a book about computer technology.

19. Jake grew (<u>gloomy</u>, gloomily) toward the end of the day.

20. The picknickers watched the dark clouds (gloomy, <u>gloomily</u>).

Lesson 39
Telling Adjectives and Adverbs Apart II

Some adjectives and adverbs demand special attention because they can be confusing. *Bad* and *good* are adjectives. They are used after linking verbs. *Badly* and *well* are adverbs. They modify action verbs. When *well* is used after a linking verb to describe a person's health, it is an adjective. *Real* and *sure* are adjectives. They describe nouns or pronouns. *Really* and *surely* are adverbs. *Most* is usually an adjective. When it is part of a superlative, it is an adverb. *Almost* is usually an adverb. When it is followed by an indefinite pronoun, it is an adjective.

ADJECTIVES	ADVERBS
The choir sounds **bad**.	She sings **badly**.
The grapes are **good**.	Grapes keep **well**.
The roses are **real**.	The roses are **really** pretty.
We are **sure** to win.	We will **surely** win.
Most people like music.	The song is **almost** too loud.

▶ **Exercise 1** **Underline the word in parentheses that best completes each sentence.**

Our cat is (real, really) fuzzy.

1. We will (sure, surely) beat the Lions tomorrow!

2. Does this milk taste (good, well) or is it sour?

3. We (most, almost) always have salad with dinner.

4. The wrestler had a (sure, surely) hold on his opponent.

5. Alex didn't feel (good, well), so he stayed home from school.

6. The boxer who landed the (most, almost) punches won the fight.

7. (Most, Almost) everyone in our class was excited about the basketball play-offs.

8. Bagels don't fit (good, well) in our toaster.

9. Don and Maria had a (real, really) good time at the party.

10. I go to (most, almost) every football game.

11. My sister and I behave (good, well) when our grandparents visit.

12. We saw a (real, really) whale when we vacationed at Cape Cod!

13. Are you (sure, surely) you are right about the time of the movie?

14. The CD sounds (<u>good</u>, well) on our new disc player.

15. (<u>Most</u>, Almost) plants need sun and water.

▶ **Exercise 2** Write in the blank the correct form of the word in italics. If the word is correct, write *C* in the blank.

_____well_____ Sheila did *good* on her English grammar test.

_____good_____ **1.** The baseball cap looked *well* on Neal's head.

_____really_____ **2.** The Mexican food was *real* spicy.

_____C_____ **3.** Jazz is *surely* popular in New Orleans!

_____almost_____ **4.** Joel *most* never watches TV on school nights.

_____well_____ **5.** With the help of my calculator, I did *good* on my math homework.

_____surely_____ **6.** We will *sure* go to the mall this weekend.

_____Most_____ **7.** *Almost* politicians have degrees in either political science or law.

_____C_____ **8.** The sound system in our school auditorium works *badly*.

_____really_____ **9.** The soccer match was *real* exciting!

_____well_____ **10.** Jasmine's grandma knits very *good*.

_____bad_____ **11.** Your messy room looks *badly*.

_____good_____ **12.** The pepperoni pizza tastes *well*.

_____sure_____ **13.** Mr. Valdez is *surely* about the results.

_____C_____ **14.** Dolphins are *really* smart mammals.

_____badly_____ **15.** The old car rattled *bad*.

▶ **Writing Link** Write one or two sentences comparing your ability to do something this year with your ability to do it last year.

_____

_____

_____

_____

_____

Lesson 40
Avoiding Double Negatives

Negative words express the idea of *not* or *no*. The adverb *not* often appears in the form of a contraction.

is + not = is**n't**	do + not = do**n't**	will + not = wo**n't**
was + not = was**n't**	did + not = did**n't**	have + not = have**n't**
were + not = were**n't**	can + not = ca**n't**	could + not = could**n't**

Negative words are the opposite of affirmative words. **Affirmative words** show the idea of *yes.* Each negative will have several opposite affirmatives.

NEGATIVE	AFFIRMATIVE	NEGATIVE	AFFIRMATIVE
never	ever, always	nobody	somebody, anybody
nothing	something, anything	nowhere	somewhere, anywhere

Using two negatives in a sentence creates a **double negative**. Avoid using more than one negative in a sentence. Correct a double negative by using an affirmative word in place of one of the negative words.

Incorrect: The teacher did**n't** grade **no** papers.
Correct: The teacher graded no papers. The teacher didn't grade any papers.

▶ **Exercise 1** Underline the word in parentheses that best completes each sentence.

We didn't see (none, <u>any</u>).

1. My father doesn't (never, <u>ever</u>) want to vacation in Florida.

2. Bill doesn't think (nothing, <u>anything</u>) is as much fun as mountain climbing.

3. My mother says she isn't (no, <u>a</u>) swimmer.

4. There weren't (no, <u>any</u>) apples on the tree.

5. There isn't (no, <u>any</u>) easy way to decide where to go.

6. Aaron wasn't (never, <u>ever</u>) able to keep up with the older boys.

7. We didn't see (nothing, <u>anything</u>) interesting at the flea market.

8. The book can't be kept (no, <u>any</u>) longer.

9. My brother didn't break (no, <u>any</u>) windows.

10. The band didn't play (nowhere, <u>anywhere</u>) last week.

11. Did you say you don't (never, <u>ever</u>) make a mistake?

12. Marcy hasn't (no, <u>any</u>) money for the book.

13. We looked for the treasure, but we didn't find (nothing, <u>anything</u>).

14. The pirates didn't intend for (no one, <u>anyone</u>) to find it.

15. Mr. Allen didn't mean (nothing, <u>anything</u>) by his comment.

16. After the picnic there weren't (no, <u>any</u>) potato chips left.

17. The broken glass wasn't (no one's, <u>anyone's</u>) fault.

18. We won't (never, <u>ever</u>) visit that theater again.

19. The police officer yelled, "Don't (nobody, <u>anybody</u>) move!"

20. There wasn't (no, <u>any</u>) popcorn for the movie.

▶ **Exercise 2 Write a negative in the blank for each of the following affirmative words. Use contractions when possible.**

ever <u>never</u>

1. will <u>won't</u>		11. can <u>can't</u>
2. one <u>none, no one</u>		12. some <u>none</u>
3. anywhere <u>nowhere</u>		13. could <u>couldn't</u>
4. did <u>didn't</u>		14. was <u>wasn't</u>
5. have <u>haven't</u>		15. someone <u>no one</u>
6. should <u>shouldn't</u>		16. would <u>wouldn't</u>
7. any <u>none</u>		17. were <u>weren't</u>
8. is <u>isn't</u>		18. anything <u>nothing</u>
9. do <u>don't</u>		19. has <u>hasn't</u>
10. always <u>never</u>		20. does <u>doesn't</u>

Unit 6 **Review**

Grammar

▶ **Exercise 1 Underline each adverb. Draw an arrow to the word it modifies.**

We practiced eagerly for two hours.

1. Rob kicked the ball well.

2. Marlo closed the door quickly.

3. The actors performed the play badly.

4. The music was really beautiful.

5. We arrived late to the movie.

6. The pool will open soon.

7. We always swim in the summer.

8. Alma cheerfully taught her little sister the game.

9. They walk to school nearly every day.

10. Their mother regularly calls them at home.

▶ **Exercise 2 Complete each sentence with the correct comparative or superlative form of the adverb in parentheses.**

Our dog obeys _____better_____ than he used to. (well)

1. The play will be held _____sooner_____ than expected. (soon)

2. Of all the animals in the world, the cheetah runs _____fastest_____. (fast)

3. This writing can be read because you pressed ____more firmly____ than before. (firmly)

4. Of all the bikers, Ralph climbed the slope ____most easily____. (easily)

5. Kendra plays checkers _____better_____ than anyone else. (well)

6. My brother plays the guitar _____worse_____ than he thinks. (badly)

Cumulative Review: Units 1–6

▶ **Exercise 1** For each complete sentence draw one line under each simple subject and two lines under each simple predicate. In each blank write *S* for simple sentence, *C* for compound sentence, or *F* for sentence fragment.

_____C_____   Our dog chased the squirrel, and the squirrel chased the mouse.

_____S_____ **1.** Our trip during spring break was a lovely cruise.

_____S_____ **2.** The weather became cool and cloudy.

_____C_____ **3.** We were unhappy with the stove, and we returned it to the store.

_____F_____ **4.** Common errors by the teacher in art class.

_____S_____ **5.** Most of the time we didn't swim in the ocean water.

_____S_____ **6.** Marcia and I went to the movie and walked to the mall.

_____F_____ **7.** Celebrating her birthday.

_____C_____ **8.** Pedro and Marta practiced their song, and they sang it for Mother and me.

_____S_____ **9.** Akeem loved the trip to the desert in Arizona.

_____F_____ **10.** For some groceries for our Thanksgiving dinner at Granddad's house.

_____S_____ **11.** Tomorrow Lance will come to the meeting.

_____C_____ **12.** Rona ate before the movie, but her brother ate afterward.

_____F_____ **13.** Angry at those rude and noisy people in the first few rows.

_____S_____ **14.** Carl sang a solo in choir last week.

_____S_____ **15.** As a child, Mark always seemed happy.

_____F_____ **16.** Susana with her father to the game.

_____C_____ **17.** The cheerleaders are planning the pep rally, but they need more help.

_____S_____ **18.** The space shuttle carried our science experiment on its last flight.

_____F_____ **19.** The contest during the last week of band practice.

_____C_____ **20.** I am looking forward to a career in space, and my brother plans as career as a

teacher.

▶ **Exercise 2 Write in the blank the plural of each noun.**

piano _pianos_

1. team _teams_
2. sister _sisters_
3. birthday _birthdays_
4. potato _potatoes_
5. visitor _visitors_
6. church _churches_
7. dog _dogs_
8. wish _wishes_
9. library _libraries_
10. market _markets_

11. donkey _donkeys_
12. puppy _puppies_
13. bee _bees_
14. boss _bosses_
15. toy _toys_
16. fly _flies_
17. fox _foxes_
18. dress _dresses_
19. bush _bushes_
20. lunch _lunches_

▶ **Exercise 3 Write _adj._ in the blank if the word in italics is an adjective. Write _adv._ if it is an adverb.**

adj. What a _lovely_ tulip!

adj. **1.** The baby has _curly_ brown hair.

adv. **2.** At _almost_ any moment, the phone may ring with the news.

adj. **3.** The _school_ band will perform at the game.

adj. **4.** There was _little_ truth to her statement.

adj. **5.** What is your _favorite_ show on television?

adv. **6.** Grace _carefully_ braided her hair.

adv. **7.** Aunt Beth has _nearly_ twenty varieties of house plants.

adv. **8.** Keith moved _rapidly_ through the grocery store.

adv. **9.** The reporter followed events _closely._

adj. **10.** I like my _new_ home very much.

adv. **11.** My father works _hard_ for a living.

adj. **12.** The new student is very _friendly._

__adv.__ **13.** Please cut the cake *quickly!*

__adj.__ **14.** The *hardest* part of redecorating my room was choosing the wallpaper.

__adv.__ **15.** A kangaroo jumps *higher* than a rabbit.

__adv.__ **16.** We *almost* always are involved in community service.

__adj.__ **17.** My sister works *long* hours delivering newspapers.

__adv.__ **18.** Abdul tiptoed *sneakily* through the house.

__adv.__ **19.** I *sometimes* curl up on the couch for a nap.

__adj.__ **20.** Juanita enjoys *most* kinds of music.

__adj.__ **21.** My mom becomes very *sleepy* after nine o'clock.

__adv.__ **22.** My family *often* goes to baseball games.

__adj.__ **23.** The jet pilot had *perfect* vision.

__adv.__ **24.** The plumber worked *long* and hard on the broken pipe.

__adj.__ **25.** Josh looked *handsome* in his new suit.

__adj.__ **26.** The backhoe dug a *deep* hole.

__adv.__ **27.** A gray seagull soared *effortlessly* in the sunny sky.

__adj.__ **28.** In a *short* while we'll be ready to go.

__adv.__ **29.** The flag fluttered *wildly* on its broken rope.

__adv.__ **30.** I hurried *downstairs.*

__adj.__ **31.** That is a *hilarious* story.

__adv.__ **32.** Elizabeth cares *deeply* about her patients.

__adv.__ **33.** This program ends *soon.*

__adj.__ **34.** That *antique* chair is fragile.

__adv.__ **35.** Please come *here* quickly.

Grammar

Unit 7: Prepositions, Conjunctions, and Interjections

Lesson 41
Prepositions

A **preposition** is a word that relates a noun or a pronoun to some other word in a sentence. Most prepositions are single words, but some are made up of two or three words. Prepositions made up of two or three words are called **compound prepositions**.

Park the tractor **behind** the barn.
Victor came **to** the meeting **instead of** Charles.

WORDS COMMONLY USED AS PREPOSITIONS

about	because of	in addition to	over
above	before	in front of	past
according to	behind	inside	since
across	below	in spite of	than
across from	beneath	instead of	through
after	beside	into	throughout
against	between	like (as)	till (until)
ahead of	beyond	near	to
along	but (except)	next to	toward
along with	by (next to)	of	under
among	despite	off	underneath
apart from	down	on	until
around	during	onto	up
as	except	on top of	upon
as well as	for	out	with
aside from	from	out of	within
at	in	outside	without

▶ **Exercise 1** **Draw a line under each preposition and compound preposition.**

Jeremiah, please stand <u>by</u> my desk.

1. Place the umbrella stand <u>beside</u> the door.

2. Lean a little <u>to</u> the left.

3. Mom, may I go skating <u>with</u> Suzi?

4. You can get extra supplies <u>from</u> the stationery store.

Grammar

5. Eileen and Miranda have been best friends <u>since</u> third grade.

6. The ground <u>under</u> the trees isn't even wet.

7. We can do this work <u>without</u> any extra help.

8. The paprika is <u>between</u> the onion powder and the pepper.

9. I can stay only <u>until</u> eight o'clock.

10. I found my homework <u>inside</u> my social studies book.

11. We ran five laps <u>around</u> the gym and then practiced shots.

12. Myra lives <u>near</u> Mr. Polumski, who is my English teacher.

13. The airplane flew <u>above</u> the storm.

14. Sprinkle the colored sugar <u>on top of</u> the frosting.

15. Meet me <u>during</u> lunch period.

16. I can meet you <u>in front of</u> the library <u>at</u> four o'clock.

17. Samantha and David ran <u>down</u> the street.

18. Alfie, my golden retriever, relaxes <u>in</u> the shade <u>under</u> the oak tree.

19. Juan shyly stood <u>apart from</u> the other new students.

20. We must be <u>on</u> the train <u>by</u> noon.

21. Jeremy sits third <u>from</u> the left <u>among</u> the other trumpet players.

22. Will you write <u>about</u> John Cabot <u>instead of</u> Abigail Adams?

23. <u>According to</u> Mr. Wolford, you performed <u>beyond</u> all expectations.

24. Everyone went <u>outside</u> the building <u>because of</u> the false alarm.

25. All <u>of</u> these papers <u>except</u> the green ones are <u>for</u> Salem Elementary.

26. Crawl <u>through</u> the tunnel, and climb <u>onto</u> the platform.

27. How did you get <u>inside</u> the house <u>without</u> your key?

28. Go <u>into</u> the stable and look <u>for</u> the saddle soap.

29. <u>During</u> my study time, I came <u>upon</u> this beautiful poem.

30. <u>On top of</u> the mountain the temperature often drops <u>below</u> zero.

31. Put this shovel <u>against</u> the wall and <u>behind</u> the lawn mower.

32. <u>Above</u> the sagging couch hung a broken lamp.

Lesson 42
Prepositional Phrases

A **prepositional phrase** is a group of words that begins with a preposition and ends with a noun or a pronoun called the **object of the preposition**.

The Adirondack Mountains are **in northern New York**. (*New York* is the object of the preposition *in*.)

I will mark the map **for you**. (*You* is the object of the preposition *for*.)

▶ **Exercise 1 Draw a line under the prepositional phrase or phrases in each sentence.**

People from countries around the world visit Yosemite each year.

1. Yosemite, in central California, is one of the best-known national parks.

2. It became a national park through the efforts of naturalist John Muir.

3. Yosemite National Park is known for its waterfalls, for its mountains and domes, and for its giant sequoia trees.

4. During the Ice Age, glaciers carved the Yosemite Valley.

5. Small side valleys, also formed by glaciers, have rivers at their bases.

6. These rivers spill over the sides of the mountains in spectacular waterfalls.

7. At 2,435 feet, Yosemite Falls is the highest waterfall in North America.

8. The water in Yosemite Creek spills over the edge in three falls.

9. Two of Yosemite's natural wonders are called El Capitán and Half Dome.

10. El Capitán is the world's largest piece of exposed granite.

11. Half Dome is a piece of granite that looks like a gumdrop cut in half.

12. The Sierra Nevadas are one huge piece of granite.

13. The park contains three separate groves of giant sequoia trees.

14. Among these groves, the Mariposa Grove of Big Trees is the most famous.

15. The largest tree in the park, the Grizzly Giant, is 3,800 years old.

16. According to historians, the name *Yosemite* means "grizzly bear."

▶ **Exercise 2** **Draw one line under each preposition and two lines under its object.**

Naturalists like John Muir left messages for people.

1. John Muir was born in Dunbar, Scotland, in 1838.

2. He was a boy when his family moved to Wisconsin in 1849.

3. When he was a young man, he walked a thousand miles from the Ohio River to the Gulf Coast.

4. Muir studied geology at a university in Wisconsin.

5. There he heard debates about the formation of the Yosemite Valley.

6. He was thirty years old when he first went to California in 1868.

7. Upon his arrival, John Muir fell in love with the land.

8. He devoted his life to the study of nature.

9. He believed erosion from glaciers caused the formation of the Yosemite Valley.

10. Muir did many studies of the Sierra Nevada Mountain Range.

11. In the 1890s, John Muir started the Sierra Club.

12. This club has been active in conservation efforts for a century.

13. John Muir was a friend of Theodore Roosevelt.

14. Teddy Roosevelt was president of the United States from 1901 to 1908.

15. In 1903 Roosevelt and Muir spent a night in Yosemite camping underneath the stars.

16. They listened to sounds of water tumbling down sheer cliffs.

17. After a campfire meal, they slept among the giant sequoias.

18. Muir wanted the valley preserved for all people.

19. Through the efforts of John Muir and with the support of Theodore Roosevelt, the valley became part of Yosemite National Park.

20. Roosevelt's administration made great efforts toward conservation.

Lesson 43
Pronouns After Prepositions

Grammar

When a pronoun is the object of a preposition, use an object pronoun, not a subject pronoun.

I backpacked with **my parents** last summer.
I backpacked with **them** last summer.

Use an object pronoun when a preposition has a compound object consisting of a noun and a pronoun or two pronouns.

Mike and Sal usually play tennis with **José** and **her.**

Pronouns in compound subjects or compound objects can be confusing. When deciding what pronoun to use, read the sentence with only the pronoun. This eliminates extra words and can help you decide if you should use a subject pronoun or an object pronoun.

Mike and Sal usually play tennis with **her.**

The pronoun *who* is a subject pronoun, and the pronoun *whom* is an object pronoun.

Who told you about the trip? From **whom** did you get the details?

Notice that *who* is the subject of the first sentence and *whom* is the object of the preposition *from* in the second sentence.

▶ **Exercise 1 Write the appropriate personal pronoun above the word or words in italics.**

him
We have to go by *Mr. Mahoney* to get out of the room.

her
1. Armand, stand next to Chico and *Jenna.*

them
2. Gordon and Sookie will play opposite *Joe and Natasha.*

her
3. Our teacher is on the second floor with *Mrs. Lane.*

her
4. Did you get the tickets from *Aunt Beatrice?*

them
5. Please give a paper to each of *the students.*

them
6. The banner will be held by *Ling and Claudia.*

her
7. Let's make room for Alicia between Amy and *Ana.*

him
8. The serpent costume with the green scales is for *Emilio.*

them

9. This award really belongs to *all the students in the sixth grade.*

him

10. For the second picture, I want Diana standing in front of Micah and *Kenneth.*

us

11. When the cheerleaders make a pyramid, Jenny is on top of *me and everyone else.*

her

12. In tonight's performance, Kitty Cain will perform instead of *Julia Rice.*

him

13. You remind me a lot of *a boy I used to know.*

them

14. We live on the sixth floor, above *the Garcias.*

her

15. Is everyone here now except *Sonia?*

him

16. Find a seat near Lydia and *Ryan.*

him

17. Jimmy, stop wrestling with *your brother.*

them

18. We will have to leave without *Paul and Mrs. Macchio.*

her

19. For this song, Audrey stands beside *Betty Jo* and faces the audience.

them

20. The fifth grade always sits in the bleachers below *the sixth grade.*

▶ **Exercise 2 Underline the pronoun in parentheses that best completes the sentence.**

First find Melissa, and Juan will be right next to (she, her).

1. I think that the Crowleys live across from (they, them).

2. According to (she, her), Monday's practice is cancelled.

3. Rodolfo, who is a new student, sits across from my sister and (I, me).

4. Stacey, I want you to help me instead of (she, her).

5. Stand back to back, lean against (he, him), and then try to sit down.

6. From (who, whom) did you get this information?

7. Jorge, will you please go to the office along with Chad and (he, him)?

8. Everyone form a circle around Mrs. Rodrigez and (we, us).

9. (Who, Whom) else is going with (they, them)?

10. Hillary is in line behind (she, her).

11. Can we rearrange the furniture in Alice's room without (she, her)?

12. (Who, Whom) wanted help from my tutor and (I, me)?

Lesson 44
Prepositional Phrases as Adjectives and Adverbs

Prepositional phrases serve as adjectives and adverbs. An **adjective phrase** is sometimes a prepositional phrase that describes a noun or a pronoun.

Castles **in Japan** were built differently from European castles. (describes the noun *castles*)
Those **in Japan** often included many courtyards. (describes the pronoun *those*)

An **adverb phrase** is sometimes a prepositional phrase that describes a verb, another adverb, or an adjective.

The first European castles were built **of earth and timber**. (describes the verb *built*)
Later **in history** castles were built out of stone. (describes the adverb *later*)
The chapel was important **in a Christian castle**. (describes the adjective *important*)

▶ **Exercise 1** **Identify the phrase in italics by writing** *adj.* **in the blank for each adjective phrase or** *adv.* **for each adverb phrase. Circle the word or phrase it modifies.**

___adv.___   Castles (served) as homes for lords and *as strongholds*.

___adv.___   **1.** How (did) people (live) *inside a medieval castle?*

___adj.___   **2.** The main (room) *in a castle* was the great hall.

___adv.___   **3.** The great hall (served) *as a bedroom, dining room, and office.*

___adj.___   **4.** Early halls had fireplaces in the (middle) *of the room.*

___adv.___   **5.** Later, wall fireplaces were introduced, and the lord's table (was) often *near the fire.*

___adv.___   **6.** The main meal was eaten (late) *in the morning.*

___adj.___   **7.** (Servants) *with pitchers* of water helped guests wash their hands before and after eating.

___adv.___   **8.** Some tables had removable legs so the room (could be used) *for many purposes.*

___adj.___   **9.** The lord's table was often the only (table) *with fixed legs.*

___adj.___   **10.** Removing the tables used for dining provided (space) *for entertainment.*

___adv.___ 11. (Later) *in the evening* straw mattresses were brought into the great hall for

sleeping.

___adv.___ 12. The floors of some castles (were decorated) *with tiles.*

___adv.___ 13. Medieval people rarely (used) carpets *as floor coverings.*

___adv.___ 14. Carpets (were regarded) *as luxuries.*

___adv.___ 15. Some carpets (hung) *on the walls* as tapestries.

___adv.___ 16. Castles (built) *after the year 1200* often had extra rooms.

___adv.___ 17. The heat for cooking (came) *from an open fire.*

___adv.___ 18. To prevent fires, halls were built (away) *from the kitchen.*

___adv.___ 19. Often the kitchen (was) *in the courtyard.*

___adv.___ 20. Later the kitchen (was connected) *to the great hall.*

___adj.___ 21. Medieval people living in castles ate a (variety) *of foods.*

___adj.___ 22. They ate beef, mutton, and many (kinds) *of wild birds.*

___adv.___ 23. They (served) venison and other game *after a hunt.*

___adv.___ 24. They (ate) fish *during Lent.*

___adj.___ 25. Many castles had (gardens) *with orchards.*

___adj.___ 26. Northern orchards provided (fruit) *like apples and pears.*

___adj.___ 27. Trenchers were flat (pieces) *of stale bread.*

___adv.___ 28. Trenchers (were used) *as plates.*

___adj.___ 29. The stale bread soaked up the (gravy) *from the meat.*

___adv.___ 30. The trenchers (could be given) *to the poor.*

___adv.___ 31. Nobles (were) usually (served) *by pages.*

___adv.___ 32. Only rich people had chairs, so most people (sat) *on benches.*

___adv.___ 33. Hunting and hawking (were enjoyed) *as entertainment.*

___adv.___ 34. In addition, the knights (participated) *in tournaments.*

___adv.___ 35. People (listened) *to musicians and storytellers.*

Lesson 45
Telling Prepositions and Adverbs Apart

Grammar

Some words can be used as either prepositions or adverbs. For a word to be a preposition, it must be part of a prepositional phrase. A preposition never stands alone in a sentence. If the word has an object, it is probably a preposition. If the word is not followed closely by a noun or a pronoun that could be an object, it is probably an adverb.

Anastasia is riding her bike **around the neighborhood.** (preposition)
Anastasia is riding her bike **around.** (adverb)

WORDS THAT CAN BE USED AS PREPOSITIONS OR ADVERBS

about	before	down	near	out	through
above	behind	in	off	outside	up
around	below	inside	on	over	

▶ **Exercise 1** Write *adv.* in the blank if the word in italics is an adverb and *prep.* if it is a preposition.

adv.   Everyone, please sit *down.*

prep. **1.** I will leave the package *outside* my front door.

adv. **2.** Kyla had a feeling that she had been here *before.*

prep. **3.** Can we hang this picture on the wall *above* my bed?

adv. **4.** Stay with the group. Don't fall *behind.*

adv. **5.** The yacht's entire crew just went *below.*

prep. **6.** Is Stephanie *in* third grade or fourth grade now?

adv. **7.** This book is so good that I can't put it *down.*

prep. **8.** Valerie made a perfect swan dive *off* the ten-foot board.

prep. **9.** Let's put the small box *inside* the larger box.

adv. **10.** Won't you please come *in* and talk?

adv. **11.** Would the children like to come *inside* for a snack?

adv. **12.** I don't see Amanda, but I'm sure she is *near.*

adv. **13.** We've put this *off* long enough.

prep.   **14.** Mom locked her keys *inside* the car.

adv.   **15.** Put your boots *on* so your feet stay dry.

adv.   **16.** Take Lucky *out* for a walk.

prep.   **17.** Do you think we can finish this *before* noon?

prep.   **18.** The rescuers climbed *up* the fire escape to the third floor.

adv.   **19.** We put the trash *outside* on Tuesday nights.

adv.   **20.** I'm glad that this project is finally *over*.

prep.   **21.** Go *through* the door, and turn left.

adv.   **22.** The crowds wouldn't let me *through*.

adv.   **23.** Button *up* before you go outside.

prep.   **24.** Most female adult gymnasts weigh *about* ninety-five pounds.

prep.   **25.** Is it possible to fly *around* the world non-stop?

prep.   **26.** Federico always has to be home *before* dinner.

prep.   **27.** A piece of paper just fell *behind* the sofa.

adv.   **28.** I'll be *around*, so call if you need me.

prep.   **29.** We can store these props in the space *below* the stage.

adv.   **30.** It's almost noon, so I'm sure she's *up*.

prep.   **31.** The Zaharis family lives *down* this street.

prep.   **32.** Hang your coat on the rack *near* the back door.

prep.   **33.** The book you want is *on* the third shelf.

adv.   **34.** We will have recess *outside* today.

prep.   **35.** Please go *out* the doors at the front of the gym.

prep.   **36.** We went *over* the hill to the picnic area.

adv.   **37.** Look *above* and below for the package.

adv.   **38.** Everything is still *up* in the air.

adv.   **39.** Carefully put the punch bowl *down* on this table.

prep.   **40.** What do you think you will be doing *in* twenty years?

Grammar

Lesson 46
Conjunctions

A **conjunction** is a word that joins single words or groups of words in a sentence. The most common conjunctions—*and, but,* and *or*—are called **coordinating conjunctions**. Coordinating conjunctions can be used to connect individual nouns, pronouns, verbs, adjectives, adverbs, prepositions, phrases, or clauses. Place a comma before the conjunction in a compound sentence.

We scoured **and** scrubbed the kitchen sink.
Simon is very relaxed **or** very lazy.
I have recovered, **but** my sister is still sick.

Correlative conjunctions are pairs of words used to connect words or phrases in a sentence. Correlative conjunctions include *both . . . and, either . . . or, neither . . . nor,* and *not only . . . but also.*

Both Wanda **and** Emily **are** right-handed.
Neither the coach **nor** Ms. Thomas **is** left-handed.

▶ **Exercise 1** **Circle each coordinating conjunction. Underline the words it connects.**

I was thrilled (and) excited when I heard your news.

1. Maureen (or) Margaret could help you.

2. Give these packages to him (and) her.

3. Broad Street runs east (and) west.

4. I really want to stay home, (but) my mom says I have to go.

5. The water was cool (and) clear.

6. Did you travel by plane (or) by car?

7. We drove over a bridge (and) through a tunnel.

8. William hemmed (and) hawed before he answered the question.

9. The flowers smell fresh (and) delicate.

10. We can write Mandy a letter tonight, (or) we can call her tomorrow.

11. Was Washington (or) Jefferson the first president?

12. The Rockies are in the West, (and) the Alleghenies are in the East.

13. This package came for you (and) me.

14. Would you like milk (or) water?

15. Are you sure of your answer, (or) do you need some time to think?

▶ **Exercise 2** Underline each coordinating or correlative conjunction.

Both Jackson <u>and</u> Austin are state capitals.

1. <u>Either</u> Danielle <u>or</u> Benjamin has the tickets.

2. My stepfather <u>and</u> mother walk two miles every day.

3. <u>Both</u> Manet <u>and</u> Monet are famous painters.

4. <u>Either</u> a salad <u>or</u> soup comes with the meal.

5. <u>Neither</u> red <u>nor</u> blue is my favorite color.

6. Ms. Torrence <u>or</u> Mr. Rodriguez teaches that course.

7. My cocker spaniel <u>and</u> cat chase each other around the tree.

8. <u>Both</u> the taxi driver <u>and</u> the bus driver drive faster than they should.

9. <u>Neither</u> fruit <u>nor</u> vegetables contain much fat.

10. <u>Either</u> the toast <u>or</u> the pie in the oven is burning.

11. The north trail <u>and</u> south trail end at the foot of the mountain.

12. <u>Neither</u> the garter snake <u>nor</u> the black snake is poisonous.

13. Do you know if <u>either</u> Li <u>or</u> Mason eats meat?

14. If it rains, <u>neither</u> the softball team <u>nor</u> the tennis team practices.

15. An open door <u>or</u> window lets in fresh air.

16. <u>Both</u> my bicycle <u>and</u> my father's car have a flat tire.

17. Can <u>either</u> girls <u>or</u> boys enter the contest?

18. <u>Neither</u> the drug store <u>nor</u> the grocery store sells notebooks.

19. Whenever you do that, Lynn <u>and</u> Morgan laugh.

20. <u>Either</u> a bacteria <u>or</u> a virus causes that disease.

Lesson 47
Interjections

An **interjection** is a word or group of words that expresses mild or strong feeling.

COMMON INTERJECTIONS

ah	congratulations	hooray	ouch
aha	good grief	phew	no
all right	great	oh	ugh
awesome	hey	oh, no	wow
bravo	hi	oops	yes

Since an interjection is not related to other words in the sentence, it is set off from the rest of the sentence by a comma or an exclamation point. Use an exclamation point after an interjection that stands alone, either before or after a sentence. Use a comma before or after an interjection that expresses a mild emotion to separate it from the rest of the sentence.

Yes! I knew you could do it!
You got front row seats! **Great!**
Congratulations, you passed the test.

▶ **Exercise 1 Underline each interjection.**

<u>No way</u>! You go first.

1. <u>Bravo</u>! You won!

2. <u>Hi</u>, I think we met at Jarrod's party.

3. <u>What</u>! You said you were bringing the money!

4. <u>Ah</u>! That sun feels good.

5. <u>Ouch</u>! You stepped on my foot.

6. <u>Yes</u>, I understand you perfectly.

7. I didn't take the last piece of cake. <u>Really</u>!

8. <u>Well</u>, it's about time you got here!

9. <u>No</u>, I haven't seen your sister.

10. <u>Whoops</u>! I didn't realize the floor was so slippery.

11. <u>Oh, no</u>! I left my homework on the bus!

Grammar

12. I only have one token left, and I need two for the subway. <u>Good grief!</u>

13. <u>My</u>, how you've grown since the last time I saw you!

14. <u>Whew</u>, that sure was a close call!

15. Do I want to go with you to see our favorite movie again? <u>Yes!</u>

16. <u>Phew!</u> That truck just missed us.

17. <u>Oh, well</u>, better luck next time!

18. <u>Rats!</u> They sold the last team sweatshirt an hour ago.

19. <u>Aha!</u> You didn't think I'd be able to find you, did you?

20. <u>Ahem</u>, I believe you're sitting in my seat.

▶ **Exercise 2 Add to each sentence an interjection that expresses the emotion in parentheses. Add appropriate punctuation.** Answers may vary.

_____Congratulations!_____ You got the part. (compliment)

1. _____Oops!_____ I didn't mean to make such a mess. (apology)

2. _____No,_____ that can't be true. (denial)

3. _____Hey,_____ that's my dessert. (call attention to)

4. _____Hooray!_____ The Eagles are winning at last. (excitement)

5. _____Ouch!_____ That really hurts! (pain)

6. _____Ugh!_____ All the snow has turned to slush. (disgust)

7. _____Good grief!_____ We are already twenty minutes late. (impatience)

8. _____Yes!_____ I'll be glad to help you. (agreement)

9. _____Wow!_____ Did you really win ten dollars? (surprise)

10. _____Hey!_____ Watch out for the car! (call attention to)

11. _____Bravo!_____ That was a great performance. (approval)

12. _____Phew!_____ The bell rang just as I got to my desk. (relief)

13. _____Oops!_____ I dropped my glass on the floor! (surprise)

14. _____Aha!_____ I finally solved the puzzle. (satisfaction)

15. _____Oh, no!_____ We were supposed to stop at the store first. (regret)

Unit 7 **Review**

▶ **Exercise 1** Identify each word in italics by labeling it *adv.* (adverb), *conj.*
(conjunction), *inter.* (interjection), or *prep.* (preposition).

       inter.   prep.   conj.
    Unbelievable! Ramón placed second *in* the first race *and* won this one.

    inter.   prep.
1. *Wow!* I am so impressed *with* your natural talent.

          prep.   conj.
2. I like most *of* this jewelry, *but* I can buy only one piece.

                    prep.   adv.
3. Have you read any stories *by* Jack London *before?*

                      prep.   conj.
4. It's supposed to snow six inches *on* Friday, *and* I don't have any boots.

    inter.   prep.
5. *Oh,* are you still practicing *for* your recital?

         prep.   prep.
6. The road *to* success is paved *with* hard work.

      conj.   prep.
7. Does Ezra *or* Camilla have the key *to* the back door?

          prep.   prep.
8. The storage shed is *behind* the garage, which is *next to* the house.

                      prep.
9. Would you rather play a board game *instead of* cards?

  inter.   prep.
10. *Uh-oh,* I'm not sure where I put the envelope *with* the money.

          prep.   conj.   prep.
11. I keep the soap *under* the sink, *but* all other cleansers belong *in* this cupboard.

  conj.   conj.   prep.
12. *Neither* Yosef *nor* Pauline recognized me *in* the costume.

  inter.   adv.   prep.
13. *Phew!* We made it *inside before* the storm.

          prep.   prep.   prep.
14. Mr. Golden lives *in* the house *on* the southeast corner *of* this block.

          prep.   conj.   prep.
15. Have you seen a jacket *with* zippers *and* snap fasteners *in* the store recently?

  inter.   prep.   conj.   prep.
16. *Oh, good!* You've got the bag *of* prizes *and* the tickets *for* the games.

          prep.   conj. adv.
17. Sandra felt weak *during* math class, *and afterward* she left for home.

         conj.   adv. prep.
18. My uncle *and* my four cousins have been *inside for* three hours.

      prep.   prep.   prep.   conj.
19. Towers *like* the one *in* this picture were used *as* watchtowers *or* storage areas.

      prep.   conj.   prep.
20. Look *underneath* the bed for my brown shoes *and* the box *with* my sweaters.

Cumulative Review: Units 1–7

▶ **Exercise 1** **Draw one line under the complete subject and two lines under the complete predicate. If the subject is understood, write _you_ in the space provided.**

__you__ Give me a chance!

_____ 1. The gate in our backyard has a lock but no key.

_____ 2. Does anyone in the audience have any questions?

__you__ 3. Roll up your sleeves.

_____ 4. You tell a good story!

_____ 5. The furniture in my bedroom came from my uncle's house.

__you__ 6. Try again.

_____ 7. Has anyone been to Grand Teton National Park?

__you__ 8. Visit with Grandma sometime this week.

_____ 9. The evergreen tree bowed under the weight of the snow.

_____ 10. Everyone but Joe was on time for the meeting.

_____ 11. Not one more thing will fit in my closet.

_____ 12. Am I speaking loudly enough?

__you__ 13. Sort these files alphabetically.

__you__ 14. Sharpen these pencils for me.

_____ 15. I won a great prize!

_____ 16. You must decide before five o'clock.

_____ 17. These instructions are confusing!

_____ 18. Can you show me that step one more time?

__you__ 19. Turn the stereo and the television off.

_____ 20. Can you believe it!

__you__ 21. Put the milk in the refrigerator right away.

_____ 22. Mark and Melissa made apple pie for tonight's dessert.

_____ 23. My mother's second cousin, April, is living with us now.

_____ **24.** Can you call my mom or dad for me?

_____ **25.** Do you ever use the new software?

► **Exercise 2** **Write in the blank the tense or form of the verb indicated in parentheses.**

Yesterday we _____walked_____ through the park at dusk. *(walk,* past)

1. Kisha _____enjoys_____ her advanced dance classes. (*enjoy*, present)

2. Fred _____is cooking_____ dinner right now. (*cook*, present progressive)

3. Opa _____pointed_____ to Germany and Ghana on the map when she was told to find

countries starting with the letter *g*. (*point*, past)

4. Mrs. Morris _____has collected_____ dolls for years. (*collect*, present perfect)

5. Elizabeth _____is jogging_____ with Barry. (*jog*, present progressive)

6. Mr. Schaffer _____typed_____ this report. (*type*, past)

7. This picture _____proves_____ my point. (*prove*, present)

8. I _____have talked_____ to Susan several times already. (*talk*, present perfect)

9. The Coles _____live_____ on Mulberry Street near High Street. (*live*, present)

10. Mr. and Mrs. Thomas _____sat_____ in the first row. (*sit*, past)

11. Joshua _____has given_____ a lot of time to this project. (*give*, present perfect)

12. Shannon _____is studying_____ for tomorrow's test. (*study*, present progressive)

13. _____Will_____ you _____swim_____ in Saturday's meet? (*swim*, future)

14. Mrs. Gunther _____had taught_____ seventh grade for ten years. (*teach*, past perfect)

15. _____Have_____ you _____gone_____ to Dallas before? (*go*, present perfect)

16. Dad _____cut_____ my hair yesterday. (*cut*, past)

17. I _____have worn_____ that shirt only once. (*wear*, present perfect)

18. Who _____broke_____ this glass? (*break*, past)

19. Jeremy's little brother _____was crying_____ . (*cry*, past progressive)

20. I _____will bring_____ flowers to my grandma next week. (*bring*, future)

▶ **Exercise 3** **Identify the word in italics by labeling it *adv.* (adverb), *conj.* (conjunction),**
***inter.* (interjection), or *prep.* (preposition).**

      inter.   conj.   prep.
     Oh, I left my books *and* my money *in* my locker.

          inter.   prep.
  1. *Congratulations!* You got the blue ribbon *for* creative arts.

  prep.   conj.
  2. *Since* my accident, I ski cross-country *but* not downhill.

                          prep.   inter.
  3. The basketball team has won its first game *in* two years. *Hooray!*

                   conj.   prep.
  4. Sylvio, can you find the Indian Ocean *or* the Bay of Bengal *on* this map?

   inter.   prep.
  5. *Ouch,* I didn't know the edge *of* the table was so sharp.

          prep.   conj.
  6. I actually ran *to* school this morning, *but* I was still late.

              adv.   prep.
  7. He left his gloves *on* when he painted the mural *on* the wall.

            conj.   prep.
  8. I vacuumed the carpets *but* still have to clean *behind* the couch.

    prep.   prep.
  9. *During* the party the dog has to stay *outside* the house.

               conj.   adv.
 10. If you can't reach my mom *or* dad, my aunt is probably *around*.

             conj.   prep.   prep.
 11. You can find an almanac *and* a dictionary *on* the shelf *in* the den.

   inter.   prep.
 12. *Oh, no!* I cracked an egg, and the shell fell *into* the batter.

  prep.   prep.   prep.
 13. *In* 1861 Lincoln offered command *of* the U.S. Army *to* Robert E. Lee.

    prep.   prep.
 14. *Along with* Jerry and Phil, I walked *toward* the opening of the cave.

         prep. conj.   prep.
 15. Put your book *down, and* listen *to* me.

   inter.   prep.   conj.
 16. *Wow!* Sam says you are fluent *in* English, Spanish, *and* German.

           adv. prep.
 17. Turn your lights *out by* ten o'clock.

   conj.   conj.   prep.   adv.
 18. *Either* close your door, *or* turn the volume *on* your stereo *down*.

Unit 8: Subject-Verb Agreement

Lesson 48
Making Subjects and Verbs Agree

The **subject** and **verb** of a sentence must agree in number. A noun that is singular must have the singular form of the verb. A noun that is plural takes the plural form of the verb.

A **cat sleeps** during the day. (singular noun *cat,* singular verb *sleeps*)
Cats sleep during the day. (plural noun *cats,* plural verb *sleep*)

▶ **Exercise 1** **Draw two lines under the verb in parentheses that agrees with the subject.**

Leroy (rides, ride) his bicycle to school every day.

1. Television (brings, bring) the world into our homes with pictures, or video, and sounds, or audio.

2. The electronic television imaging device (was, were) invented in the 1920s.

3. The first practical TV system (was demonstrated, were demonstrated) at the New York World's Fair in 1939.

4. Early television sets (was, were) crude black and white models.

5. Today, technical advancements (gives, give) us high-quality color pictures.

6. Also, most programs now (comes, come) with stereo sound.

7. Television programs (is based, are based) on movies, plays, books, original screenplays, and short stories.

8. The subjects (remains, remain) the same, yesterday and today.

9. *I Love Lucy* still (serves, serve) as the example for all family shows.

10. *The Mickey Mouse Club* (was, were) first broadcast to "Mouseketeers" throughout America in 1955.

11. Today, their grandchildren (watches, watch) a new program with the same name.

12. Both *Mickey Mouse Club* shows (has, have) music, games, information, and humor.

13. The original *Mickey Mouse Club* (<u><u>seems</u></u>, seem) almost foreign to viewers of today's show.

14. However, each show (<u><u>presents</u></u>, present) the popular styles of the day.

15. Until the 1960s, a city (<u><u>was given</u></u>, were given) only four or five TV channels.

16. Thirty years later, cable TV (<u><u>brings</u></u>, bring) many channels into your set.

17. Entire channels (focuses, <u><u>focus</u></u>) on one subject.

18. Experts (predicts, <u>predict</u>) 500-channel cable systems in the next few years.

19. Television sets can (shows, <u><u>show</u></u>) more than just TV programs.

20. The "Information Superhighway" (<u><u>combines</u></u>, combine) computer data, programs, games, and communications.

▶ **Exercise 2** **Underline the subject of each sentence. Then, choose the verb in parentheses that agrees with the subject and write it in the blank.**

Many <u>individuals</u> _____**use**_____ television to view the news. (uses, use)

1. A television <u>newscast</u> _____**relies**_____ on the efforts of many different persons. (relies, rely)

2. The on-air <u>newscasters</u> _____**are**_____ a small part of a large, mostly unseen team. (is, are)

3. News <u>programs</u> _____**begin**_____ with a producer. (begins, begin)

4. The <u>producer</u> _____**decides**_____ which stories to cover. (decides, decide)

5. The assignment desk <u>dispatcher</u> _____**sends**_____ reporters and video photographers to different parts of the city. (sends, send)

6. News <u>photographers</u> _____**carry**_____ video cameras to tape whatever stories they cover. (carries, carry)

7. Back at the station, electronic news gathering (ENG) <u>editors</u> _____**combine**_____ different videotapes and scenes to tell a story. (combines, combine)

8. Each news <u>tape</u> _____**lasts**_____ between twenty and ninety seconds. (lasts, last)

9. Live <u>newscasts</u> _____**are**_____ broadcast from a studio. (is, are)

10. A typical <u>studio</u> _____**has**_____ about thirty powerful spotlights. (has, have)

Lesson 49
Subject Pronouns and Verb Agreement

Subject pronouns (*I, you, he, she, it, we, they*) must also agree with the verb.

I **walk.** (First person, singular)   We **walk.** (First person, plural)
You **walk.** (Second person, singular)   You **walk.** (Second person, plural)
He, she or it **walks.** (Third person, singular)   They **walk.** (Third person, plural)

The verbs *have, do,* and *be* can be main verbs or helping verbs. They must agree with the subject whether they are used as main verbs or helping verbs.

I **am** asleep. (main verb)   I **am** walking. (helping verb)
She **does** good work. (main verb)   They **do** like their work. (helping verb)
You **have** three dollars. (main verb)   You **have** met our new teacher. (helping verb)

▶ **Exercise 1** **Draw two lines under the verb in parentheses that agrees with the subject.**

I (hopes, hope) the movie isn't sold out.

1. Before beginning to eat, they (thanks, thank) their hostess.

2. We always (has, have) to wait for Anne to arrive.

3. She (is, are) planning to read *Little Women* this summer.

4. On the top shelf you (finds, find) the basket of fruit.

5. It (is, are) obvious that the picnic will have to be postponed.

6. He (lives, live) in a town called Woodsfield.

7. Walking up to the plate, I (prepares, prepare) to bat.

8. They (has, have) seen the new art exhibit.

9. We usually (packs, pack) our suitcases the day before we leave on a trip.

10. Since it is so late, he (is, are) coming with us.

11. Today you (seems, seem) even happier than usual.

12. Gretchen was going to organize a softball game, but now it (looks, look) like rain.

13. I (practices, practice) singing every day.

14. She (visits, visit) the neighbors twice a week.

15. He (says, say) the park is filled with flowers.

Grammar

16. We (is, <u>are</u>) waving to the boaters from the bridge.

17. When shopping for gifts, they (searches, <u>search</u>) for practical items.

18. You (paints, <u>paint</u>) beautifully, Irene.

19. I (has, <u>have</u>) enjoyed learning to play chess.

20. It (<u>is</u>, are) the prettiest garden we have ever seen!

21. They (likes, <u>like</u>) to go camping on weekends.

22. She (<u>is</u>, are) thinking about buying Christina a new watch.

23. Beyond the horizon he (<u>sees</u>, see) the glow of a gorgeous sunset.

24. Singing joyously, we (marches, <u>march</u>) toward the stage.

25. You (has, <u>have</u>) heard Danny's new composition, haven't you?

26. It (<u>startles</u>, startle) me when the wind chimes sound unexpectedly.

27. We often (stays, <u>stay</u>) at Grandpa's farm during the summer.

28. After running five miles, I (<u>am</u>, are) ready for a rest.

29. They (laughs, <u>laugh</u>) whenever they look at themselves in the carnival mirrors.

30. He (<u>cooks</u>, cook) delicious Italian meals.

31. This month we (is, <u>are</u>) learning how to polka.

32. Drew, you (picks, <u>pick</u>) the colors for the decorations.

33. He (<u>waits</u>, wait) in the airport restaurant, hoping his plane will arrive soon.

34. It (<u>appears</u>, appear) as if the understudy will have to go on tonight.

35. Smiling, I (greets, <u>greet</u>) the new member of the class.

▶ **Writing Link** **Write a short paragraph about your favorite team sport. Use at least two subject pronouns, and be sure each subject and verb agree.**

_____

_____

_____

_____

_____

Lesson 50
Locating the Subject

Sometimes a prepositional phrase comes between the subject and the verb. The verb must agree with the subject of the sentence and not with the object of the preposition.

The **rooms** near the entrance **have** new windows.
The **air** in the mountains **contains** little oxygen.

In the first sentence, *near the entrance* is a prepositional phrase. The subject of the sentence is *rooms,* which is plural; therefore, the verb that agrees with it, *have,* is also plural. In the second sentence, *in the mountains* is a prepositional phrase. The singular verb *contains* agrees with *air,* which is a singular subject.

You can check for subject-verb agreement by removing the prepositional phrase.

The rooms have new windows.   The air contains little oxygen.

Some sentences begin with *there* or *here.* These words are never the subject of a sentence. Look for the subject after the verb.

There **are** many palm **trees** in Florida.   Here in the city **is** a large **building**.

To make finding the subject easier, rearrange these sentences by placing the subject before the verb in the usual manner.

Many palm **trees are** there in Florida.   A large **building is** here in the city.

▶ **Exercise 1** **Draw one line under the subject. Draw two lines under the verb in parentheses that agrees with the subject.**

<u>Each</u> of the girls (has, have) her own locker.

1. The <u>monkeys</u> in the zoo (climbs, climb) trees all day long.

2. <u>Students</u> from all over the country (attends, attend) day camp every spring.

3. <u>Cookies</u> fresh from the oven (tastes, taste) delicious.

4. <u>Drivers</u> from the freight company (travels, travel) across the country.

5. A <u>truckload</u> of band uniforms (arrives, arrive) Saturday.

6. <u>Millions</u> of persons (listens, listen) to radio every day.

7. A <u>sergeant</u> from the police department (teaches, teach) bicycle safety at our school.

8. <u>Roots</u> from the mesquite tree (extends, <u>extend</u>) far below the ground.

9. A <u>ticket</u> for front-row seats (<u>costs</u>, cost) too much.

10. The <u>restaurant</u> with the chairs and tables in front of it (<u>serves</u>, serve) authentic Hawaiian food.

11. <u>Suitcases</u> with an extra pouch (holds, <u>hold</u>) extra clothes.

12. The <u>fireworks</u> at the city park (begins, <u>begin</u>) at 9:30 P.M.

13. <u>Patterns</u> from the Smith Clothing Catalog (requires, <u>require</u>) careful cutting.

14. <u>Teams</u> in the City League (scores, <u>score</u>) more touchdowns than any other teams in the county.

15. Here (<u>is</u>, are) the <u>book</u> that belongs to Kim.

16. The <u>president</u> of the United States (<u>lives</u>, live) in the White House.

17. <u>Hamburgers</u> at this restaurant (comes, <u>come</u>) with tomatoes, lettuce, and cheese.

18. <u>Trees</u> near the top of the mountain (needs, <u>need</u>) more water.

19. The <u>glue</u> on postage stamps (<u>contains</u>, contain) flavoring to make it taste better.

20. The <u>photographer</u> from the school paper (<u>wants</u>, want) us to smile for the class picture.

21. <u>All</u> of the visitors to the museum (receives, <u>receive</u>) a souvenir.

22. The school <u>year</u> in this district (<u>lasts</u>, last) nine months and two weeks.

23. The <u>lockers</u> in this building (stands, <u>stand</u>) more than six feet high.

24. The <u>core</u> of Earth (<u>contains</u>, contain) molten iron.

25. There (is, <u>are</u>) reptile <u>eggs</u> in that leathery covering.

26. <u>Each</u> of the birds in the wetlands (<u>wears</u>, wear) an identification tag.

27. The <u>leader</u> of the circus clowns (<u>works</u>, work) in a bank during the week.

28. The <u>organist</u> in Rhonda's church also (<u>plays</u>, play) at the baseball stadium.

29. The <u>cider</u> from Washington apples (<u>has</u>, have) a pleasant aroma.

30. Class <u>pictures</u> from the 1980s (hangs, <u>hang</u>) in the halls.

31. <u>Light</u> from the sun (<u>reaches</u>, reach) Earth in eight minutes.

32. The <u>sound</u> of the crickets (<u>interrupts</u>, interrupt) the quiet night.

Lesson 51
Agreement with Compound Subjects

A **compound subject** is two or more subjects that have the same verb. When two or more subjects are joined by *and*, the verb is plural.

William **and** Sandy **live** on the same block.
Both trees **and** flowers **require** sunlight.
Elaine **and** her brothers **play** in the band.

Compound subjects can also be joined by *or, either...or,* and *neither...nor.* In these cases, the verb must agree with the subject that is closer to it.

Dana **or** Maria **knows** the answer.
Either Dana **or** his study partners **know** the answer.
Neither the fifth-graders **nor** Dana **knows** the answer.

▶ **Exercise 1 Draw two lines under the verb in parentheses that agrees with the subject.**

Both Florida and Hawaii (has, have) beautiful beaches.

1. Neither shoes nor jackets (fits, fit) in these lockers.

2. Tomas and his brothers (runs, run) in the marathon every year.

3. Both the mayor and the governor (has, have) offices downtown.

4. Either cotton or wool (feels, feel) comfortable.

5. Elephants and rhinos (lives, live) in the jungles of Africa.

6. Both the orchestra conductor and the musicians (studies, study) classical music for years.

7. Either newspapers or a magazine (contains, contain) advertisements.

8. Martha and Jean (walks, walk) to school when the weather is warm.

9. Neither snow nor ice (stays, stay) on the ground after the spring thaw.

10. Blisters and bruises may (appears, appear) on one's hands after doing yardwork.

11. Heat or smoke by the door (warns, warn) of a fire on the other side.

12. Both badminton and tennis (uses, use) a net to divide the two halves of the court.

13. Bowlers and gymnasts (competes, compete) indoors.

14. Neither skateboards nor roller skates (is permitted, <u>are permitted</u>) in the parking area.

15. In many cities, cars and bicycles (shares, <u>share</u>) the same road.

16. Both glass and plastic (holds, <u>hold</u>) water.

17. Neither the dancers nor the instructor (<u>thinks</u>, think) the stage is too slippery.

18. Palm trees and bushes (provides, <u>provide</u>) shade.

19. Dolphins and whales (belongs, <u>belong</u>) to the same order of mammals.

20. Mrs. Trinh and Mr. Walton (teaches, <u>teach</u>) at City College in the summer.

21. Orange juice or grapefruit juice (<u>has</u>, have) plenty of Vitamin C.

22. Carpenters and electricians (serves, <u>serve</u>) apprenticeships before starting their own businesses.

23. Either the ocean or the pool (<u>is</u>, are) a pleasant place to relax.

24. Electric bulbs and candles (creates, <u>create</u>) light.

25. African elephants and Indian elephants (has, <u>have</u>) different facial features.

26. Yarn and silk (is used, <u>are used</u>) for embroidery.

27. Both the arcade and the amusement park (closes, <u>close</u>) after Labor Day.

28. A map or a navigation chart (<u>shows</u>, show) where to find the coral reef.

29. Billboards and posters (advertises, <u>advertise</u>) new movies.

30. Neither wood nor bricks (keeps, <u>keep</u>) out all of the cold weather.

31. Both dogs and cats (enjoys, <u>enjoy</u>) running in the park.

32. Joel and Adam (plays, <u>play</u>) video games on weekends.

33. Neither boots nor galoshes (leaks, <u>leak</u>) in wet weather.

34. Gerbils and hamsters (runs, <u>run</u>) on stationary wheels.

35. A calculator or a computer (<u>solves</u>, solve) difficult math problems.

36. Kanisha and John (sings, <u>sing</u>) a duet in the school play.

37. A postcard or an entry form (<u>is</u>, are) acceptable.

38. A pitcher and a catcher (communicates, <u>communicate</u>) with hand signals.

39. Neither a mop nor a sponge (<u>absorbs</u>, absorb) all the water.

40. Water and oil (does, <u>do</u>) not mix.

 Unit 8 **Review**

▶ **Exercise 1 Draw two lines under the verb in parentheses that agrees with the subject.**

There by the building (<u>is</u>, are) a large tree.

1. The Amazon River basin (<u>covers</u>, cover) one-third of Brazil.

2. A cool breeze (<u>chills</u>, chill) the air on a hot summer day.

3. Sharks (roams, <u>roam</u>) the oceans looking for things to eat.

4. Yoshi (<u>plays</u>, play) the clarinet in the school band.

5. We (has seen, <u>have seen</u>) this movie before.

6. Ashley (<u>prefers</u>, prefer) French fries to potato chips.

7. Our teacher (<u>goes</u>, go) to the beach every summer.

8. Cartoons (has, <u>have</u>) many hand-drawn scenes.

9. Young children (imitates, <u>imitate</u>) the actions of their parents, sisters, and brothers.

10. Professional athletes (trains, <u>train</u>) for years to learn their sport.

11. A bugle (<u>sounds</u>, sound) similar to a trumpet.

12. Toni (<u>wants</u>, want) to play goalie next quarter.

13. Birds (flies, <u>fly</u>) from one tree to another.

14. She (<u>sings</u>, sing) in the church choir.

15. Mushrooms (grows, <u>grow</u>) in damp, dark forests.

16. A canoe (<u>holds</u>, hold) one or two people.

17. My city (<u>has</u>, have) a large fireworks display every Fourth of July.

18. Cactus plants (retains, <u>retain</u>) water.

19. I (rides, <u>ride</u>) the number 8 bus to go to school.

20. The theater (<u>shows</u>, show) a new movie every two weeks.

21. The leaders of every country (talks, <u>talk</u>) to each other once a year.

22. A hike up the mountain (<u>requires</u>, require) plenty of strength.

Grammar

Cumulative Review: Units 1–8

▶ **Exercise 1** **Draw one line under each complete subject. Draw two lines under each complete predicate.**

The fish in the pond <u>swam back and forth.</u>

1. Everyone at the party <u>had a great time.</u>

2. This book <u>has many interesting facts.</u>

3. Each contestant <u>chose a category and answered a question.</u>

4. A bubbling brook <u>meandered through the mountains.</u>

5. Christopher <u>opened the mysterious box,</u> but Lisa <u>closed it quickly.</u>

6. The rally <u>ended with two stirring speeches and the singing of the national anthem.</u>

7. An explosion <u>came from the chemistry lab.</u>

8. Sixteen teams <u>will play in the annual tournament.</u>

9. Cardinals and blue jays <u>are common in this area.</u>

10. The Tylers <u>are moving to Chicago in February.</u>

11. We <u>will study black holes in science class today.</u>

12. Some television programs <u>seem educational as well as entertaining.</u>

13. Our field hockey team <u>won the championship last year,</u> and they <u>may win again this year.</u>

14. Dad <u>tells funny jokes at the dinner table.</u>

15. You <u>should try white-water rafting sometime.</u>

16. Talia <u>asked about the value of the gemstones.</u>

17. The cooking instructor <u>taught us a recipe for beef burgundy.</u>

18. The recreation center <u>has an indoor swimming pool.</u>

19. Jackie <u>is flying home for her grandma's birthday.</u>

20. Silence <u>reigned throughout the large library.</u>

▶ **Exercise 2** Write the part of speech of the italicized word in the blank. Use these abbreviations: *N* (noun), *V* (verb), *pro.* (pronoun), *adj.* (adjective), *adv.* (adverb), *prep.* (preposition), *conj.* (conjunction), and *int.* (interjection).

adj.   We have *three* maple trees in our backyard.

_V_   **1.** Todd *raced* to the corner store.

prep.   **2.** Pictures *in* the museum hang on special hooks.

_N_   **3.** *Conservation* of rare animals requires careful planning.

prep.   **4.** The pedals *on* a bicycle spin in both directions.

adv.   **5.** Student athletes are *constantly* working, either in the classroom or on the playing field.

int.   **6.** *Wow!* That band plays great music.

conj.   **7.** Alison *and* Sydney rode the roller coaster twice.

pro.   **8.** *He* always brings his lunch in a brown paper sack.

adj.   **9.** Mom bought a *blue* sweater to wear with her white skirt.

adv.   **10.** Carrie *often* stops at the music store after school.

_N_   **11.** Give your ticket to the *usher*.

pro.   **12.** Yesterday *we* tried the new Mexican restaurant.

_V_   **13.** Roberto really *enjoyed* his trip to the planetarium.

conj.   **14.** The letter contained valuable information, *but* Nora did not know what to do with it.

int.   **15.** *Well,* I always thought he would come back to his hometown.

adv.   **16.** Lucia was *truly* surprised at the reception she received.

prep.   **17.** The ball of yarn rolled *under* the dining room table.

adj.   **18.** The poem was *long,* but it was also quite beautiful.

_V_   **19.** The firecracker *exploded* into a hundred twinkling lights.

_N_   **20.** Jasmine adored the playful *puppy* in the pet shop window.

Grammar

▶ **Exercise 3** **Draw two lines under the verb in parentheses that agrees with the subject.**

The men in my family (has, <u>have</u>) red hair.

1. Members of the soccer team (wears, <u>wear</u>) special shoes for wet fields.

2. Squirrels in the park (gathers, <u>gather</u>) nuts for the winter.

3. The announcer on TV (<u>says</u>, say) it is going to rain this weekend.

4. A camel's water supply (<u>lasts</u>, last) for many days.

5. The cans of paint (weighs, <u>weigh</u>) seven pounds each.

6. Vacations by the beach (ends, <u>end</u>) too quickly.

7. The runners on sleds easily (glides, <u>glide</u>) over fresh snow.

8. Libraries and museums (adds, <u>add</u>) culture to a city.

9. Hot chocolate or soup (<u>warms</u>, warm) you up on a cold winter day.

10. Old trunks and treasure chests (hides, <u>hide</u>) many interesting things.

11. Oil and gas (forms, <u>form</u>) underground.

12. Both Democrats and Republicans (campaigns, <u>campaign</u>) for political offices.

13. Neither rivers nor streams (runs, <u>run</u>) uphill.

14. Factories and mills (manufactures, <u>manufacture</u>) products for people to buy.

15. Both frogs and toads (croaks, <u>croak</u>) in the swamps.

16. A bell or chimes (rings, <u>ring</u>) on the hour.

17. The space shuttle and satellites (orbits, <u>orbit</u>) Earth.

18. Neither Will nor his sisters (rides, <u>ride</u>) our school bus this year.

19. Sand and cactus plants (bakes, <u>bake</u>) in the desert sun.

20. Both butterflies and moths (goes, <u>go</u>) through several stages of development.

21. Either a coat or a parka (<u>provides</u>, provide) warmth in the winter.

22. Dolphins and tuna (swims, <u>swim</u>) in groups.

23. Either a rainbow or floods (follows, <u>follow</u>) a storm.

24. Both decorations and ornaments (brightens, <u>brighten</u>) up a room.

25. Statues and monuments (honors, <u>honor</u>) outstanding individuals.

Unit 9: Diagraming Sentences

Lesson 52
Diagraming Simple Subjects and Simple Predicates

To diagram a sentence, first draw a long horizontal line. Then draw a short vertical line that crosses the horizontal line. Write the simple subject to the left of the vertical line. Write the simple predicate to the right of the vertical line. When diagraming sentences, use capital letters as they appear in the sentence, but do not use punctuation.

Dynamite explodes.

| Dynamite | explodes |

Write only the simple subject and the simple predicate in this part of the diagram. Remember that the simple predicate can include a helping verb.

The dynamite will explode on schedule.

| dynamite | will explode |

▶ **Exercise 1 Diagram only the simple subject and the simple predicate of each sentence.**

1. The store opens early on Saturday.   **2.** My aunt works as a chemist.

| store | opens |

| aunt | works |

3. A torch lit the way.

4. The football team burst onto the field.

team | burst

5. The Giraldis traveled through Italy last summer.

Giraldis | traveled

6. The heavy rainfall soaked the dry soil.

7. They named the collie pups Wynken, Blynken, and Nod.

They | named

8. Tazu came to the library.

Tazu | came

9. This movie is almost three hours long.

movie | is

10. The sixth-grade girls won the volleyball tournament.

girls | won

Lesson 53
Diagraming the Four Kinds of Sentences

The simple subject and the simple predicate of four kinds of sentences are diagramed below. Notice that the location of the simple subject and the simple predicate in a sentence diagram is always the same, regardless of word order in the sentence. In an interrogative sentence the simple subject often comes between the two parts of a verb phrase. In an imperative sentence the simple subject is understood to be *you*.

Declarative: The house has central heat.

house	has

Interrogative: Does it have air conditioning?

it	Does have

Imperative: Turn down the thermostat at ten o'clock.

(you)	Turn

Exclamatory: How warm it is in this room!

it	is

▶ **Exercise 1 Diagram only the simple subject and the simple predicate.**

1. Eli Whitney invented the cotton gin.

2. The ice cream will melt there.

Eli Whitney	invented

ice cream	will melt

Grammar

Name _____ Class _____ Date _____

3. How much money do you need?

you	do need

4. Why did Sally call the emergency squad?

Sally	did call

5. What caused the stain on the living room rug?

What	caused

6. What a good movie that was!

that	was

7. How odd this is!

this	is

8. Put the leftovers in the refrigerator.

(you)	Put

182   *Grammar and Language Workbook, Grade 6*

Lesson 54

Diagraming Direct and Indirect Objects and Predicate Words

Grammar

In a sentence diagram, the direct object is placed to the right of a vertical line after the action verb.

Marissa threw the ball.

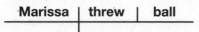

Similarly, place the predicate noun to the right of the linking verb. Draw a slanted line to separate the verb from the predicate noun.

Today's special is blackened swordfish.

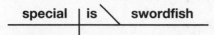

Diagram a predicate adjective just as you would diagram a predicate noun.

Edmund seems confused.

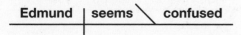

In a diagram, the indirect object sits on a line below and to the right of the verb. Draw a slanted line to connect the indirect object to the verb.

Marissa threw Jake the ball.

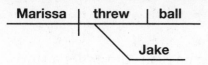

▶ **Exercise 1** **Diagram the simple subject, simple predicate, direct or indirect object, and predicate noun or adjective.**

1. The library needs volunteers.

2. Yoshitaka finished the pizza.

| library | needs | volunteers |

| Yoshitaka | finished | pizza |

3. Mom gave me a hug.

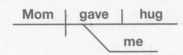

6. Aunt Eleanor bought me tickets.

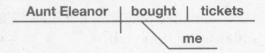

4. The sudden rain soaked the ground.

rain | soaked | ground

7. This watermelon tastes so sweet!

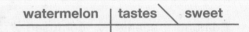

5. Please hand me that bowl.

8. Katherine read Alexandra a story.

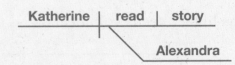

Lesson 55
Diagraming Adjectives and Adverbs

An **adjective** modifies a noun or a pronoun. In a diagram write the adjective on a slanted line beneath the noun or the pronoun it modifies. Diagram possessive nouns and pronouns and the articles *a, an,* and *the* just as you would diagram other kinds of adjectives.

The sturdy house withstood the violent storm.

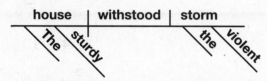

An adverb can modify a verb, an adjective, or another adverb. Notice how adverbs are diagramed.

The extraordinarily loud noise woke us immediately.

▶ **Exercise 1 Diagram each sentence.**

1. The beautiful cherry blossoms attract many visitors.

2. The bright colors caught the infant's attention.

3. Anne slept late yesterday.

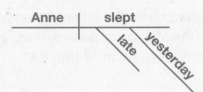

6. Do not give me so much spaghetti!

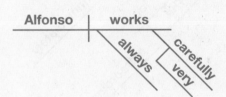

4. The wren chirped merrily.

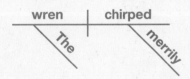

7. Alfonso always works very carefully.

5. The long, curvy road suddenly disappeared.

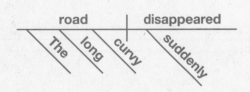

8. This lesson confuses me somewhat.

Lesson 56
Diagraming Prepositional Phrases

All prepositional phrases, whether used as an adjective or as an adverb, are diagramed the same way.

Used as an adjective: The boxes under the stairs are full.

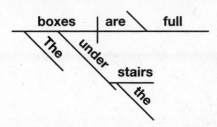

Used as an adverb: Hector put the boxes under the stairs.

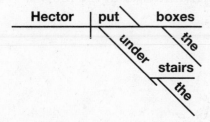

▶ **Exercise 1 Diagram each sentence.**

1. Toni's letter from Italy arrived earlier.

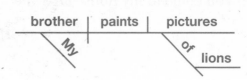

2. The garden under the grape arbor is Grandma's favorite.

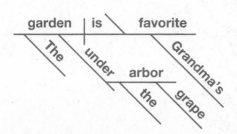

3. My brother paints pictures of lions.

4. Put your coat on a hook by the back door.

5. The shelves beneath the books hold family heirlooms.

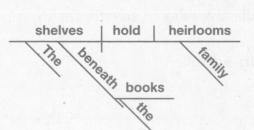

6. The brick house above the river's delta was built in the last century.

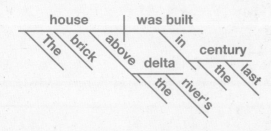

7. Can you come to my house after the game?

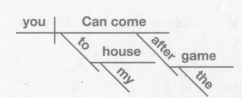

8. Mr. Larkspur's surprise was the package outside the classroom door.

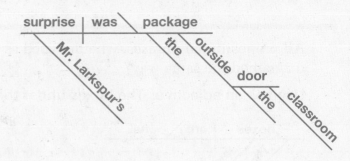

9. The flags of all the participating countries fluttered in the breeze.

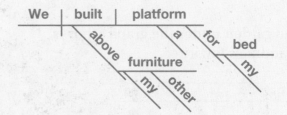

10. We built a platform for my bed above my other furniture.

Lesson 57
Diagraming Compound Sentence Parts

When you diagram compound parts of a sentence, place the second part of the compound below the first.

Compound Subject: Casaba and cantaloupe are melons.

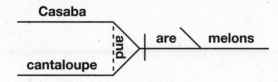

Compound Predicate: Fruit trees grow and blossom.

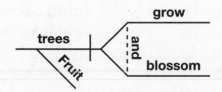

Compound Sentence: Some fruits are sweet, but some have a tart taste.

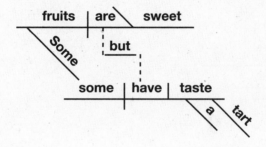

▶ **Exercise 1 Diagram each sentence.**

1. Geanna or Rodolfo could do the artwork.

2. The library and the post office close at noon on Saturday.

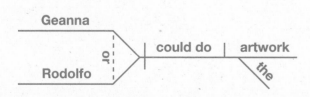

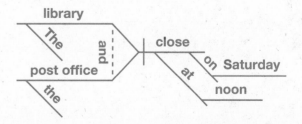

3. It rains often and hails seldom.

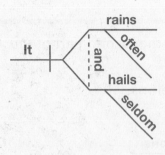

6. Irene and Hoshi raked the leaves, and Toshiko and Olivia carried them.

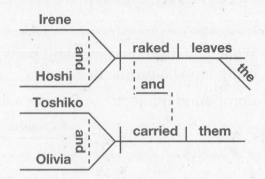

4. Peter pushed the door, but it was heavy.

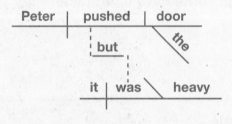

7. Bright colors and unusual shapes will help these posters.

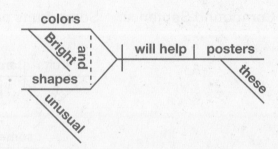

5. Dad vacuumed and dusted.

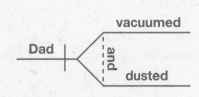

8. Sharps and flats can change the mood of the music.

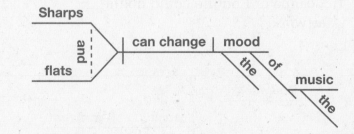

Unit 9 **Review**

▶ **Exercise 1 Diagram each sentence.**

1. Do you know Mr. Sweeney?

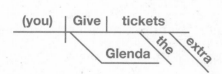

2. Mrs. Peterson sent us six blankets for the refugees.

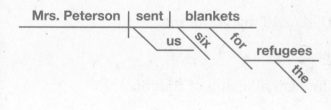

3. Give Glenda the extra tickets.

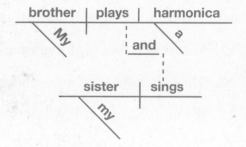

4. The excited children scampered quickly into the decorated room.

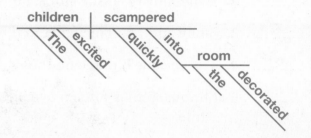

5. My brother plays a harmonica, and my sister sings.

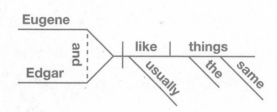

6. Eugene and Edgar usually like the same things.

Grammar

Cumulative Review: Units 1–9

▶ **Exercise 1** Write *S* if the sentence is a simple sentence, *C* if it is compound, or *frag.* if it is a sentence fragment.

_____ C _____ Robins sing, and turkeys gobble.

_____ C _____ 1. Cats meow, and dogs bark.

_____ C _____ 2. Wind moves sailing ships, but a motor powers a speedboat.

_____ S _____ 3. Jenny and Francine went to the Somerset County Fair together.

_____ frag. _____ 4. The antique biplane on the wide cement runway.

_____ C _____ 5. Miriam studies French every day, but Askalu studies Swahili only once in a while.

_____ S _____ 6. My brand-new computer has a hard drive and a modem.

_____ frag. _____ 7. Growing in the garden, down by the old broken birdbath.

_____ C _____ 8. The grass needs mowing, and the garage needs painting.

_____ S _____ 9. I forgot all about that big history test on Monday.

_____ frag. _____ 10. The brand-new notebook and the dirty blue jacket.

_____ C _____ 11. I shall seal this big envelope, and Darla will mail it for me.

_____ S _____ 12. Those bananas are growing browner every day.

_____ S _____ 13. My aunt Kanya still reads to me from her collection of storybooks.

_____ S _____ 14. The gray clouds made the day dreary.

_____ S _____ 15. Jeff saw his friends Tommy and Jamal in the park.

_____ C _____ 16. Lightning flashes frighten me, but I like the sound of thunder.

_____ S _____ 17. Why is the road crew working in front of our house again?

_____ S _____ 18. In spite of its appearance, our old car runs pretty well.

_____ S _____ 19. Do you remember the Smith family: Michael, Brandon, Sara, and Elizabeth?

_____ frag. _____ 20. Bright red robin on the long, twisted tree branch.

_____ S _____ 21. Your new ten-speed bicycle flies down the road so swiftly and smoothly!

_____ C _____ 22. I smell that delicious apple pie, and I can almost taste it.

_____ frag. _____ 23. Exciting stories about actual events and real heroes.

_____S_____ **24.** Cindy and Carla quite often practice their music after school.

_____C_____ **25.** Glenn could come tomorrow, but he cannot make it today.

_____S_____ **26.** The canary's song is soothing.

_____C_____ **27.** Mr. Raintree sings one part, and we follow with ours.

_____frag._____ **28.** A stormy sea and high winds, black sky and occasional lightning.

▶ **Exercise 2** Write *P* if the verb is in the present tense, *pres. prog.* if present progressive, *pres. perf.* if present perfect, *past* if past tense, *past prog.* if past progressive, and *past perf.* if past perfect.

_____pres. perf._____ The puppy *has stolen* one of Dad's new blue slippers.

_____past prog._____ **1.** Ms. Johnson *was giving* a test in the next room.

_____P_____ **2.** The hours *creep* by slowly on rainy afternoons.

_____pres. prog._____ **3.** I *am drawing* a picture for art class.

_____past perf._____ **4.** Sally *had woven* that scarf before her twelfth birthday.

_____pres. perf._____ **5.** *Have* you ever *ridden* a horse?

_____past_____ **6.** I *woke* up at four in the morning.

_____pres. perf._____ **7.** The flowers *have grown* fast in this wet weather.

_____P_____ **8.** Your voice *reminds* me of someone else.

_____past_____ **9.** Conor *threw* the final strikeout pitch in our game against Central.

_____pres. perf._____ **10.** Who *has seen* my old green jacket?

_____P_____ **11.** I *collect* rocks, stamps, and old coins.

_____past_____ **12.** The fans *stared* at their favorite actor as he walked in.

_____P_____ **13.** Sharon *sings* in the choir.

_____pres. perf._____ **14.** That dog *has bitten* people before.

_____pres. perf._____ **15.** They *have weathered* many storms throughout their years together.

_____pres. prog._____ **16.** *Are* you *leaving* soon?

_____past perf._____ **17.** Paul *had swept* the room carefully.

_____P_____ **18.** The maple trees *provide* shade on a hot day.

_____pres. perf._____ **19.** Mrs. Baughman *has paid* me for mowing her yard.

Grammar

pres. prog.	**20.** I *am holding* the ladder steady.
pres. perf.	**21.** The snow *has come* at last!
P	**22.** The wind *rattles* the window panes.
P	**23.** My bird feeder *hangs* on a limb outside my bedroom window.
past	**24.** The baron *rose* and stood by the window, dreaming of his princess.
past perf.	**25.** The meat *had* not *frozen* properly.
pres. prog.	**26.** I'm *teaching* my puppy to sit, roll over, and fetch.
pres. perf.	**27.** That tree *has stood* there for hundreds of years.
P	**28.** The little field mouse *hides* timidly under the tulip leaves.

▶ **Exercise 3** Write *pro.* if the italicized noun is a proper noun, *com.* if it is a common noun, or *col.* if it is a collective noun. For nouns that are both common and collective, wirte *col.*

col.	The *group* has decided not to pay for a new slide projector.
col.	**1.** The *family* will buy this land for a new store.
pro.	**2.** *Mrs. Smith* will teach our class next week.
pro.	**3.** *Dr. Johnson* says a lot of funny things when I visit him.
col.	**4.** When will the *legislature* vote on that bill?
com.	**5.** The Carlson's *dog* is always in our yard.
pro.	**6.** *Tom Sawyer* is one of my favorite story characters.
col.	**7.** The cheerleading *squad* will practice after school on Tuesday.
com.	**8.** What's the name of the *actor* who played the butler?
pro.	**9.** *President Abraham Lincoln* is my favorite American leader.
col.	**10.** According to Bob, our *class* will go on a field trip next week.
com.	**11.** The *alligator* crossed the road right in front of us!
com.	**12.** The giant *battleship* is now a war memorial for our state.
col.	**13.** My brother's army *battalion* will pass through our town today.
com.	**14.** The *clouds* looked like white feathers on the underwing of the sky.
com.	**15.** Although *cricket* is played with a ball and a bat, it is different from baseball.

*U*sage
Glossary

Unit 10: Usage Glossary

Lesson 58
Usage: *accept* to *a lot*

Words that are similar are sometimes misused.

accept, except *Accept* means "to receive." *Except* means "other than."

Linda accepted the award.   **Kim knew all of the answers except two.**

all ready, already *All ready* means "completely prepared." *Already* means "by this time."

The Flints were all ready for their vacation.   **I already mowed the lawn.**

all together, altogether *All together* means "in a group." *Altogether* means "completely."

The puppies ran all together.   **Albert was altogether sure of the song's title.**

a lot *A lot* means "very much." It is always two words. Because *a lot* is unclear, it is better to use words such as *often*, *many*, or *much*.

Mr. Alvarez called the hospital often.   **She showed much courage.**

▶ **Exercise 1 Underline the word or words in parentheses that best complete each sentence.**

Mitsuyo did not (<u>accept</u>, except) money for weeding her grandmother's garden.

1. Our clothes were (all together, <u>altogether</u>) ruined by the old washing machine.

2. My mother makes spaghetti for dinner (a lot, <u>often</u>).

3. (Accept, <u>Except</u>) for tying my shoes, I was (<u>all ready</u>, already) to go.

4. My aunts and uncles could not remember the last time they were (<u>all together</u>, altogether).

5. Emilio is (all ready, <u>already</u>) studying for the test.

6. It rains (a lot, <u>often</u>) in the summer.

7. Cody had (all ready, <u>already</u>) eaten breakfast by the time we woke up.

8. The marching band got (a lot of, <u>very much</u>) exercise.

9. Dana was (all together, <u>altogether</u>) surprised by the birthday party.

10. (Accept, <u>Except</u>) for a few loyal fans, the stadium was empty.

11. The deer were (<u>all ready</u>, already) to protect their young.

12. Does the arcade (<u>accept</u>, except) tokens or coins?

13. By the time Mom arrived to pick us up, we had (all ready, <u>already</u>) left.

14. My friends and I go to (a lot of, <u>many</u>) movies.

15. The village was (all together, <u>altogether</u>) destroyed by the floods.

▶ **Exercise 2** **Write in the blank the correct form of the word or words in italics. If the sentence is correct, write C in the blank.**

_____already_____ When we arrived, the party had *all ready* begun.

_____accept_____ **1.** The vending machine will not *except* dollar bills.

_____C_____ **2.** Our drama teacher asked if we would rather practice *all together* or alone.

_____already_____ **3.** The sun had *all ready* set when we left the picnic.

_____C_____ **4.** *All together* we earned fifteen dollars.

_____accept_____ **5.** It was hard for the basketball team to *except* the defeat.

_____all ready_____ **6.** Our backpacks full, Ted and I were *already* for the long hike.

_____Except_____ **7.** *Accept* for the lima beans, my sister eagerly ate everything on her plate.

_____all ready_____ **8.** Dinner was *already* when we got home.

_____C_____ **9.** My cousin was *already* walking by the time she was nine months old!

_____except_____ **10.** The camp was quiet *accept* for the chirping of crickets.

_____altogether_____ **11.** We were *all together* stunned by the news.

_____very much_____ **12.** We liked the new Russian exchange student *a lot*.

_____C_____ **13.** The frisky puppy was *all ready* for the walk.

_____except_____ **14.** We rode every roller coaster at the park *accept* one.

_____all together_____ **15.** The CDs are piled *altogether* on the shelf in my closet.

Usage

Name _____ Class _____ Date _____

Lesson 59
Usage: *beside* to *chose*

---

beside, besides *Beside* means "next to." *Besides* means "in addition to."

The ducklings waddled **beside** their mother.
Besides the goldfish, we have only one pet.

among, between Use *between* for two people, things, or groups. Use *among* for three or more people, things, or groups.

The pizza place is **between** the laundromat and the drugstore.
A little boy was **among** those hurt in the accident.

choose, chose *Choose* means to "to select." *Chose* is the past tense of *choose*.

Harriet didn't know which drink to **choose**.
Yesterday the kitten **chose** the ball of string to play with.

Usage

▶ **Exercise 1** Underline the word in parentheses that best completes each sentence.

(Beside, <u>Besides</u>) my coat, I wore gloves and a hat.

1. Because I couldn't do both, I had to choose (among, <u>between</u>) piano and flute lessons.

2. Kesia (choose, <u>chose</u>) two challenging computer games to play.

3. The contest was (among, <u>between</u>) our two classes.

4. Marty carefully (choose, <u>chose</u>) a book from the library.

5. The yellow bus parked (<u>beside</u>, besides) the football field.

6. A picture of my grandparents appeared (<u>among</u>, between) the photographs in the attic.

7. Last Saturday we (choose, <u>chose</u>) a shady spot for our picnic.

8. (Beside, <u>Besides</u>) Kim, who else will volunteer to pass out tests?

9. (Among, <u>Between</u>) the two cities was an old bridge.

10. Cheng-Yu is standing (<u>beside</u>, besides) the water fountain.

11. The little boy knew he had to (<u>choose</u>, chose) a balloon.

12. I will (<u>choose</u>, chose) a movie everyone will like.

13. (Beside, <u>Besides</u>) skating, I also like swimming.

14. (Among, Between) the books at the library were several about the Civil War.

15. The chair (beside, besides) me was empty.

▶ **Exercise 2** Write in the blank the correct form of the word in italics. If the italicized word is correct, write *C* in the blank.

_____beside_____	The boy standing *besides* me in the picture is my cousin Tom.
_____C_____	**1.** To earn money for college is *among* the reasons my brother got a summer job.
_____Among_____	**2.** *Between* all the flowers in the garden was a patch of weeds.
_____chose_____	**3.** The squirrel *choose* a hiding place for its nuts.
_____Besides_____	**4.** *Beside* an entertaining elephant act, the circus also presented a funny clown show.
_____C_____	**5.** Meagan *chose* chocolate ice cream for dessert.
_____beside_____	**6.** Tara left her glasses on the table *besides* the bed.
_____choose_____	**7.** The magician told me to *chose* any card from the deck.
_____C_____	**8.** Last night Tonya *chose* the runt of the litter as her new puppy.
_____between_____	**9.** The exciting soccer game *among* the two schools ended in a tie.
_____choose_____	**10.** The whole family will *chose* a name for the kitten.
_____C_____	**11.** Dad took a picture of me standing *beside* the Liberty Bell.
_____among_____	**12.** A seashell was *between* the many souvenirs I brought home.
_____C_____	**13.** Because it was so hot yesterday, Akira and I *chose* to go swimming.
_____Besides_____	**14.** *Beside* soccer, Michael also plays hockey.
_____between_____	**15.** My book fell into the space *among* the couch and the wall.

▶ **Writing Link** Choose one or two of the word pairs in this lesson. Write a humorous sentence that will help you remember how to use those words correctly.

_____

_____

_____

_____

Usage

Lesson 60
Usage: *in* to *learn*

in, into *In* means "inside." *Into* indicates an action toward the inside.

The pie was baking **in** the oven.   The batter hit the ball **into** the outfield.

its, it's *Its* is the possessive form of it. *It's* is the contraction of *it is*.

The cat licked **its** paws after eating.   **It's** a good idea to exercise.

lay, lie *Lay* means "to place." *Lie* means "to recline."

I always **lay** my jacket on the chair.   The doctor told the patient to **lie** on the cot.

learn, teach *Learn* means to "to gain knowledge." *Teach* means "to give knowledge."

We **learned** a new Spanish word.   Edward **teaches** his brother basketball plays.

▶ **Exercise 1** **Underline the word in parentheses that best completes each sentence.**

(Its, It's) not often that we see a raccoon in our backyard.

1. Our cat likes to (lay, lie) on the windowsill and look outside.

2. Ellen slowly poured the milk (in, into) a glass.

3. The dog wagged (its, it's) tail when I scratched its ears.

4. Tomorrow our teacher will (learn, teach) us about the layers of Earth's crust.

5. Miyoki is putting the cookie dough (in, into) the oven.

6. (Its, It's) important to get a good education.

7. Because I've never used a printer before, I asked Mrs. Vega to (learn, teach) me how.

8. (Lay, Lie) your pencils down after finishing the quiz.

9. My mom keeps a big old trunk (in, into) our basement.

10. The cheetah was (laying, lying) in the cool grass.

11. Children can (learn, teach) to swim at a very young age.

12. The monkey scratched (its, it's) stomach and screeched with pleasure.

13. Mark began to (lay, lie) the dishes on the counter.

14. Cheryl dove (in, <u>into</u>) the water with a huge splash.

15. Do you think (its, <u>it's</u>) harder to get up early when it is cold outside?

▶ **Exercise 2** **Write in the blank the correct form of the word in italics. If the italicized word is correct, write *C* in the blank.**

_____into_____   My mother drove the car *in* the garage.

_____teach_____   **1.** Elliot tried to *learn* his baby parakeet to say "Hello."

_____C_____   **2.** We raked the leaves and put them *into* big bags.

_____lay_____   **3.** If you *lie* the marshmallow on a hot surface, it will melt.

_____learn_____   **4.** Marsha wants to *teach* several French words before she goes to Quebec.

_____in_____   **5.** The festival was held *into* the school's gymnasium.

_____lay_____   **6.** We know better than to *lie* wet towels on the floor.

_____C_____   **7.** Juan played chess with his friends *in* the living room.

_____into_____   **8.** I got goosebumps as we walked *in* the cold movie theater.

_____C_____   **9.** Florida has Tallahassee as *its* capital city.

_____teach_____   **10.** Can you *learn* me to do that neat card trick?

_____It's_____   **11.** *Its* too late in the season to go bird watching.

_____C_____   **12.** Laura is *learning* to play the piano.

_____its_____   **13.** The watchdog bared *it's* sharp, white teeth.

_____lie_____   **14.** After the race we were ready to *lay* down and rest.

_____C_____   **15.** Alfonso is sitting *in* the dentist's waiting room.

▶ **Writing Link** **Write a brief paragraph describing your house or apartment. Include the words *in*, *into*, *its*, *it's*, *lay*, and *lie*.**

_____

_____

_____

_____

_____

_____

Usage

Lesson 61
Usage: *leave* to *sit*

---

leave, let *Leave* means "to go away." *Let* means "to allow."

Don't **leave** before saying good-bye.   The guard won't **let** them inside the fence.

loose, lose *Loose* means "not firmly attached." *Lose* means "to misplace" or "to fail to win."

Mike's clothes were **loose** after he lost weight.   Did you **lose** the video game?

raise, rise *Raise* means "to cause to move up." *Rise* means "to move upward."

The cat **raises** its head when the door opens.   Dough **rises** slowly.

set, sit *Set* means "to place" or "to put." *Sit* means "to place oneself in a seated position."

Fido likes to **set** his chin on my knee.   Jason was grateful to **sit** down.

▶ **Exercise 1** **Underline the word in parentheses that best completes each sentence.**

The team could not afford to (loose, <u>lose</u>) another game.

1. Ricardo will (<u>set</u>, sit) the oars inside the canoe.

2. Dad will (leave, <u>let</u>) me help him paint the fence in our backyard.

3. I always (<u>raise</u>, rise) the blinds in my room, rain or shine.

4. My little sister's front tooth is (<u>loose</u>, lose).

5. The curtain in the auditorium squeaks when it (raises, <u>rises</u>).

6. Our group sometimes (sets, <u>sits</u>) in the library for long periods of time.

7. My sister (leaves, <u>lets</u>) me interview her for my school project.

8. Warm air always (raises, <u>rises</u>).

9. The (<u>loose</u>, lose) shutters flapped in the breeze.

10. If we (<u>leave</u>, let) by six, we can make it to the early movie.

11. Jill will (sit, <u>set</u>) her books down so that she can help Angel with her crutches.

12. The candidate will (<u>raise</u>, rise) many issues if she is elected.

13. If your shoestrings are too (<u>loose</u>, lose), you could fall and get hurt.

Usage

14. Will your parents (leave, <u>let</u>) you camp out in the backyard?

15. (Sit, <u>Set</u>) a bowl of milk on the floor for the kitten.

16. Luis was careful not to (loose, <u>lose</u>) his lunch money.

17. We were often reminded to (<u>sit</u>, set) up straight.

18. Dad had to (<u>leave</u>, let) work early to pick us up.

19. The fog seemed to (raise, <u>rise</u>) off the ground.

20. As we hike we are careful to watch for (<u>loose</u>, lose) rocks.

▶ **Exercise 2** **Write in the blank the correct form of the word in italics. If the italicized word is correct, write *C* in the blank.**

_____rise_____   Hot-air balloons *raise* from the ground.

_____C_____ **1.** Mom will *let* me watch TV if my homework is done.

_____raise_____ **2.** We *rise* the flag every morning.

_____sits_____ **3.** My dad always *sets* at the head of the table.

_____C_____ **4.** Paul is careful not to *lose* his door key.

_____let_____ **5.** I often *leave* my brother ride my bike.

_____loose_____ **6.** Our dog sometimes gets *lose.*

_____rise_____ **7.** The cake we baked never seemed to *raise.*

_____C_____ **8.** Can we *leave* the party early?

_____lose_____ **9.** Do you think we will *loose* the gymnastics meet?

_____set_____ **10.** I helped my brother *sit* the table.

_____leave_____ **11.** Please *let* your bike in the bike rack.

_____C_____ **12.** Zach always seems to *lose* his radio.

_____let_____ **13.** Will you *leave* me ride your skateboard?

_____C_____ **14.** The chain on her bike is always *loose.*

_____rise_____ **15.** The day we went fishing we saw the sun *raise.*

_____C_____ **16.** My dad has to *leave* by seven to go to work.

_____sit_____ **17.** I always *set* on a beanbag chair when I read.

_____C_____ **18.** The mechanics had to *raise* the car to see under it.

Usage

Lesson 62
Usage: *than* to *whose*

---

than, then *Than* introduces the second part of a comparison. *Then* means "at that time" or "after that."

A viola is larger **than** a violin.   Let's eat dinner, and **then** we'll play tennis.

their, they're *Their* is the possessive form of *they*. *They're* is the contraction of *they are.*

They put on **their** uniforms.   **They're** playing basketball tonight.

to, too, two *To* means "in the direction of." *Too* means "also" or "to an excessive degree." *Two* is the number after one.

We go **to** the bank.   May I go, **too**?   The soup is **too** hot.
Jo drank **two** glasses of juice.

who's, whose *Who's* is the contraction of *who is*. *Whose* is the possessive form of *who.*

Who's going to the movie?   **Whose** tickets are these?

▶ **Exercise 1** **Underline the word in parentheses that best completes each sentence.**

Australia is the only country that is a continent (to, <u>too</u>).

1. Australia is smaller (<u>than</u>, then) any of the other continents.

2. It is bordered by (too, <u>two</u>) oceans, the Indian Ocean and the Pacific Ocean.

3. Australia is made up of five mainland states, one island state, and (too, <u>two</u>) territories.

4. Captain James Cook, (<u>whose</u>, who's) voyages led him (<u>to</u>, too) Australia, claimed it for Great Britain in 1770.

5. Australians were influenced by the English in (they're, <u>their</u>) language and customs.

6. If you go to Australia, (than, <u>then</u>) you must drive on the left side of the road!

7. Animals native (<u>to</u>, too) Australia include kangaroos, platypuses, koalas, and wallabies.

8. For Australians, wheat is one of (<u>their</u>, they're) main crops.

9. Mining is an important economic activity, (two, <u>too</u>).

10. Australia has a different type of government (<u>than</u>, then) the United States.

11. It is a commonwealth (<u>whose</u>, who's) legislative body is a parliament.

12. Canberra, Australia's capital, is smaller (<u>than</u>, then) most state capitals.

13. Sydney, which is home (<u>to</u>, too) the Sydney Opera House, is the largest and oldest city.

14. The interior of the country, called the *outback*, is where people have (they're, <u>their</u>) cattle and sheep farms.

15. There are few paved roads for these farm families, so (their, <u>they're</u>) quite isolated.

▶ **Exercise 2** **Write in the blank the correct form of the word in italics. If the italicized word is correct, write *C* in the blank.**

_____who's_____ An Aborigine is a person *whose* native to Australia.

_____they're_____ **1.** Today, however, *their* only a small portion of the Australian population.

_____to_____ **2.** Before the Europeans came *too* Australia, the Aborigines made up a large part of Australia's population.

_____C_____ **3.** Nearly five hundred different groups, speaking many different languages, existed *then*.

_____C_____ **4.** The Aborigines were nomads *whose* migratory way of life allowed them to have few belongings.

_____two_____ **5.** They existed by doing *to* things—hunting and gathering.

_____too_____ **6.** Religion was a large part of their culture, *to*.

_____Their_____ **7.** *They're* belief was that humans were a part of nature.

_____They're_____ **8.** *Their* part of a society based on a kinship system.

_____C_____ **9.** *Their* artistic productions included ritual objects, cave paintings, and engravings.

_____C_____ **10.** Drama, dance, and poetry played an important role in their culture, *too*.

_____Then_____ **11.** *Than*, after Europeans arrived about 1788, Aboriginal societies diminished.

_____whose_____ **12.** Those *who's* societies continued were unable to maintain their cultures.

_____than_____ **13.** Australian Aborigines are now more a part of modern Australia *then* they used to be.

_____They're_____ **14.** *Their* entitled to the same rights as other Australian citizens.

_____C_____ **15.** *They're* people whose identity and heritage are important to them.

Usage

Unit 10 **Review**

▶ **Exercise 1** Underline the word in parentheses that best completes each sentence.

I reminded Leah not to (<u>leave</u>, let) without saying good-bye.

1. The plane moved (in, <u>into</u>) the hangar for repairs.

2. Swimmers had to choose (among, <u>between</u>) morning or afternoon practices.

3. (Beside, <u>Besides</u>) being fun, tennis is also good exercise.

4. Darryl (choose, <u>chose</u>) the striped scarf instead of the plain one.

5. After school I sometimes (lay, <u>lie</u>) down and take a nap.

6. Alejandra wants to (learn, <u>teach</u>) kindergarten someday.

7. We (all ready, <u>already</u>) had plans when Aunt Karen called.

8. Tammy is almost ready to (<u>accept</u>, except) the responsibility of baby-sitting.

9. We were (all together, <u>altogether</u>) exhausted after a day at the science museum.

10. (Its, <u>It's</u>) not unusual to find harmless snakes in the woods.

11. Taking the subway is quicker (<u>than</u>, then) taking the bus.

12. Randy (leaves, <u>lets</u>) me borrow his new CD.

13. (<u>Whose</u>, Who's) umbrella was left on the bus?

14. (<u>Raise</u>, Rise) your hand if you're interested in going on the field trip.

15. Candy always (sets, <u>sits</u>) with us at lunch.

16. The youth groups are holding (<u>their</u>, they're) annual picnic.

17. Ana is (to, <u>too</u>) sick to want to go to the movie.

18. (Whose, <u>Who's</u>) in charge of taking attendance?

19. Our neighbors have a bicycle made for (too, <u>two</u>).

20. He will attend college and (than, <u>then</u>) go on to medical school.

Cumulative Review: Units 1–10

▶ **Exercise 1** Draw a vertical line between each subject and predicate. Draw one line under each simple subject and two lines under each simple predicate.

The marching band | will play at the parade.

1. Corinne | sings in the choir at church.

2. The crying child | was calmed by his mother.

3. The ice cream | melted in the sun.

4. The pizza parlor | becomes busy every Friday night.

5. Our math teacher | rarely gives us homework.

6. All of the sixth graders | are going on a field trip.

7. Several inches of snow | fell overnight.

8. Tracy | forgot her lunch today.

9. Most meteor showers | come from the debris of comets.

10. Mark Twain | was the pen name of the author Samuel Clemens.

11. Mark, Isaiah, Shana, and Micah | met Mr. Lee on their way to the new mall.

12. The ocean water | tasted salty.

13. The families in our neighborhood | save and recycle their cans and newspapers.

14. The salad with the artichoke hearts | tasted delicious.

15. The black stallion | ran away and jumped over the fence.

16. Our team | did well in the game on Saturday.

17. Bala | is my sister's science tutor.

18. The student committee | voted for a car wash on Saturday.

19. The soccer team | won its third game in a row.

20. My uncle's job | a car and a uniform.

Name _____ Class _____ Date _____

▶ **Exercise 2** Draw two lines under each verb or verb phrase. In the blank write the tense or form of the verb: *present, past, future, pres. prog.* (present progressive), *past prog.* (past progressive), *present perfect,* or *past perfect.*

_____future_____ Kelly will go to the museum with her sister.

_____past_____ 1. Yumiko arrived after dinner.

_____past perfect_____ 2. By the age of five, Jen had learned many songs on the piano.

_____present_____ 3. We visit my grandfather once a week.

_____past prog._____ 4. The members of the orchestra were tuning their instruments.

_____present perfect_____ 5. I have already finished my homework.

_____pres. prog._____ 6. My aunt is flying in from Kansas tonight.

_____past perfect_____ 7. Chuck had been a Boy Scout for two years.

_____past prog._____ 8. The frog was jumping from rock to rock.

_____future_____ 9. I will have a paper route next year.

_____present_____ 10. Terry auditions for all the school plays.

_____pres. prog._____ 11. Where is Wendy playing tennis?

_____past_____ 12. Kevin sprained his ankle during the basketball game.

_____present perfect_____ 13. I have never bowled before.

_____past perfect_____ 14. The cat had eaten its dinner early.

_____past prog._____ 15. The gymnasts were practicing their dismounts.

▶ **Exercise 3** Fill in the blank with the correct pronoun. Then circle the antecedent of the pronoun.

(Brenda) could use some help with her homework. _____She_____ is falling behind.

1. The (Shermans) visited last summer. _____They_____ have five children.

2. We read that (book) in English. _____It_____ is an interesting one.

3. (José) was involved in many sports. _____He_____ had to find time to finish his essay.

4. The track (coach) broke his leg, so _____he_____ will be out for a month.

5. (Brian and Takeo) played tennis. Jill and I watched _____them_____ .

6. (Judy) put her glasses in her backpack because _____she_____ didn't want to lose them.

7. The chipmunk buried the (nuts.) It would need _____ **them** _____ in the winter.

8. (Mi Ling) lost her pen, so I gave ____ **her** _____ mine.

9. The (dogs) were barking, and _____ **they** _____ woke me up.

10. The (monkeys) at the zoo were very playful. _____ **They** _____ entertained us for an hour.

11. (Moisha and I) solved the mystery. _____ **We** _____ were proud of ourselves.

12. (Mrs. Lopez) went to aerobics class every Sunday. It helped ____ **her** _____ stay healthy.

13. We took the (recipes) out of the box and organized _____ **them** _____.

14. My (mom and I) finished shopping, and then the bus took _____ **us** _____ home.

15. (Rafael) had a sore throat, so his dad took _____ **him** _____ to the doctor.

▶ **Exercise 4** **Underline each adjective and circle each adverb. Ignore the articles *a*, *an*, and *the*.**

I was (very) glad I could fix the old bicycle.

1. My family (finally) bought a new minivan.

2. Julie described Boston as a beautiful city.

3. Benito (already) has a positive attitude.

4. Liz works (extremely) (hard) to get good grades.

5. A large rock (partially) covered the entrance to the cave.

6. Museums (typically) display rare paintings.

7. We walked (quickly) toward the warm campfire.

8. The red car stopped (abruptly) in front of the house.

9. The unique gift (completely) surprised Olivia.

10. Kevin (carefully) carved the wood into a small horse.

11. The open gate thumped (loudly) against the post.

12. Would the red cover look better than the blue one?

13. The band concert ended with a fast march.

14. Priscilla ran (fast) to catch the early bus.

15. The autumn leaves fell (early) this year.

Usage

*M*echanics

· ·

Unit 11: Capitalization

Lesson 63
Capitalizing Sentences, Quotations, and Salutations I

To **capitalize** means to begin a word with a capital letter. Capitalize the first word of every sentence.

This assignment is due early next week.

The first word of a direct quotation is capitalized if the quotation is a complete sentence.

Mrs. Crawford said, "**S**tart with the dictionary."

Sometimes other words interrupt a direct quotation. Do not capitalize the beginning of the second part of an interrupted quotation unless the second part begins a new sentence.

"Start with the dictionary," said Mrs. Crawford, "**w**here you can find a lot of useful facts."

"Start with the dictionary," said Mrs. Crawford. "**Y**ou can find a wealth of useful facts in the dictionary."

▶ **Exercise 1** **Draw three lines under each lowercase letter that should be capitalized. Write *C* in the blank if the sentence is correct.**

_____ "do you know," asked Mrs. Crawford, "anybody in history named Webster?"

___C___ **1.** "Daniel Webster," answered Mark, "lived a long time ago."

_____ **2.** "yes, he did," responded the teacher. "do you know another Webster?"

_____ **3.** "I do," ventured Tasha. "did he write *Webster's Dictionary?*"

_____ **4.** the other students did not add anything to the discussion.

_____ **5.** everyone knew a project was waiting to be assigned.

_____ **6.** "who wants to research dictionaries?" thought Arnoldo. "i certainly don't."

___C___ **7.** Noah, however, thought that words were interesting to study.

___C___ **8.** "I want everyone to look in an encyclopedia," said Mrs. Crawford.

_____ **9.** she suggested topics such as "dictionary," "lexicographer," and "Noah Webster."

_____ 10. "hey," thought Noah, "maybe Noah Webster invented the English language.

that's where I'm going to start."

_____ 11. "then," Mrs. Crawford added, "write five sentences."

_____ 12. "give them to me on Friday," the teacher said. "on Monday we will share our

information."

___C___ 13. Noah decided to start right away.

_____ 14. first Noah looked in the encyclopedia under "Noah Webster."

___C___ 15. He didn't see anything about Noah Webster's inventing the English language.

_____ 16. however, the article noted that Noah Webster was an American lexicographer.

___C___ 17. "'Lexicographer' is one of the suggested topics," Noah said to himself.

___C___ 18. "I don't know what that word means," said Noah out loud, "but I'm going to

find out."

___C___ 19. "Then I will know what's so important about Noah Webster," he continued.

___C___ 20. Noah looked for the word *lexicographer* in the dictionary.

_____ 21. "well, what do you know?" whistled Noah. "a lexicographer writes dictionaries!"

___C___ 22. Noah read some interesting articles about Noah Webster.

_____ 23. he was eager to share information in class on Monday.

___C___ 24. Noah also wanted to hear what the other students had learned.

_____ 25. on Monday the teacher asked for volunteers.

_____ 26. Kofi reported, "he was born in Connecticut in 1758."

_____ 27. "he fought with Washington in the Revolutionary War," added Jeff.

___C___ 28. Marianne added that he wrote a spelling book and a dictionary.

___C___ 29. "*Webster's Dictionary* was the first American dictionary," contributed Noah.

_____ 30. he further explained, "Webster put new words in his dictionary, and he

changed the spelling and pronunciation of others."

_____ 31. "webster wanted his book to be a dictionary of American English."

_____ 32. "the really important thing that Noah Webster did," Noah said, "was to help

make American English its own language."

Lesson 64
Capitalizing Sentences, Quotations, and Salutations II

Remember to capitalize the first word of a sentence and the first word of a direct quotation that is a complete sentence.

"My pen pal," said Mark, "lives in Germany."
"How long have you been writing to him?" asked Thad. "Does he have a friend?"

Do not capitalize the first word of an indirect quotation. An indirect quotation does not appear in quotation marks and does not give a person's exact words.

Thad said that he had been writing to Karl for a year.

Capitalize the first word in the salutation of a letter. Capitalize the title and the name of the person you are addressing. Capitalize the first word in the closing of a letter.

Dear President Lincoln,   Yours very truly,

▶ **Exercise 1** Draw three lines under each lowercase letter that should be capitalized. Draw a slash (/) through each capital letter that should be lowercase. Write *C* if the item is correct.

_____   Marty said That he appreciated our help.

_____ **1.** dear Mrs. lamont,

_____ **2.** Harriet said that You would help me with my report.

__C___ **3.** "Did Juan finish raking your leaves yesterday?" asked Mrs. Perez.

_____ **4.** "yes," said Mr. Sakamoto, "And he did a fine job."

_____ **5.** Your Friend,

_____ **6.** Sara Jane said She liked the movie we saw.

_____ **7.** Jeff wants to know If You will go with him.

_____ **8.** Zorah shouted, "watch out below!"

_____ **9.** Who said, "give me Liberty or give me death"?

_____ **10.** Dear senator Smith,

__C___ **11.** Sincerely yours,

_____ **12.** did you ask your mother If I could stay overnight?

Mechanics

_____ **13.** The principal told us To do our best.

_____ **14.** dear aunt Jo and Uncle bill,

__C__ **15.** Bess told me her grandmother never learned to drive.

_____ **16.** Respectfully Yours,

_____ **17.** "have you seen the new science teacher, Beth?" asked Randy.

_____ **18.** "I met her this morning," replied Beth. "she seems very smart."

_____ **19.** someone told me She used to teach at a university.

__C__ **20.** Dear friends and relatives,

_____ **21.** Did you suggest that I Give up my paper route?

_____ **22.** no one knows Those children have never seen a real cow.

_____ **23.** "have you decided what to get Mom for her birthday?" asked Meg.

_____ **24.** "she might like an embroidered sweater," suggested Drew, "Or maybe a wallet."

__C__ **25.** Yours affectionately,

_____ **26.** I had never heard That Sandra was a champion marbles player.

_____ **27.** Dear Grandma and grandpa Wilson,

_____ **28.** Has anyone mentioned that There will be a test in math tomorrow?

_____ **29.** she said You would help her study.

_____ **30.** with love and gratitude,

▶ Writing Link **Write a paragraph about your favorite summer activity. Capitalize
sentences correctly.**

_____

_____

_____

_____

_____

_____

Lesson 65
Capitalizing Names and Titles of Persons I

Capitalize names of people and initials that stand for names.

Bonnie Morris   **Carl M. Lustek**   **P. J. Carter**

Capitalize the names and abbreviations of academic degrees and professional titles that follow a person's name. Capitalize *Jr.* and *Sr.*

Raul Espinoza, **B**achelor of **S**cience   Nelson Davies, **D.D.S.**
Kate Strong, **R**egistered **D**ietitian   Lester Linston **S**r.

Capitalize words that show family relationships when used as titles but not when they follow an article or a possessive noun or pronoun.

Uncle **F**rankie   Diane's grandmother   my sister   an aunt

Always capitalize the pronoun *I.*

Are you really interested in what **I** think?

▶ **Exercise 1** **Draw three lines under each lowercase letter that should be capitalized. Draw a slash (/) through each capital letter that should be lowercase. Place a check (✔) before each sentence with correct capitalization.**

_____   For years Kaya has taken piano lessons from Mrs. ̲c̲arter.

_____ **1.** My interest in names comes naturally; my F̸ather's name is Jonathon Apple.

_____ **2.** Most people can hardly believe that ̲m̲om's name is Carmel.

___✔___ **3.** They are really amazed when they hear that my name is Candy.

_____ **4.** I never bother telling them about ̲g̲randma and ̲g̲randpa MacIntosh!

___✔___ **5.** I think it's interesting, too, that sometimes a person's name matches his or her job.

_____ **6.** For example, we bought my glasses from Arthur Sites, ̲o̲.̲d̲.

_____ **7.** My U̸ncle's knee surgery was performed by Inez Bonecutter, M.D.

_____ **8.** I know it's hard to believe, but I've seen a sign for James McCracken, ̲d̲octor of ̲c̲hiropractic.

_____ **9.** My favorite, though, is William R. Crooks, ̲s̲heriff of Fayette County, Ohio.

Mechanics

_____✔____ **10.** Sometimes a perfectly ordinary name becomes special when you see the last name first.

_____✔____ **11.** For example, Susan Jolly is listed in the phone book as Jolly Susan!

_____ **12.** Through using the phone book, i've uncovered many great names.

_____✔____ **13.** Henry Reeder holds a doctorate in literature.

_____✔____ **14.** Jackie Ford Jr. owns a car dealership.

_____ **15.** Sometimes i see an interesting last name and wonder where it comes from.

_____✔____ **16.** I guessed the origin of the last name *Pretty* had to do with appearance.

_____ **17.** According to the *New Dictionary of American Family Names*, the name *pretty* is an English name that means "the crafty, cunning man."

_____ **18.** The dictionary also revealed that the name *mondello* comes from the Italian for "the little, cute, clean man."

_____✔____ **19.** *Frid* comes from the Swedish word for "peace."

_____ **20.** From the Polish language comes the name *sobota*, "one who always does something on Saturday."

_____ **21.** Surely you can see by now why i collect names.

_____✔____ **22.** If you'd like to collect names, too, let other people know that you are a collector.

_____ **23.** Aunts, Uncles, and other family members often are willing to help out.

_____ **24.** My Cousin Lisa told me about a classmate whose name is Bea Cool.

_____ **25.** grandpa's name, godfrey, is German for "God's peace."

▶ **Writing Link Write five sentences about someone in the news. Include his or her title if you can. Use proper capitalization in each sentence.**

_____

_____

_____

_____

_____

_____

Lesson 66
Capitalizing Names and Titles of Persons II

A general rule to follow is to capitalize proper nouns but not common nouns.

Frederick Douglas   **writer**

Capitalize a title when it comes before a person's name or when it is used in direct address but not a title that follows a person's name.

Mayor Jean Dean   **Capt. John Gray**   **Mr. Ralph Rivera**
The reporter asked, "**Mr. President**, when is your next meeting?"
Bill Clinton was elected president in 1992.

▶ **Exercise 1 Draw three lines under each lowercase letter that should be capitalized.**

Kosey will eat lunch with capt. williams and then meet the mayor.

1. Mrs. kimi hayashi recommends dr. jack grady.

2. Louisa may alcott wrote the book *Little Women.*

3. The dentist's sign advertised "mara klein, d.d.s."

4. Jamal interviewed commissioner brown yesterday.

5. England's reigning queen is elizabeth II.

6. Josie, have you ever met lieutenant martinez?

7. Mayor harold jones and capt. bernadette henley met this morning.

8. What does the "s" in "harry s truman" stand for?

9. Are peggy, meg, and maggie all nicknames for margaret?

10. Address the letter to dr. alejandra castillo.

11. Why does the program refer to dr. cruz as rey cruz, m.d.?

12. Which president is known as f.d.r.?

13. Charlie, chuck, and chas are all nicknames for charles.

14. When did eric the red and the Vikings sail from Norway?

15. Grandma, aunt stephanie, and uncle floyd will stay for a week.

16. My uncle, hector salazar, is running for mayor this year.

17. Is it king henry VIII of England who was married to six queens?

18. Please tell mrs. gustafson that mr. swensen is here.

19. Was winston churchill the prime minister of England in 1944?

20. Her full legal name is rebecca jane katherine stevenson.

▶ **Exercise 2** **Draw three lines under each lowercase letter that should be capitalized. Draw a slash (/) through each capital letter that should be lowercase. Write *C* in the blank if the sentence is correct.**

_____ How long is your grandmother staying with mrs. grossman?

_____ **1.** Will mr. bowman consider running for mayor next year?

_____ **2.** Please send this report to both the Teacher and the Principal.

___C___ **3.** Perhaps you will meet the senator today.

_____ **4.** The Police Officer's name is Amanda Rogers.

___C___ **5.** A woman is the lieutenant governor of our state.

_____ **6.** This is lieutenant governor bernardo mansa.

___C___ **7.** Next summer I will visit my aunt in Mexico.

_____ **8.** Show these pictures of major sullivan to Grandma Rose.

_____ **9.** First my dad took me to see dr. norton, who is an Internist.

_____ **10.** This lawyer advertises himself as morey walsh, j.d.

_____ **11.** It's been more than two years since I've seen uncle Roberto.

_____ **12.** Abraham lincoln was the sixteenth President of the United States.

_____ **13.** Was Andrew Johnson or Andrew Jackson Vice President under Lincoln?

_____ **14.** Maria's Aunt spoke to my class about safety.

_____ **15.** Did you locate the information, captain?

_____ **16.** Mr. mayor, will you be in your office this afternoon?

___C___ **17.** For my social studies report, I have to interview the mayor and one of his assistants.

_____ **18.** Harriet Snelling is our family Doctor.

Mechanics

Lesson 67
Capitalizing Names of Places I

Capitalize the names of cities, counties, states, countries, continents, geographical features such as mountains and rivers, and sections of a country.

Mount Vernon	Westchester County	New Jersey
Ethiopia	Africa	Indian Ocean
the Grand Canyon	Bering Strait	Olentangy River
Bay of Bengal	Cape of Good Hope	Ohio River Valley
Mount Everest	the Northwest	New England

Capitalize the names of streets and highways as well as the names of specific buildings, bridges, and monuments.

Royal Forest Boulevard	Avenue of the Americas	Pulaski Skyway
World Trade Towers	Golden Gate Bridge	Lincoln Memorial

Do not capitalize words like *city, state, mountain, river, street,* and *bridge* if they are not part of a specific name.

On our trip we drove through ten states and five major cities, but we did not see any mountains.
Turn left at the next street, and take the bridge over the river.

▶ **Exercise 1 Draw three lines under each lowercase letter that should be capitalized.**

Names like illinois and arizona remind us of our country's beginnings.

1. Many place names in the united states are spelled in a way that made sense to

    someone from france or england or spain.

2. The mississippi river is named from a word meaning "great river."

3. Explorers in the southwest asked the Pimas what they called the area.

4. The Pimas used the word *arishoonak*; that name later became arizona.

5. One group in the south cleared thickets to make room for food.

6. The group gave their name to the state of alabama; the word for which this state

    was named means "thicket clearers."

7. The word *mesikami* became the word for the state of michigan and lake michigan.

8. The Sioux word for *friends* was translated into the names for north dakota and south dakota.

9. The Iroquois called one River *oheo*, which means "beautiful."

10. Do you recognize this word as the name of Ohio and the Ohio river valley?

11. The Ute people gave their name to one of the western states, utah.

▶ **Exercise 2** **Draw three lines under each lowercase letter that should be capitalized. Draw a slash (/) through each capital letter that should be lowercase.**

Do you know why the city of baltimore is in the State of Maryland?

1. We can learn some history by investigating the names of our Cities and streets, Mountains and rivers.

2. Ask yourself why there is a crockett st. in san antonio, texas.

3. Why is a lake in Northern New York called lake champlain?

4. Why is the city of pontiac in michigan while joliet is in illinois?

5. The hudson river is in New York.

6. Then why is there a hudson bay in northern Canada?

7. Is there a story behind williamsburg, virginia?

8. In what city is the empire state building?

9. Where do you think the benjamin franklin bridge is?

10. Why do many names in the southwest come from spain?

11. Sometimes the name of a City, such as *jamestown,* tells us when it was named.

12. jamestown was founded in 1607 when James Stuart was king of england.

13. Who ruled england when charleston and williamsburg were named?

14. Names such as *pittsburgh* and *pennsylvania* refer to important people.

15. William Penn founded pennsylvania; pittsburgh was named for William Pitt.

16. Even names of Streets can tell us about a City's early history.

17. Many cities have a street named main street or broad street.

18. These Streets were probably the major Street or the broadest Street in town.

Mechanics

Lesson 68
Capitalizing Names of Places II

Capitalize compass points when they refer to a specific section of the country but not when they indicate direction. Do not capitalize adjectives formed from words showing direction.

the **West Coast**   the **Southeast**   **n**orth of **At**lanta   **s**outhern **e**xposure

Capitalize the names of specific places but not the articles and prepositions that are part of geographical names.

Tucson, Arizona   the **West Indies**   the **United States of America**

▶ **Exercise 1** **Draw three lines under each lowercase letter that should be capitalized. Draw a slash (/) through each capital letter that should be lowercase. Write *C* in the blank if the sentence is correct.**

_____   We live ~~S~~outh of indianapolis, Indiana.

_____ **1.** You will find lake Erie to the ~~N~~orth of Ohio.

_____ **2.** Look for the northeast in Maine, New Hampshire, and Vermont.

_____ **3.** I would like to see ~~T~~he Missouri river someday.

_____ **4.** We traveled through santa fe, New Mexico, last August.

___C___ **5.** My house sits to the east of Main Street.

_____ **6.** The Grand canyon has many wonderful views for the tourist to marvel at.

_____ **7.** Did you hear about the earthquake in ~~T~~he San Fernando valley?

_____ **8.** The ~~N~~orthwestern part of my ~~S~~tate is fairly flat.

___C___ **9.** Samantha lives northwest of Carson City, Nevada.

_____ **10.** We went fishing in ~~T~~he Columbia River last year.

_____ **11.** Southwestern Kansas is not much different geographically than ~~S~~outheastern

Kansas, I'd say.

___C___ **12.** My friends live on the broad coastal plain of northern Germany.

_____ **13.** The country of Colombia lies to the ~~S~~outh of Panama.

_____ **14.** That ~~N~~ortherly breeze cools off everything in the valley.

_____ **15.** Search for the great Salt lake within the boundaries of the state of Utah.

_____ **16.** I would like to travel to the south Pacific one day.

_____ **17.** Travel west from Ohio, and you will find indiana.

_____ **18.** The Atlas mountains rise on the Western edge of the Sahara.

_____ **19.** My grandfather came from Hunan Province, located in the Southeastern area

of central China.

_____ **20.** The famous train known as the *Orient Express* ran Eastward from Paris to

Istanbul, turkey.

_____ **21.** Aunt Sally was born in duluth, Minnesota.

_____ **22.** My uncle has a house on cape Cod, which I would like to visit one day.

__C__ **23.** What states make up the American Midwest?

_____ **24.** My great-great-grandmother came through the Cumberland gap, located in

Northeastern Tennessee.

_____ **25.** We traveled North from London, england, to Edinburgh, scotland, in one day.

_____ **26.** My friend Rosanna is from montevideo, the capital of uruguay.

_____ **27.** The state of south Australia has a Capital named Adelaide.

__C__ **28.** Sri Lanka is a large island to the south of India.

_____ **29.** The famous town of timbuktu developed beside a river in Western Africa.

_____ **30.** Ancient galatia is now part of North Central Turkey.

▶ **Writing Link Write three sentences about the land features in your community.
Include names of buildings, streets, or geographical features.**

_____

_____

_____

_____

_____

_____

Lesson 69
Capitalizing Other Proper Nouns and Adjectives I

Capitalize proper nouns and adjectives but not common nouns and adjectives.

Mark Klees   a punctuation **m**ark   **New York City**   a **c**ity in New York

Capitalize the names of clubs, organizations, businesses, institutions, and political parties. Capitalize brand names but not the nouns following them.

the **Rotary Club**   **Girl Scouts of America**   **Imperial Products, Inc.**
Rockefeller Foundation   the **Republican** party   **Spinoff** yarn

Capitalize the names of important historical events and periods of time. Capitalize the names of days of the week, months of the year, and holidays, but not the names of the seasons.

the **Civil War**   the **Ice Age**   summer
Saturday   **August**   the **Fourth of July**

▶ **Exercise 1 Draw three lines under each lowercase letter that should be capitalized.**

We will start the book on <u>m</u>onday.

1. Tony joined the <u>b</u>oy <u>s</u>couts last <u>s</u>eptember.

2. President Kennedy founded the <u>p</u>eace <u>c</u>orps in the 1960s.

3. What do you think of <u>a</u>nna's <u>a</u>rt <u>w</u>ork as a name for my store?

4. Hashim goes to <u>f</u>ranklin <u>m</u>iddle <u>s</u>chool; Lenny goes to Reeseville <u>h</u>igh.

5. Will you be a <u>d</u>emocrat or a <u>r</u>epublican when you are old enough to vote?

6. We buy only <u>s</u>ummer's <u>b</u>ounty frozen vegetables.

7. Teddy Roosevelt led the Rough Riders in the <u>s</u>panish <u>a</u>merican <u>w</u>ar.

8. Did the <u>b</u>ronze <u>a</u>ge come before or after the <u>i</u>ron <u>a</u>ge?

9. I would like to see her by <u>t</u>hursday.

10. I think of <u>m</u>emorial <u>d</u>ay, <u>l</u>abor <u>d</u>ay, and the <u>f</u>ourth of <u>j</u>uly as summer holidays.

11. My brother joined the <u>u</u>nited <u>s</u>tates <u>n</u>avy last <u>m</u>ay.

12. The <u>t</u>asty <u>c</u>ompany makes pretty good snacks.

13. My father works for sunny products corporation.

14. Mom registered our dog with the American kennel club.

15. My brother applied to two colleges, kenyon college and miami university.

16. Our Aunt Nellie belongs to the local chapter of the green thumbs garden club.

17. People living in the stone age made beautiful things from a variety of rocks.

18. The war of 1812 occurred between 1812 and 1815.

19. England has two major political parties, the conservative party and the labor party.

20. We learned about the middle ages in a history class.

21. My favorite time of the year is fall.

22. Robert E. Lee commanded the army of northern virginia in the Civil War.

23. The handy help company repaired the damaged portions of our roof.

25. The revolutionary war involved many famous soldiers and statesmen.

26. Are new movies first shown on tuesday or on wednesday?

28. I love winter in january, with its snow, deep blue sky, and silent nights.

▶ **Exercise 2 Draw three lines under each lowercase letter that should be capitalized. Draw a slash (/) through each capital letter that should be lowercase. Write *C* in the blank if the sentence is correct.**

_____   Maybe we will visit you in april instead of march.

_____ **1.** Have you ever heard of a Club called The knights Of columbus?

___C___ **2.** Ichiko is writing a paper on the Mexican-American War.

_____ **3.** Bob's new Store, party machine, sells trinkets for democrats and republicans.

_____ **4.** My first School was north broadway preschool.

_____ **5.** Our Spring Vacation starts on friday, march 27.

_____ **6.** The Fashion show featured designs from bangles and beads boutique.

_____ **7.** We speak spanish at home and english Everywhere else.

_____ **8.** Joni and I bought Hats from mexico at sombrero sam's.

_____ **9.** The scientific method was developed during the age of reason.

_____ **10.** My birthday falls in the spring on april 19.

Lesson 70
Capitalizing Other Proper Nouns and Adjectives II

Capitalize the first word, the last word, and all important words in titles.

Charlotte's Web	*Romeo and Juliet*	"The Ransom of Red Chief"
"Old King Cole"	*Gone with the Wind*	*Sesame Street*
National Geographic	the *New York Times*	Chapter 7

Capitalize the names of ethnic groups, nationalities, and languages as well as proper adjectives formed from these names.

Mexican Americans	the Slavic countries
speaking Portuguese	Italian food

▶ **Exercise 1** **Draw three lines under each lowercase letter that should be capitalized. Draw a slash (/) through each capital letter that should be lowercase. Write *C* in the blank if the sentence is correct.**

_____ The C̸ookbook *Kids can cook* aims to teach kindergartners basic cooking skills.

_____ **1.** We will finish reading the book *little women* on Tuesday.

_____ **2.** I would like to hang a copy of the declaration of independence on my B̸edroom wall.

_____ **3.** Did you read the magazine *ranger rick* when you were younger?

_____ **4.** We have a T̸est on chapter 3 and chapter 4 tomorrow.

_____ **5.** Jeremy told me about a M̸agazine called *cobblestones*.

__C__ **6.** My great-grandfather worked on the famous newspaper *New York World*.

_____ **7.** My mom really liked the M̸ovie *fiddler on the roof*.

_____ **8.** My N̸ame is russian, but my mother is french.

_____ **9.** Kata really can't decide which she likes better, mexican food or italian food.

_____ **10.** I am learning the german language, but Otto is learning japanese.

_____ **11.** Cousin Carlos writes for a spanish language newspaper.

_____ **12.** The book *wind in the willows* is one of my favorites.

_____ **13.** Did you know that the W̸orld's oldest restaurant is a chinese one?

__C__ **14.** The ancient Hittites lived between the Greeks and the Persians.

Mechanics

_____ **15.** We get a Newspaper called the *miami herald* delivered to our door.

___C___ **16.** An Inuit poem known as "Eskimo Chant" vividly tells about the change of

seasons.

_____ **17.** My Family loves watching *the sound of music.*

_____ **18.** My favorite humorous poem is "casey at the bat."

_____ **19.** The scottish author Sir Walter Scott wrote the novel *ivanhoe.*

_____ **20.** Director Kenneth Branagh made shakespeare's play *much ado about nothing*

into a beautiful Movie.

_____ **21.** My Favorite Book is *Gulliver's travels.*

_____ **22.** I am sure that you've Read *the tale of peter rabbit.*

___C___ **23.** If only I could learn to speak the Greek language.

___C___ **24.** My dad has seen the movie *The Maltese Falcon* fifteen times.

_____ **25.** Joel Chandler Harris wrote the Book *nights with uncle remus.*

_____ **26.** I've studied chapter 10 very Thoroughly.

_____ **27.** A belgian horse has many useful duties as a Farm workhorse.

___C___ **28.** She worked hard to solve the Hungarian puzzle.

_____ **29.** Aunt Elizabeth will teach me to Speak a little swedish.

___C___ **30.** The magazine *Zillions* is one of my favorites.

▶ **Writing Link** **Make a list of several titles of books, movies, and TV shows that you like. Check that you have capitalized words correctly.**

_____

_____

_____

_____

_____

_____

_____

_____

☑ Unit 11 **Review**

▶ **Exercise 1** **Draw three lines under each lowercase letter that should be capitalized.**

our girl scout meetings are the first monday of each month.

1. joel and meg are going to visit their cousins during their spring vacation.

2. "just give it a try," encouraged joe. "i think you'll like it."

3. "use sunscreen," aunt bea insisted, "to protect your skin."

4. mrs. wehinger suggested that i get a tutor to help me with english.

5. the museum of american folk art is featuring native american art.

6. roald dahl wrote the poem "aunt sponge and aunt spiker."

7. *saris* are the traditional indian dress for women.

8. great-grandma gray came from norway in 1900 and settled in north Carolina.

9. i met hilda when i visited my aunt in kokomo last summer.

10. i've already read *the bridge to terabithia* six times.

11. mom lived in wauwatosa, wisconsin, before i was born.

12. the matterhorn is a famous mountain in western europe.

13. northern alaska's climate is different from southern alaska's climate.

14. alabama and florida are southern states.

15. ohio and indiana are in the midwest.

16. you'll see signs for the new jersey turnpike just west of the bridge.

17. you can see the empire state building from the george washington bridge.

18. abraham lincoln delivered the gettysburg address at the dedication of a cemetery.

19. school starts on the last monday in august.

20. in the united states thanksgiving day is the fourth thursday in november.

Mechanics

Cumulative Review: Units 1–11

▶ **Exercise 1** **Identify the type of sentence by writing in the blank *dec.* for declarative, *int.* for interrogative, *imp.* for imperative, or *exc.* for exclamatory.**

__dec.__   The Civil War began in 1861.

__dec.__   **1.** Emile broke his arm last week.

__int.__   **2.** Have you read any good books lately?

__imp.__   **3.** Turn off the television.

__exc.__   **4.** What a terrific job you did!

__dec.__   **5.** Chapter 5 begins on page 46.

__exc.__   **6.** What fun we had last Sunday!

__int.__   **7.** Can I play on this team?

__imp.__   **8.** Try to finish by Saturday morning.

__dec.__   **9.** The basketball season opens in early December.

__int.__   **10.** When will you know the details?

__exc.__   **11.** What good weather we had for our picnic!

__imp.__   **12.** Come to my house right after school tomorrow.

__int.__   **13.** Do you know how to keep score for volleyball?

__int.__   **14.** Is there any news from Rachel?

__dec.__   **15.** Lauren sang a solo in the spring concert.

__imp.__   **16.** Answer the questions at the end of the chapter.

__imp.__   **17.** Turn left at the stop light.

__exc.__   **18.** How easy it is to make a baby smile!

__dec.__   **19.** The flood waters disappeared rapidly.

__exc.__   **20.** How tired you look!

__dec.__   **21.** Jane shared her friendship bread with us.

__int.__   **22.** Is there some way to turn this radio off?

__imp.__   **23.** Don't forget Mara's birthday is tomorrow.

__exc.__   **24.** We're finished!

Mechanics

Name _____ Class _____ Date _____

▶ **Exercise 2** Identify each word in italics. Write above the word *prep.* for preposition, *conj.* for conjunction, and *inter.* for interjection.

                prep.
Plants turn *toward* the sun.

1. Hagos threw the ball *from* the foul line. — prep.

2. *Ouch!* My head hurts. — inter.

3. Zina can sing *and* dance. — conj.

4. *Congratulations!* I knew you could do it. — inter.

5. I really want to go with you, *but* I can't. — conj.

6. Keep your eye *on* the ball. — prep.

7. Emily saw Shawnda *and* Denise *before* school. — conj. prep.

8. *Help!* My shoe is stuck *in* the mud. — inter. prep.

9. I can't remember whether I wore my heavy coat *or* my light coat *to* school. — conj. prep.

10. *Wow!* You won the race *without* any effort! — inter. prep.

11. The box *of* costumes is *in* the closet *underneath* the stairs. — prep. prep. prep.

12. My parents will meet *with* Mr. Kenworth *in* the library *at* seven. — prep. prep. prep.

13. Throw the ball *into* the basket three times *in* a row. — prep. prep.

14. *Oh no!* I forgot *about* the test *on* Tuesday. — inter. prep. prep.

15. Our plans changed again *after* my talk *with* Jamal. — prep. prep.

16. Go *past* the gas station *on* the corner, *and* then turn left. — prep. prep. conj.

17. Choose a topic *for* your report, *or* you will not finish *on* time. — prep. conj. prep.

18. My grandma *and* grandpa went *to* Europe *for* three months last year. — conj. prep. prep.

19. John Adams *and* his son, John Quincy Adams, were both presidents *of* the United States. — conj. prep.

20. *Shucks!* I left my homework *on* the kitchen table again. — inter. prep.

21. *Plop!* The ball landed *in* the toddler's lap. — inter. prep.

22. Drink a mixture *of* hot tea *and* honey *for* your sore throat. — prep. conj. prep.

23. Step lively, *and* look alert! — conj.

24. Stuart always whistles the theme song *from* that old TV show. — prep.

▶ **Exercise 3** **Draw three lines under each lowercase letter that should be capitalized.**

the rainbow bridge spans the niagara river.

1. abraham lincoln was president of the united states during the civil war.

2. to get to arlington, cross ross bridge and turn north onto route 16.

3. the official start of spring is march 21.

4. chapter 7 of the book *charlotte's web* by e. b. white is called "bad news."

5. part of the border between new york and new jersey is the hudson river.

6. the ridge of the rocky mountains forms the north american great divide.

7. cleveland is in cuyahoga county, which borders lake erie.

8. "take a deep breath," said officer ling, "and then tell me what happened."

9. every thursday i read articles from two magazines, *newsweek* and *reader's digest,* to mr. boyd.

10. the jefferson memorial is by the potomac river in washington, d.c.

11. i have to memorize the gettysburg address for the veterans day assembly.

12. "we have nothing to fear," said f.d.r., "but fear itself."

13. the five great lakes are in the northern midwest.

14. sandra said the empire state building is on fifth avenue at 34th street.

15. my uncle's name is emmitt ian clark jr., but we call him uncle mitty.

16. "i am interested in howard university," stated edgar. "what do you know about it?"

17. can you tell me how to get to hayden planetarium, officer?

18. in new york city, little italy is just a block north of chinatown.

19. i was very young when i first saw the movie *101 dalmatians.*

20. the song "memory" is from andrew lloyd webber's play *cats.*

21. Wayne named his boat *water baby.*

22. Those african violets need watering.

23. "You may have won first prize in the lump of loot sweepstakes," the electronic voice broadcast throughout the mall.

24. *The Peasant Girl's Dream* by George MacDonald is set in the scottish highlands.

Mechanics

Unit 12: Punctuation

Lesson 71
Using the Period and Other End Marks

Use a **period** at the end of a declarative sentence.

Marvelous inventions make our lives easier.

Use a period at the end of an imperative sentence.

Please hand me that wrench.

Use a question mark at the end of an interrogative sentence.

Where would the world be without inventors?

Use an exclamation point at the end of an exclamatory sentence or an interjection.

What a great idea that is! Fantastic!

▶ **Exercise 1** Write *dec.* in the blank if the sentence is declarative, *imp.* if it is imperative, *int.* if it is interrogative, and *exc.* if it is exclamatory. Add the correct end mark to each sentence.

___int.___   Do you know who invented suspenders?

___dec.___   **1.** I believe it was Mark Twain.

___exc.___   **2.** Wow, that was a great idea!

___int.___   **3.** Does that information surprise you?

___dec.___   **4.** Without Howe's sewing machine, people would have to sew by hand.

___dec.___   **5.** I'm sure clothing would cost more.

___int.___   **6.** How did people keep their ears warm before earmuffs were invented?

___imp.___   **7.** Thank Chester Greenwood for making the first earmuffs.

___int.___   **8.** Where would we be without the safety pin?

___dec.___   **9.** That was the bright idea of Walter Hunt.

___int.___ **10.** What did Robert Goddard invent?

___dec.___ **11.** He developed the first rocket engine.

Mechanics

dec. **12.** I used Sarah Boone's invention this morning.

int. **13.** Didn't she design the first ironing board?

int. **14.** What is your favorite invention?

dec. **15.** I couldn't get along without a library card.

dec. **16.** Philo Farnsworth invented television in 1930.

int. **17.** Do you think Farnsworth would like _The Simpsons_?

dec. **18.** The first popular comic strip, _Hogan's Alley_, appeared in 1895.

dec. **19.** The first zippers replaced buttons on high-button shoes.

int. **20.** Did it take a long time to button those shoes?

dec. **21.** Sometimes it took as long as fifteen minutes.

exc. **22.** Whew, that's a long time!

dec. **23.** Long ago, people bathed with a mixture of ashes and water.

dec. **24.** Then they applied oil or grease.

dec. **25.** Finally they rinsed with clean water.

imp. **26.** Try it sometime to see if it works.

exc. **27.** My goodness, what a strange way to get clean!

dec. **28.** Actually, the chemicals in ashes and grease are similar to those in modern soap.

dec. **29.** Early people probably got themselves quite clean.

imp. **30.** Compare that method with the one we use today.

imp. **31.** Think of William Addis the next time you brush your teeth.

dec. **32.** The history of the toothbrush is very interesting.

dec. **33.** William Addis invented the toothbrush in 1770.

dec. **34.** He bored a hole in a small piece of bone and glued in some bristles.

exc. **35.** What a clever man Addis was!

dec. **36.** If it weren't for him, we'd still be cleaning our teeth with rags.

dec. **37.** Someday somebody might invent a machine that turns off gravity.

exc. **38.** Hey, that would be fun!

Mechanics

Lesson 72
Using Commas I

Commas make sentences easier to understand because they signal a pause or a separation between sentence parts.

Use commas to separate three or more items in a series.

No one knows whether Bigfoot is a man, a myth, or a monster.

Use a comma to show a pause after an introductory word.

No, Bigfoot has never been captured.

Use a comma after two or more prepositional phrases at the beginning of a sentence.

Despite years of searching, no one has gotten close to Bigfoot.

Use commas to set off words that interrupt the flow of thought in a sentence.

That doesn't mean, however, that people will stop trying.

Use commas to set off names used in direct address.

Bethany, what would you do if you saw Bigfoot?

▶ **Exercise 1 Add commas where needed. Write *C* if the sentence is correct.**

_____ Bigfoot has thick fur, wide shoulders, and huge feet.

_____ **1.** Most people, naturally, would love to see Bigfoot.

__C___ **2.** James, do you think you'd be afraid?

_____ **3.** No, Dr. Rico, I'd shake his hand.

__C___ **4.** Some people, of course, think that Bigfoot is just a man dressed in an ape suit.

__C___ **5.** People in the Himalayas tell stories of a creature called *yeti.*

__C___ **6.** Yes, the yeti is similar to Bigfoot.

_____ **7.** "Wild men" have also been seen in Nepal, China, and Australia.

__C___ **8.** The beast is called a *yowie* in Australia.

_____ **9.** Most strange creatures, fortunately, are seen in unsettled areas.

__C___ **10.** No one, I think, has sighted a Bigfoot on a subway train.

_____ **11.** Have you ever heard of the Loch Ness monster, Juan?

_____ **12.** Loch Ness, of course, is in Scotland.

_____ **13.** On a map of Scotland, you'll see that Loch Ness is huge.

__C__ **14.** It is also, some people feel, deep enough to hide a monster.

_____ **15.** Beth, Lauro, and Heather wrote a report on Loch Ness.

_____ **16.** They decided, I believe, that the creature doesn't exist.

__C__ **17.** However, no one believed rumors about the Komodo dragon, either.

_____ **18.** On a remote island in Indonesia, many Komodo dragons were found.

_____ **19.** Modern scientists, it seems, are searching Loch Ness.

__C__ **20.** The truth about the creature is hard to pin down, however.

_____ **21.** As a matter of fact, some people think that a prehistoric animal survives in Loch Ness.

_____ **22.** The beast, it appears, looks like the plesiosaur.

_____ **23.** The plesiosaur, if you'll remember, was a water reptile whose limbs looked like paddles.

_____ **24.** Could it be, Juan, that this ancient animal is not really extinct?

_____ **25.** In the movies and on television, prehistoric animals are often seen.

__C__ **26.** In 1938 a coelacanth was caught off the South African coast.

_____ **27.** This fish, it was thought, had been extinct for 70 million years.

__C__ **28.** Do you conclude, Dr. Rico, that other prehistoric animals may yet be found?

__C__ **29.** Yes, I believe that the world holds many surprises.

_____ **30.** Besides, there are many unexplored areas of the world.

_____ **31.** Believe it or not, scientists frequently find new species of life.

__C__ **32.** In the Amazon, I read somewhere, there is a bird whose chicks have claws on their wings.

_____ **33.** Well, a prehistoric bird also had claws on its wings.

_____ **34.** Nevertheless, this does not mean that anyone will find a dinosaur.

Mechanics

Lesson 73
Using Commas II

Use a **comma** before *and*, *or*, and *but* when they join simple sentences.

Felicia constructed the model, **and** Paul painted it.
Daniel wants to go to the movies, **but** he has to do his homework.
You can come with us, **or** you can stay home and read.

Use a comma after the salutation of a friendly letter and after the closing of both a friendly letter and a business letter.

Dear Beth,   With love,   Sincerely,

Use a comma to prevent misreading.

Instead of three, four o'clock is a better time.

▶ **Exercise 1 Add commas where needed in the following letter.**

Dear Alicia,

    I wanted to write to you yesterday, but I didn't have time. We're finally on our class trip,

and it's a lot of fun. Since 1990 three classes have gone to New York. Instead of New

York, Boston was our choice.

    When we got here, some of us rested, but most of us went for a walk. I read for a while,

and Antonia took a nap. Between three and four o'clock, five of us went to the aquarium. It

was a holiday, so many children were there. The aquarium shop was great, and I bought a

couple of souvenirs. I almost bought a poster, but I got a book instead. It would be a nice

present for Andi, or I could give it to Juan. Antonia bought two sharks' teeth, and she also

bought a seashell.

    Now it's suppertime, and we're getting ready to go out. I just combed my hair, but I

haven't brushed my teeth yet. I plan to wear slacks, and Antonia wants to wear a dress.

She's hoping for seafood, but I'd rather have pizza. Afterward we might see a movie, or we

could walk around town.

Mechanics

If you talk to Jess, Antonia says to tell her hello. I'll call you when I get home, and maybe we can get together.

Love, Kimmie

▶ **Exercise 2** **Add commas where needed. Write *C* in the blank before each correct sentence.**

_____   Some people like lima beans, but Jim can't stand them.

_____ **1.** Hakeem weeded the garden, and his mom picked the vegetables.

___C___ **2.** The lightning hit the barn, but it didn't catch fire.

_____ **3.** Is it raining, or did you just wash your hair?

_____ **4.** I've been to Kansas, but I've never seen Oklahoma.

___C___ **5.** The cat is napping on the chair, and the dog is sleeping under the bed.

___C___ **6.** Felipe's first language is Spanish, and André speaks French.

_____ **7.** Ana's favorite subject is geography, but she's better at math.

___C___ **8.** We wanted to buy that tape, but the store was sold out.

_____ **9.** Instead of twelve, six players got new uniforms.

_____ **10.** I'd talk louder, but I'm afraid I'd wake the baby.

___C___ **11.** Can you babysit tonight, or do you already have plans?

_____ **12.** You bring the bat and ball, and Joe will bring the mitt.

___C___ **13.** The violin was scratchy, but the trumpet sounded sweet and clear.

_____ **14.** Do you have relatives in Mexico, or is your whole family here?

_____ **15.** One twin was dressed in purple, and the other wore pink.

___C___ **16.** Does Jaime want juice with supper, or would he rather have milk?

_____ **17.** Janelle came in first, four seconds ahead of Sonya.

_____ **18.** Heather was a scarecrow at the costume party, and Jill was a movie star.

_____ **19.** Ali was invited to dinner, but he didn't feel well.

___C___ **20.** Do you know how to do this problem, or shall I help you?

_____ **21.** That looks like a kangaroo, but I think it's a wombat.

___C___ **22.** The clown tripped on her shoelace, and the children laughed loudly.

Mechanics

Lesson 74
Using Commas III

In dates, use **commas** after the day of the month and the year. Do not use a comma if only the month and the year are given.

Shama arrived in this country on July 6, 1989, with her family.
She became a citizen in January 1996.

Use commas before and after the name of a state or country when it is used with the name of a city. Do not use a comma after the state if the state name is followed by a zip code.

She used to live in Chicago, Illinois, but now she lives in Detroit, Michigan.
His address is 296 S. Pacific Avenue, Pittsburgh, Pennsylvania 15211.

Use a comma or a pair of commas to set off an abbreviated title (except *Jr.* and *Sr.*) or a degree following a person's name.

Lou Szupinski, Ph.D., wrote the book about fossils.

▶ **Exercise 1   Add commas where needed. Write *C* if the sentence is correct.**

_____ Send your questions on health to Dr. Chris Boyd, M.D.

___C___ **1.** His address is 1402 Michigan Boulevard, Chicago, Illinois 60606.

_____ **2.** We had a huge blizzard on February 18, 1989.

___C___ **3.** Our largest blizzard before that was in January 1953.

___C___ **4.** Pat Hoyt, D.V.M., is the veterinarian.

___C___ **5.** The Pittsburgh Press is at 34 Boulevard of the Allies, Pittsburgh, Pennsylvania

15230.

___C___ **6.** On graduation day my sister will be Alma Lopez, B.A.

_____ **7.** We crossed the bridge into Brooklyn, New York.

___C___ **8.** The lawyer talking to the judge is Marion Ling, J.D.

___C___ **9.** Francisco was born in Guanajuato, Mexico.

_____ **10.** The Sistine Chapel is in Vatican City, Italy.

_____ **11.** Portland, Maine, is the home of the Portland Sea Dogs.

___C___ **12.** Abraham Lincoln was born in February 1809.

Mechanics

_____C_____ **13.** New Bedford, Massachusetts, was famous for whaling.

_____C_____ **14.** El Morro castle is in San Juan, Puerto Rico.

_____C_____ **15.** On March 23, 1904, her grandfather was born in Moscow, Russia.

_____ **16.** The sweater was made in Belfast, Ireland.

_____C_____ **17.** The *Titanic* struck an iceberg on April 14, 1912.

_____C_____ **18.** The priest who said mass was Terry O'Brien, S.J.

_____ **19.** The president delivered his speech in Washington, D.C.

_____C_____ **20.** Paul Revere made his famous ride in April 1775.

_____ **21.** Write to the Weather Channel at 2840 Mt. Wilkinson Parkway, Atlanta, Georgia 30339.

_____ **22.** On December 8, 1941, the United States entered World War II.

_____C_____ **23.** Chuck was born on January 26, 1984.

_____ **24.** October 13, 1994, was an important day in her life.

_____ **25.** The Prado, a famous art museum, is in Madrid, Spain.

_____C_____ **26.** My parents were married on June 12, 1980.

_____ **27.** Did you read about that big earthquake in Mexico City, Mexico?

_____ **28.** August 14, 1989, was the last time the circus came to our town.

_____C_____ **29.** The Library of Congress is in Washington, D.C.

_____ **30.** The Harvard University Library is in Cambridge, Massachusetts.

_____C_____ **31.** Write to the National Baseball Hall of Fame at Post Office Box 590, Cooperstown, NY 13326.

_____ **32.** She lived in Los Gatos, California, before she moved here.

_____C_____ **33.** We ate at El Churrasco, a fine restaurant in Cordoba, Spain.

_____C_____ **34.** The cave paintings in Lascaux, France, date to the last Ice Age.

_____ **35.** The Basketball Association is at 645 Fifth Avenue, New York, New York.

_____C_____ **36.** Palm Springs, California, was once called *Agua Caliente*.

_____ **37.** Davy Crockett fought at the Alamo in San Antonio, Texas.

_____C_____ **38.** The Valley of the Tombs of the Kings is near Luxor, Egypt.

Mechanics

Lesson 75
Using Commas IV

Use a comma or a pair of commas to set off a direct quotation.

Brer Rabbit said, "I am the smartest animal on this earth."
"There's not a creature in this woods," he went on, "who can outsmart me."

▶ **Exercise 1 Add commas where needed to the sentences below.**

"My favorite story," said LaToya, "is called 'The Moon in the Mill Pond.'"

1. "One night Brer Rabbit and Brer Terrapin were talking by the fire," LaToya said.

2. "A terrapin is like a turtle," she explained.

3. She went on, "They heard a sound in the woods behind them."

4. "Brer Rabbit," she said, "knew that Brer Fox and Brer Bear were sneaking up on them."

5. She explained, "Those two wanted to catch Brer Rabbit and Brer Terrapin and eat them for dinner."

6. "Brer Rabbit," she said, "winked at Brer Terrapin and started fussing with the fire."

7. She continued, "He started talking about how hot the fire had to be to cook up their feast."

8. "Just then," she said, "Brer Fox and Brer Bear walked out of the woods."

9. "Brer Rabbit welcomed them to the feast," she said.

10. LaToya went on, "Brer Fox and Brer Bear asked what the feast was."

11. "Brer Rabbit," she explained, "said that the feast was at the mill pond."

12. "He told them," she said, "that the pond held a fine mess of fish."

13. "Brer Rabbit said that all they had to do was reach out their paws and grab the fish from the water," LaToya went on.

14. "Well," LaToya continued, "they all walked down to the mill pond."

15. "When they got there," she said,"Brer Rabbit saw that the full moon was shining on the water. He got an idea."

16. "Brer Rabbit acted as if he had just seen something awful," LaToya said.

17. "He told Brer Fox and Brer Bear that the moon had fallen into the mill pond," she went on.

18. "He was going to have to get the moon out of the mill pond because it was scaring the fish away," she said.

19. "Brer Rabbit ran to get a net to scoop the moon out of the mill pond," LaToya continued.

20. She said,"While he was gone, Brer Terrapin told Brer Fox that there was a pot of gold in the mill pond, right where the moon was."

21. "Finally, Brer Rabbit got back with the net," she said.

22. "Brer Fox and Brer Bear grabbed it from him," she said excitedly.

23. "They jumped into the mill pond and dragged the net around," she said.

24. LaToya said,"Brer Rabbit kept telling them to go out further."

25. "Finally," she said,"they fell into a big hole and got tangled in the net."

26. "Brer Rabbit and Brer Terrapin laughed and laughed," LaToya said.

27. "They were happy that they outsmarted Brer Fox and Brer Bear," she explained.

28. "And they were especially happy that they hadn't been eaten," she ended.

29. "Do you think," asked Ben,"that there really was gold in the mill pond?"

30. "No," answered LaToya. "That was just a trick."

31. "It was a smart trick," laughed Ben.

32. "Sometimes small animals have to be extra smart," pointed out Jerome.

33. "Otherwise," he said,"they'd get caught by the bigger ones."

34. "Brer Rabbit was clever," said Sal, "and so was Brer Terrapin."

35. "I wonder what other adventures they had," said Ben.

36. Sal said,"Here's one about how Brer Terrapin beats Brer Rabbit in a race."

Lesson 76
Commas in Review

▶ **Exercise 1** **Add commas where needed. Write *C* if the item is correct.**

_____ At school we learn to read, write, and do math.

_____ **1.** Excuse me, Mr. Ogura, did you drop this book?

_____ **2.** In case of fire, go out through the rear door.

__C__ **3.** Josie, did you hear what I said?

__C__ **4.** Susan graduated from college in June 1996.

__C__ **5.** Bring some old magazines or newspapers to class.

_____ **6.** In baseball you have to throw, hit, and catch the ball.

_____ **7.** Jason, have you eaten lunch yet?

__C__ **8.** Gorillas are large, but they are very shy.

_____ **9.** The *Titanic* sank, and hundreds of lives were lost.

_____ **10.** For the test we had to do problems 3, 6, and 9.

_____ **11.** Like Bill, Andy tried out for the lead in the play.

__C__ **12.** Inside the cage a small, fluffy animal was eating seeds.

_____ **13.** On the first Saturday in June, the pool will open.

_____ **14.** The box held three marbles, a button, and a ticket stub.

_____ **15.** Bill's dog, Ana discovered, had found the missing sock.

__C__ **16.** As a matter of fact, I was about to do my homework.

__C__ **17.** Robert, may I use the computer after you?

__C__ **18.** My red shirt was wrinkled, but I wore it anyway.

_____ **19.** Along the highway into town, you will pass several horse farms.

_____ **20.** Instead of nine, ten o'clock is when the children went to bed.

__C__ **21.** On the beach Ali and Jessica were building a sand castle.

__C__ **22.** Just inside the door her faithful cat was waiting.

____C____ **23.** For supper we had mashed potatoes, peas, and chicken.

_____ **24.** For the first time in my life, I actually won something!

_____ **25.** Please turn down the radio, Kim.

_____ **26.** Dear Aunt Millie,

_____ **27.** I'm not sure, however, that I am willing to help you with your math homework.

____C____ **28.** Nadine, are you going to the grocery store?

_____ **29.** Besides the United States, Canada exports a lot of wheat.

____C____ **30.** The address is 803 Church Street, Honesdale, Pennsylvania 18431.

____C____ **31.** Al didn't go on the class trip, and he wishes he had.

_____ **32.** Robert Capozza, Ph.D., wrote this book on fossils.

_____ **33.** His doctor is Denita Thurgood, M.D.

_____ **34.** Throughout the world, war devastates many lives.

____C____ **35.** "Well done, my lad," said the captain.

_____ **36.** Tim cried out, "I wish I had never run away to sea!"

____C____ **37.** "There's a cyclone coming, Em," said Uncle Henry.

_____ **38.** December 4, 1982, was the date on the yellowed newspaper.

_____ **39.** "Sit down, Clyde, and put your feet up," said Hari.

_____ **40.** Anita shouted, "Call the fire department!"

_____ **41.** "The cat," Alicia said, "is scratching the furniture."

____C____ **42.** Uncle Josh asked, "Is it hot enough for you?"

_____ **43.** "Fellow citizens," said Abraham Lincoln, "we cannot escape history."

_____ **44.** Are you reading about Naples, Maine, or Naples, Italy?

____C____ **45.** Look in the December 1992 issue of *National Geographic*.

Lesson 77
Semicolons and Colons

Use a **semicolon** to join parts of a compound sentence when a conjunction such as *and, but,* or *or* is not used.

Belinda likes oatmeal for breakfast; I prefer cream of wheat.

Use a **colon** to introduce a list of items that ends a sentence. Use words such as *these, the following,* and *as follows* to introduce lists.

English words that come from Spanish include the following: *ranch, corral,* and *stampede.*

Do not use a colon immediately after a verb or a preposition.

Jaime likes to read, play basketball, and dance.

Use a colon to separate the hour and the minute.

School begins at 8:15 on the dot.

Use a colon after the salutation of a business letter.

Dear Professor D'Amico: To whom it may concern:

▶ **Exercise 1   Add semicolons and colons where needed. Write *C* if a sentence or phrase is correct.**

____C____   Devin is my brother; he's my best friend, too.

____C____ **1.** At the grocery store Mom bought milk, fruit, and cereal.

_____ **2.** Meet me at the corner at 12:30.

____C____ **3.** Pete loves flowers; roses are his favorite.

_____ **4.** The forecast called for rain; it snowed instead.

_____ **5.** The green shoes are pretty; the red ones are more comfortable.

____C____ **6.** She may get a parrot; she may not.

_____ **7.** For the class trip you'll need the following: raincoat, boots, pencil, paper or pen, and lunch.

____C____ **8.** Earth is the third planet from the sun; Mars is the fourth.

_____ **9.** We had chicken last night; tonight we'll have fish.

_____C_____ **10.** Robert Frost wrote poems; L. Frank Baum wrote books.

_____ **11.** The last episode was great; the next will be even better.

_____C_____ **12.** Say "thank you" in Spanish as follows: "Gracias."

_____ **13.** The following dogs received honorable mention: Spot, Blaze, Nathan, and

Maggie.

_____C_____ **14.** Be here by 7:10 so we'll have plenty of time.

_____ **15.** The spelling test will focus on these words: *spectacles, decimal, shrill,* and

fantastic.

_____C_____ **16.** Dear Dr. Washington:

_____C_____ **17.** This store is sold out of batteries; we'll have to look elsewhere.

_____ **18.** Ladybugs are helpful insects; so are bees.

_____ **19.** The show starts at 7:30; we should try to get there earlier.

_____C_____ **20.** Lionel is a good writer; he draws well, too.

_____C_____ **21.** Put a stamp in the upper right corner; put your return address in the upper left.

_____C_____ **22.** These students please report to the office: Sally, Geno, and Basil.

_____C_____ **23.** The movie only costs $2.25; you gave him $2.50.

_____ **24.** My mom's not home; please call back later.

_____C_____ **25.** The cat has green eyes; the dog's are brown.

_____C_____ **26.** Cuba is a warm country; Canada is colder.

_____ **27.** For drinks we have the following: milk, juice, water, and soda.

_____C_____ **28.** The baby eats mashed potatoes, carrots, and bananas.

_____ **29.** This is a picture of my mom; my dad is standing behind her.

_____C_____ **30.** One of the twins has short hair; the other twin's hair is long.

_____C_____ **31.** Read this book about pirates; it's the best I've come across.

_____ **32.** This fruit juice is delicious; you should try it.

_____C_____ **33.** I can't reach the top shelf; it's too high.

_____ **34.** The wastebasket is full; please empty it.

Lesson 78
Quotation Marks

Use **quotation marks** before and after a direct quotation.

"How very strange this is!" cried Alice.

Use quotation marks before and after each part of an interrupted quotation.

"With those broken shutters," said Carter, "this place looks deserted."

Use a comma or commas to separate a phrase such as *she said* from the quotation itself. Place the comma outside opening quotation marks but inside closing quotation marks.

The White Rabbit said, "Oh, dear! Oh, dear! I shall be too late!"
"It was much more pleasant at home," thought Sarah.

Place a period inside closing quotation marks.

Clarisse said, "I read a good book last weekend."

Place a question mark or an exclamation mark inside the quotation marks when it is part of the quotation.

"What exactly did you see?" asked Detective Keeler.

Place a question mark or an exclamation mark outside the quotation marks when it is part of the entire sentence but not part of the quotation.

Did you hear him shout "Carumba!"?

▶ **Exercise 1 Add quotation marks and other punctuation marks as needed.**

"This book," said Toni, "is the best I have ever read."

1. "What a great car!" exclaimed Ricardo.

2. Robin asked the lady, "Would you like to sit down?"

3. Did Ms. Mercado say, "Read the first three chapters"?

4. "No, thank you," said Tomás, "I don't want any more mashed potatoes."

5. Colleen said, "May I use the phone when you're finished with it?"

6. Juan said, "Chris is two inches taller than Pete."

7. Fidel said to Ahmed, "Could you lend me a pencil?"

Mechanics

8. Mom asked, "Who wants to go to the store with me?"

9. Tom yelled, "The boat is sinking!"

10. I think he said, "No talking during a fire drill."

11. "Three strikes and you're out," said the umpire.

12. "Does anyone here," asked Michele, "know how to spell *embarrass*?"

13. Did you hear him yell, "You're out"?

14. Dad asked, "Would you rather have hamburgers or chicken for supper?"

15. "That," said Penny, "is the silliest joke I've ever heard."

16. "After you log on to the computer," said Aiko, "choose a game from the menu."

17. "Uh-oh," said Jill, "we're out of cat food."

18. "Here's the two dollars I owe you," said Diego.

19. "My cat," said Jack, "weighs eighteen pounds."

20. "That's a mighty big cat," said Beth.

21. Carl asked, "Is English your favorite subject?"

22. "The ancient Greeks," Mr. Hassan said, "were famous for their cleverness."

23. "I'm going to be an astronaut," Jane said proudly.

24. "President Abraham Lincoln," my dad told me, "liked to tell funny stories."

25. "I have to go," Derek said. "There's a call waiting."

26. Terri shouted, "Let's get out of here!"

27. Karne called and said, "When are you coming?"

28. "A penny saved is a penny earned," Ben Franklin said.

▶ **Writing Link** **Write about a conversation you have had with a friend or a family member. Use quotation marks and other punctuation as needed.**

_____

_____

_____

_____

_____

Mechanics

Lesson 79
Quotation Marks and Italics

Use italics (underlining) to identify the title of a book, play, film, television series, magazine, newspaper, or name of a ship, train, or plane.

The Wind in the Willows (book)
Home Improvement (television series)

Use quotation marks for the title of a short story, essay, poem, song, magazine or newspaper article, or book chapter.

The poem "Jabberwocky" is in the chapter entitled "Looking-Glass House."

▶ **Exercise 1 Read each title. Add quotation marks or underline for italics.**

<u>Mysterious Tales of the New England Coast</u> (book)

1. <u>Old Yeller</u> (film)

2. <u>Old Yeller</u> (book)

3. <u>The Sword in the Stone</u> (book)

4. "Caring for Your Pet" (magazine article)

5. "Jingle Bells" (song)

6. <u>Pittsburgh Post-Gazette</u> (newspaper)

7. <u>Cricket</u> (magazine)

8. <u>The Adventures of Huckleberry Finn</u> (book)

9. "Mamma Sewing" (essay)

10. "The Tale of the Tiger's Paintbrush" (short story)

11. "The Great Eclipse" (magazine article)

12. "Love Song for a Jellyfish" (poem)

13. <u>Jump! The Adventures of Brer Rabbit</u> (book)

14. <u>Mayflower</u> (ship)

15. <u>Time</u> (magazine)

16. <u>The Longest Journey</u> (film)

Mechanics

17. "Hurt No Living Thing" (poem)

18. Grandpa and the Statue (play)

19. "The Doctor of Literature" (book chapter)

20. "America, the Beautiful" (song)

21. Portland Press Herald (newspaper)

22. "The Cowardly Lion" (book chapter)

23. "The Weaving Contest" (short story)

24. "Old McDonald Had a Farm" (song)

25. "A Cellar and an Attic" (poem)

26. Titanic (ship)

27. The Silver Chair (book)

28. The Thief of Baghdad (film)

29. Highlights for Children (magazine)

30. "Langston Terrace" (essay)

31. "Money" (book chapter)

32. The Dick Van Dyke Show (television series)

33. The Last Battle (book)

34. Miss Louisa and the Outlaws (play)

35. "The Fun They Had" (short story)

▶ **Writing Link** Write five sentences about your two favorite books and their most interesting chapters.

_____

_____

_____

_____

_____

_____

Lesson 80
Apostrophes

Use an **apostrophe** and an *s* ('s) to form the possessive of a singular noun.

boy + **'s** = boy**'s**   horse + **'s** = horse**'s**

Use an apostrophe and an *s* ('s) to form the possessive of a plural noun that does not end in *s*.

children + **'s** = children**'s**   sheep + **'s** = sheep**'s**

Use an apostrophe alone to form the possessive of a plural noun that ends in *s*.

monkeys + **'** = monkey**s'**   libraries + **'** = librarie**s'**

Do not use an apostrophe in a possessive pronoun.

His dad baked the cake.   **Ours** made the cookies.

Use an apostrophe to replace letters that have been omitted in a contraction.

there is = there**'s**   cannot = can**'t**

▶ **Exercise 1 Add apostrophes where needed. Write *C* if the sentence is correct.**

_____ Blackbeard's name is an infamous one in history.

___C___ **1.** His real name was Edward Teach.

_____ **2.** Blackbeard commanded the *Queen Anne's Revenge.*

_____ **3.** Blackbeard's cruelty was legendary.

_____ **4.** His men's hearts were filled with fear of their captain.

___C___ **5.** Theirs was a hard and dangerous life.

___C___ **6.** Many books have been written about Blackbeard and other pirates.

_____ **7.** Some pirates' treasures have never been found.

___C___ **8.** Each pirate crew's code was to share treasure equally.

_____ **9.** Its not true that many pirates had to walk the plank.

___C___ **10.** What's more likely is that many were marooned on islands.

_____ **11.** Sometimes women put on men's clothing and ran away to sea.

_____C_____ **12.** Robert Louis Stevenson's book about pirates is called *Treasure Island*.

_____ **13.** Although a movie was made of the book, it can't compare to the book.

_____ **14.** It tells the tale of the pirates' attempts to recover a treasure.

_____ **15.** In the book, a sea captain's belongings include a treasure map.

_____C_____ **16.** The map leads Captain Smollet and the members of his crew to Treasure Island.

_____ **17.** The name of the ship's cook is Long John Silver.

_____C_____ **18.** Silver's plan is to seize the treasure first.

_____ **19.** He's foiled by Ben Gunn, who was marooned on the island three years earlier by Silver and his band of pirates.

_____ **20.** Scotland's most famous pirate was William Kidd.

_____ **21.** Captain Kidd's death by hanging was a warning to other pirates.

_____C_____ **22.** The pirate Grace O'Malley's name is famous in Ireland.

_____ **23.** She's known for her love of the sea.

_____ **24.** One of China's most famous pirates was Koxinga.

_____ **25.** Koxinga's father had been a pirate, too.

_____ **26.** His father's death at the hands of the Manchus made Koxinga angry.

_____ **27.** He fought many battles against the Imperial Navy's ships.

_____C_____ **28.** The English pirate John Rackam's wife was the pirate Anne Bonny.

▶ **Writing Link Write five sentences about a visit to the beach. What would you like to see and do? Use apostrophes where needed.**

_____

_____

_____

_____

_____

_____

_____

Lesson 81
Hyphens

Use a **hyphen** to show the division of a word at the end of a line. Always divide a word between syllables.

The Big Dipper is probably the most familiar of all the constella-tions.

Use a hyphen in compound numbers from twenty-one through ninety-nine.

Use a hyphen or hyphens in certain compound nouns. Check a dictionary.

father-in-law   sisters-in-law

▶ **Exercise 1**   **Add hyphens where needed. Write *C* if the sentence needs no changes.**

___C___   He peeled twenty-three apples for the pies.

___C___   **1.** I have thirty-five dollars to spend.

_____   **2.** Drew's great-grandmother knows a lot of interesting stories.

_____   **3.** Gregorio's dad turns thirty-five tomorrow.

_____   **4.** Jack Benny always said he was thirty-nine.

___C___   **5.** This company produces fifty-seven kinds of soup.

_____   **6.** The latitude of Chicago is forty-two degrees.

_____   **7.** The mother of my sister's husband is my sister's mother-in-law.

___C___   **8.** Did you climb all ninety-one steps?

_____   **9.** The produce store has twenty-seven kinds of vegetables.

_____   **10.** The piano has eighty-eight keys.

___C___   **11.** Jeanna has exactly seventy-three cents in her pocket.

_____   **12.** The speed limit on the highway is fifty-five miles an hour.

_____   **13.** The woman over there is my sister-in-law.

___C___   **14.** She lives in Boonetown; he lives thirty-three miles away.

_____   **15.** There are thirty-eight desks in the room.

_____   **16.** She's never been more than seventy-five miles from home.

_____C_____ **17.** A slice of bread has only forty-two calories.

_____C_____ **18.** There must be at least eighty-five cows in the field.

_____C_____ **19.** Can I buy a good radio for twenty-five dollars?

_____ **20.** The bottle has forty-one vitamin pills in it.

_____C_____ **21.** The alphabet has twenty-six letters.

_____ **22.** Alfonso counted sixty-eight jelly beans in the basket.

_____ **23.** The temperature is thirty-four degrees.

_____ **24.** There are one hundred and forty-two steps between my house and yours.

_____ **25.** The pie in the nursery rhyme had twenty-four blackbirds in it.

_____ **26.** Her birthday is the thirty-first of March.

_____ **27.** Four score and seven is the same as eighty-seven.

_____ **28.** Not too many years ago there were only forty-eight states.

_____ **29.** The cheese sandwich costs eighty-five cents.

_____ **30.** Are there enough books for twenty-eight students?

▶ **Writing Link Write three or four sentences of a plot for a book that stretches over several generations. Give the character's relationships and ages.**

_____

_____

_____

_____

_____

_____

_____

_____

_____

_____

_____

Mechanics

Lesson 82
Abbreviations I

Use the abbreviations *Mr., Mrs., Ms.,* and *Dr.* before a person's name. Abbreviate *Junior (Jr.)* and *Senior (Sr.)* after a person's name. Abbreviate professional or academic degrees that follow a person's name.

Ida Ames, Ph.D. (doctor of philosophy)   **Sid Poff, M.F.A.** (master of fine arts)

Use all capital letters and no periods for abbreviations that are pronounced letter by letter or as words. Exceptions are U.S. and Washington, D.C. which do use periods.

FBI (Federal Bureau of Investigation)   **ROM** (read-only memory)
PSAT (Preliminary Scholastic Aptitude Test)

Use the abbreviations A.M. (*ante meridiem,* "before noon") and P.M. (*post meridiem,* "after noon") for exact times. For dates use B.C. (before Christ) and, sometimes, A.D. (anno Domini, "in the year of the Lord," after Christ.)

10:25 A.M.   4:30 P.M.   300 B.C.   A.D. 50

Abbreviate calendar items (days of the week, months of the year) only when they appear in charts and lists.

Sun.	Mon.	Tues.	Wed.	Thurs.	Fri.	Sat.	
Jan.	Feb.	Mar.	Apr.	Aug.	Sept.	Oct.	Nov.	Dec.

▶ **Exercise 1 Complete each sentence with the abbreviation of the word or words in parentheses. Write *C* if no abbreviation should be used.**

Samuel Smith _____Jr._____ is the principal's name. (Junior)

1. _____Mr._____ Alfredo will give you the information you need. (Mister)

2. This piece of pottery dates back to 500 _____B.C._____. (before Christ)

3. _____Mr._____ O'Malley is here to pick up his daughter. (Mister)

4. Belinda is usually home at 6:15 _____P.M._____ every day. (*post meridiem*)

5. The tool dates from about _____A.D._____ 618. (after Christ)

6. _____Fri._____, _____Sat._____, and _____Sun._____ are abbreviations for days of the week.

   (Friday, Saturday, Sunday)

7. Alma Romero will be here at 3:00 _____P.M._____ to take over. (after noon)

Mechanics

8. Alicia and Cheryl have birthdays in _____C_____. (February)

9. This article was written by Brad Frank of _____UPI_____. (United Press International)

10. The date on the letter was _____C *or* Oct._____28, 1996. (October)

11. _____Dr._____ Benito prescribed medicine for Sarah's sore throat. (Doctor)

12. My hat carries the insignia of _____NASA_____. (National Aeronautics and Space Administration)

13. Marla Todd, _____Ph.D_____, is how my mom's name is written on her business cards. (doctor of philosophy)

14. In 44 _____B.C._____ Julius Caesar was assassinated. (before Christ)

15. Promptly at 7:10 _____A.M._____ the bus arrives. (*ante meridiem*)

▶ **Exercise 2** **Write the abbreviation for each italicized word or phrase.**

1. *Mister* Adams _____Mr._____

2. *Wednesday* _____Wed._____

3. *Doctor* DiFillipo _____Dr._____

4. 8:00 *ante meridiem* _____A.M._____

5. *December* _____Dec._____

6. 952 *after Christ* _____A.D._____

7. *Food and Drug Administration*
FDA _____

8. 3:00 *post meridiem* _____P.M._____

9. 22 *before Christ* _____B.C._____

10. *Medical Doctor* _____M.D._____

11. *Friday* _____Fri._____

12. *January* _____Jan._____

13. *November* _____Nov._____

14. Juan Lopez *Senior* _____Sr._____

15. *Public Broadcasting Service*
PBS _____

16. Barry Castwell, *Master of Social Work*
MSW _____

17. *Thursday* _____Thurs._____

18. *North Atlantic Treaty Organization*
NATO _____

19. *Tuesday* _____Tues._____

20. *American Medical Association*
AMA _____

21. Carl Cook *Junior* _____Jr._____

22. *Central Intelligence Agency*
CIA _____

23. 11:00 *in the evening* _____P.M._____

24. *International Olympic Committee*
IOC _____

AMA _____

Lesson 83
Abbreviations II

In charts, graphs, and tables abbreviate units of measure.

ounce(s) **oz.**   pound(s) **lb.**   yard(s) **yd.**   mile(s) **mi.**   gallon(s) **gal.**
meter(s) **m**   foot (feet) **ft.**   inch(es) **in.**   liter(s) **l**   kilometer(s) **km**

On envelopes abbreviate the words that refer to street names.

Street **St.**   Boulevard **Blvd.**   Avenue **Ave.**   Road **Rd.**   Court **Ct.**

On envelopes use Postal Service abbreviations for the names of states.

Massachusetts **MA**   Oregon **OR**   West Virginia **WV**   Iowa **IA**
Wisconsin **WI**   Ohio **OH**   Maine **ME**   Nevada **NV**
Mississippi **MS**   Indiana **IN**   New York **NY**   Texas **TX**

▶ **Exercise 1** **Rewrite the following addresses, using abbreviations as they would appear on envelopes.**

Juan Lopez
1557 Rochester Boulevard
Boston, Massachusetts 13799

Juan Lopez
1557 Rochester Blvd.
Boston, MA 13799

Susan Ming
375 Fredericks Street
Salem, Oregon 10227

Susan Ming
375 Fredericks St.
Salem, OR 10227

Adrien Frank
879 Meander Court
Youngstown, Ohio 11337

Adrien Frank
879 Meander Ct.
Youngstown, OH 11337

▶ **Exercise 2** **Using the form on the next page, rewrite the following chart, substituting abbreviations for the words in parentheses.**

Approximate Equivalent Measurements

16 (ounces)	= 1 (pound)	= 453.6 (grams)
1 (gallon)	= 4 (quarts)	= 3.8 (liters)
12 (inches)	= 1 (foot)	= .3 (meter)
3 (feet)	= 1 (yard)	= .9 (meter)
5,280 (feet)	= 1 (mile)	= 1,609 (meter)
3,279 (feet)	= .62 (mile)	= 1 (kilometer)

Mechanics

Approximate Equivalent Measurements

16 oz.	= 1 lb.	= 453.6 g
1 gal.	= 4 qt.	= 3.8 l
12 in.	= 1 ft.	= .3 m
3 ft.	= 1 yd.	= .9 m
5,280 ft.	= 1 mi.	= 1,609 m
3,279 ft.	= .62 mi.	= 1 km

▶ **Exercise 3** **Write the abbreviation for each italicized word.**

3 *pounds* __lb._____

1. Galveston, *Texas* __TX_____

2. Oak *Road* __Rd._____

3. Portland, *Maine* __ME_____

4. Easy *Street* __St._____

5. 15 *miles* __mi._____

6. 16 *yards* __yd._____

7. Tuscon *Avenue* __Ave._____

8. 42 *inches* __in._____

9. Indianapolis, *Indiana* __IN_____

10. Dayton, *Ohio* __OH_____

11. 17 *liters* __l_____

12. Biloxi, *Mississippi* __MS_____

13. 20 *kilometers* __km_____

14. Carson City, *Nevada* __NV_____

15. Buffalo, *New York* __NY_____

Mechanics

Lesson 84
Writing Numbers I

In charts and tables always write numbers as figures. However, in sentences numbers are sometimes spelled out and sometimes written as numerals.

Spell out numbers that can be written in one or two words.

There are **twenty-two** days until my birthday.

Use numerals for numbers of more than two words.

I think the answer is **333**.

Spell out any number that begins a sentence, or reword the sentence.

Five thousand two hundred people watched the eclipse from the park.

Write a very large number as a numeral followed by *million* or *billion*.

The sun is about **93 million** miles from Earth.

▶ **Exercise 1** **Write the correct form of the number in each sentence. Write *C* if the sentence is correct.**

___thirteen___	Buffalo has won 13 games so far this year.
___C___	**1.** Tickets to the game cost six dollars.
___C___	**2.** The population of Avon is about four thousand.
___Fourteen thousand___	**3.** 14,000 people signed the petition.
___608___	**4.** Last year the shelter found homes for six hundred eight cats.
___four___	**5.** The blizzard dumped 4 feet of snow on our town.
___C___	**6.** Light travels at about 186,000 miles per second.
___C___	**7.** The planet Saturn is about 900 million miles from the sun.
___C___	**8.** Crater Lake in Oregon is more than 1,950 feet deep.
___three___	**9.** I've seen that movie 3 times.
___C___	**10.** In 1990 this country imported about 2 million cars from Japan.
___C___	**11.** The Grand Canyon is about one mile deep.

Mechanics

_____ C _____ **12.** Nevada is about 490 miles long from north to south.

_____ 5 _____ **13.** About five million people have seen this movie.

_____ two hundred _____ **14.** The meeting room will hold 200 people.

_____ C _____ **15.** The Ohio River is about 981 miles long.

▶ **Exercise 2 Draw a line under the correct form.**

   (40, <u>forty</u>) minutes

1. (<u>6</u>, six) billion cats

2. (8, <u>eight</u>) cars

3. (20, <u>twenty</u>) inches

4. (<u>642</u>, six hundred forty-two) miles

5. (12, <u>twelve</u>) inches

6. (2, <u>Two</u>) bikes are parked there.

7. (<u>3</u>, three) million dollars

8. (81, <u>eighty-one</u>) feet high

9. (60, <u>sixty</u>) meters wide

10. (13, <u>thirteen</u>) years old

11. (20, <u>twenty</u>) minutes

12. (3, <u>three</u>) phone calls

13. (88,000, <u>eighty-eight thousand</u>) pounds

14. A yard is shorter than (1, <u>one</u>) meter.

15. Is the answer (<u>15</u>, fifteen) million or billion?

Mechanics

Lesson 85

Writing Numbers II

If one number in a sentence must be written as a numeral, use all numerals, even though you might spell out one of the numbers if it appeared alone.

Jessica has **305** points, and Cleon has **300** points.

Spell out ordinal numbers (*first*, *second*, and so forth).

Alaina was first in line to buy tickets to the concert.

Use words for amounts of money that can be written in one or two words, for the approximate time of day, and for the time of day when A.M. or P.M. is not used.

ten cents   half past **six**   a quarter past **five**   two **o'clock**

Use numerals for dates, for decimals, for house, apartment and room numbers, for street or avenue numbers, for telephone numbers, for page numbers, for percentages, for amounts of money involving both dollars and cents, to emphasize the exact time of day, or when A.M. or P.M. is used.

May **9, 1996**   **20** percent   **$45.75**   **1:12** P.M.

▶ **Exercise 1 Write the correct form of the number in each sentence. Write *C* if the sentence is correct.**

_____96_____	Central finished the game with ninety-six points, but South had 104 points.
_____C_____	**1.** There will be a partial eclipse of the moon on May 15.
_____C_____	**2.** The eclipse begins at 2:15 P.M.
_____first_____	**3.** She was the lst in her family to go to college.
__48 percent__	**4.** About forty-eight % of the students bring their lunches to school.
_____60_____	**5.** This slice of bread has 120 calories; that one has sixty.
_____C_____	**6.** I think she lives at 20 St. James Place.
_____21_____	**7.** My grandmother lives in Apartment twenty-one.
_____C_____	**8.** He dropped his books for the second time that day.
_____C_____	**9.** The telephone number of the planetarium is 787-2112.
_____third_____	**10.** Did you do the 3rd problem yet?

Mechanics

_____six_____ **11.** Mom got home at around 6 o'clock.

_____C_____ **12.** Alabama has 53 miles of coastline; Florida has 770.

_____53_____ **13.** Please open your book to page fifty-three.

_____C_____ **14.** When it's ten o'clock in Ohio, it's seven o'clock in California.

_____C_____ **15.** I've seen that movie three times.

_____C_____ **16.** Twenty-five percent of all our customers are under sixteen years old.

_____forty-five_____ **17.** Can you lend me 45 cents until tomorrow?

_____5:25_____ **18.** Supper is at five-twenty-five P.M. sharp.

_____third_____ **19.** Last night we had spaghetti for the 3rd time this week.

_____33_____ **20.** Send your postcards to thirty-three Exchange St.

_____C_____ **21.** Massachusetts entered the Union on February 6, 1788.

_____first_____ **22.** Delaware was the lst state to enter the Union.

_____4000_____ **23.** People began writing in about four thousand B.C.

_____1_____ **24.** In A.D. one there were about 200 million people in the world.

_____fifteen_____ **25.** Is fifteen miles longer than 15 kilometers?

_____C_____ **26.** This is the sixth episode of the show that I've seen.

_____eight_____ **27.** Is it 8 o'clock already?

_____percent_____ **28.** We are 100% ready.

_____C_____ **29.** The movie starts at 6:20 P.M. and ends at eight o'clock.

_____C_____ **30.** Confucius lived around 500 B.C.

Mechanics

☑ Unit 12 **Review**

▶ **Exercise 1 Add punctuation marks where needed. Underline words or phrases that should be in italics.**

Terri, you're in charge of refreshments for our next meeting.

1. Usually on Saturday nights my family eats at a restaurant, goes to a movie, or plays a board game at home.

2. For the first time in his life, he went to Disneyland.

3. No, he wasn't a bit afraid of the roller coaster. *or* !

4. Terry wore a green-striped shirt, and Jerry wore a polka-dotted one.

5. The Children's Hour is popular on our local cable channel.

6. "Get out of the way!" yelled Jeff.

7. December 1, 1968, is Aunt Barbie's birthday.

8. What an exciting movie!

9. Gerald moved to Indianapolis, Indiana, just before school started.

10. The grand total of Lisa's savings was twenty-seven cents.

11. My oldest sister graduated on June 9, 1995, and her title is now Jean Stewart, M. D.

12. On New Year's Eve I resolved the following: get plenty of sleep, exercise daily, and eat nothing but chocolate for the rest of the day! *or* .

13. I planned to get up at 6:00 A.M.; I arose at seven.

14. Mary asked, "Where are you going?"

15. Tranh's favorite movie is Angels in the Outfield.

16. Alisha, your mother is here to take you home.

17. Why couldn't the coin's inscription be 4 B.C.?

18. Mr. Cline works at NASA as an engineer.

Cumulative Review: Units 1–12

▶ **Exercise 1** **Draw a line under the correct word in parentheses.**

I gave my sketches (<u>to</u>, two) Akira.

1. (Their, <u>They're</u>) flying to Canada next week.

2. We had (all ready, <u>already</u>) finished the homework.

3. Gene has (<u>two</u>, too) pet turtles.

4. I (<u>accept</u>, except) your apology.

5. Let's toast the marshmallows and (than, <u>then</u>) play cricket.

6. The problem is this (<u>loose</u>, lose) wire.

7. Put the bike (in, <u>into</u>) the garage.

8. (Its, <u>It's</u>) a shame that you missed the parade.

9. Karen went to (lay, <u>lie</u>) down.

10. I bought a tape that teaches Spanish because I like to (<u>learn</u>, teach) other languages.

11. Will you (<u>let</u>, leave) me go horseback riding with Steve?

12. Sophie was bobbing up and down (<u>in</u>, into) the pool.

13. (Beside, <u>Besides</u>) math, I enjoy band and science.

14. If I have to (<u>choose</u>, chose) the dog's name, it's going to be "Arfie."

15. Gail is (<u>all ready</u>, already) for the recital.

16. (<u>Lay</u>, Lie) the bottle of sunscreen on the beach.

17. Everyone in our family (accept, <u>except</u>) Alex had a cold last weekend.

18. A lilac bush grows (<u>between</u>, among) the house and the garage.

19. The sad-eyed puppy licked (<u>its</u>, it's) paw.

20. (Sit, <u>Set</u>) the box on top of the washer.

Mechanics

Name _____ Class _____ Date _____

▶ **Exercise 2** **Draw a line under each prepositional phrase and write whether it is used as an adjective (*adj.*) or adverb. (*adv.*). Insert a comma if the sentence requires it.**

_____adv._____   From the doorway I heard the phone ringing.

adv., adv.   **1.** After the movie, we went to Burger Heaven.

____adv.____   **2.** The newfallen snow glittered in the moonlight.

____adv.____   **3.** The choir is singing at the mall.

____adj.____   **4.** The song of whales is beautiful.

____adv.____   **5.** The bay was filled with smog.

____adv.____   **6.** Because of the storm we stayed inside.

____adv.____   **7.** The sunset leaked gold accents across the deep purple sky.

____adv.____   **8.** The car emerged from the garage.

____adv.____   **9.** The lightning crashed into the tree.

____adj.____   **10.** The dog from next door followed me home.

____adv.____   **11.** The breeze carried Camilla's voice across the lake.

____adv.____   **12.** Melisa left the room before the bell.

____adj.____   **13.** Carol, write a poem about our town.

____adv.____   **14.** Do you see the colorful oriole in that big tree?

____adv.____   **15.** East of town the circus will be held.

adj., adv.   **16.** The echoes of a faraway bell spread across the remote valley.

____adv.____   **17.** The baby birds were chirping inside of their nest.

____adv.____   **18.** The toddler spilled lemonade on Jenifer's new slacks.

____adv.____   **19.** Bart splashed the cool water against his face.

____adv.____   **20.** Does anyone know why Victor is flying to Texas?

____adj.____   **21.** I want the chair next to Gloria.

____adj.____   **22.** The teapot with the broken lid was never used.

adv., adj.   **23.** After the rehersal on Wednesday, the director felt discouraged.

____adv.____   **24.** Across the street rolled the empty wagon.

____adv.____   **25.** The lion cub tumbled down the hill.

▶ **Exercise 3 Place the correct punctuation mark after each sentence.**

What do you think of my haircut?

1. We did it! *or* .

2. Where did you put my eyeshadow?

3. I left my bike under the shade tree.

4. Madras is coming! *or* .

5. Mr. Dubois is ready to judge the Science Fair.

6. Gary, what did you do with my history book?

7. Close the refrigerator door.

8. Who ate all the fudge?

9. I want to write like Roald Dahl.

10. My parents decided to unplug the TV for one whole week.

11. Did Tio Jorge call?

12. Let Daniel come with us to Garcy Park to play baseball.

13. Is that story about a Trojan horse based on fact?

14. Henny Penny warned, "The sky is falling!"

15. Get out of there fast! *or* .

16. How can you not like that band?

17. I've already read that book.

18. The hamster got out! *or* .

19. My bike needs new tires and a paint job.

20. Eat healthful foods, and get plenty of exercise.

21. The sailor in the crow's nest shouted, "Land ahoy!"

22. The kindergartners listened closely to Carlene's story.

23. Was first prize a computer?

24. Tom added a Ted Williams card to his baseball card collection.

25. First, line up in alphabetic order.

Vocabulary and Spelling

Unit 13: Vocabulary and Spelling

Lesson 86

Building Vocabulary: Learning from Context

Context clues are words and sentences around an unfamiliar word that explain its meaning. Three types of context clues are definition, example, and general context. The definition, or meaning, of the unfamiliar word may be given in the sentence. Clue words such as *that is*, *in other words*, or *which means* tell you that a definition is following. Sometimes examples are given to explain an unfamiliar word. The clue words *like*, *for example*, *including*, or *such as* often come before an example. If there are no special clue words in the sentence, you can use the general context. That is, you can use the details in the words or sentences around the new word to determine its meaning.

Darla is a philatelist, *which means* that she collects stamps. (The clue words *which means* tell you that the word *philatelist* means "stamp collector.")

Bovines, *including* domestic cattle and the American bison, are an important source of food for many cultures. (The word *including* introduces examples of bovines. From the examples you can guess that bovines are members of the cattle family.)

Armand took the rough stones to a lapidary. She was going to cut, grind, and polish the stones so that they could be set in silver bracelets. (The general context tells you that a lapidary has something to do with making jewelry. A lapidary is a person who works with gemstones.)

▶ **Exercise 1** **Write in the blank the meaning of the word in italics.**

Arnold is good at *ciphering*, which is an old way of saying he is good at math.

<u>using numbers as in math</u>

1. Wolves are *carnivores*, which means they are meat eaters. <u>animals that eat meat</u>

2. Fina owns several large *implements* such as a tractor, a combine, and a baler.

   <u>tools</u>

3. Ms. Chien praised our *deportment*, or in other words, our behavior.

   <u>behavior, manner</u>

4. Jerry's father filled the spaces between the tiles with *grout,* that is, thin finishing plaster.

a plaster or cement used to hold tiles in place

5. *Primates,* such as apes and humans, usually have well-developed brains.

a high order of mammals

6. The motel offered many *amenities,* such as a pool and free soda.

special added features

7. Marla grew up in a *parsonage,* that is, a minister's home.

a home provided for a pastor

8. The sisters cleaned the vacant lot *gratis;* in other words, they were not paid.

for free

9. We just finished a unit on famous *edifices,* such as cathedrals and skyscrapers.

large, imposing buildings

10. Jingdan is quite *meticulous;* that is, she pays attention to every detail.

very exact and accurate

11. Marco played several *percussion instruments,* including snare drum, tympani, and

xylophone. instruments that produce sound by being struck

12. Chicago hosted a convention of *numismatists,* who are people who collect coins.

coin collectors

13. The crowd *guffawed;* in other words, they laughed loudly.

laughed loudly

14. A good chef uses many *herbs,* such as basil and garlic.

plants used for seasoning

15. Mr. Ramirez has sports *memorabilia* such as his ticket stub from the 1956 World Series.

objects that bring memories

16. The picnic grounds were very *tranquil.* No traffic noise interrupted us. The wind was

calm. Even the birds were quiet. peaceful, relaxed

Vocabulary and Spelling

Lesson 87
Building Vocabulary: Prefixes

A **prefix** is a word part that is added to the beginning of a word and changes its meaning. An understanding of prefixes and their meanings will help you learn new words.

The king was dethroned. (The prefix *de-* means "remove from" or "reduce"; therefore, the king was removed from his throne.)

PREFIX	MEANING	EXAMPLE	MEANING
in-	not	**in**direct	not direct
non-	without	**non**stop	without stopping
	not	**non**salable	unable to be sold
un-	opposite of, not	**un**clean	not clean
	to reverse	**un**tie	to loosen
pre-	before	**pre**pay	to pay in advance
de-	remove from	**de**throne	remove from the throne
	reduce	**de**grade	to make lower
dis-	opposite of, not	**dis**agree	not agree

▶ **Exercise 1** Underline the prefix of each word. Using the meaning of the prefix, write in the blank the meaning of the word. Use a dictionary if you are uncertain of the meaning.

preselect _____to select in advance_____

1. devalue _____to lower in value_____

2. disassemble _____to take apart_____

3. unfit _____not proper or qualified_____

4. preview _____to view in advance_____

5. inactive _____not active, at rest_____

6. nonverbal _____without speech_____

7. defrost _____to remove frost_____

8. unfold _____to remove the folds, to open up_____

9. prewar _____before the war_____

10. disbud _____to remove a plant's buds_____

11. nonsense _____without reason or sense_____

12. preheat _____to heat in advance_____

13. deactivate _____to stop action_____

14. undo _____to reverse what has been done_____

15. discourage _____to take away one's courage_____

16. insensitive _____not sensitive, unfeeling_____

17. disadvantage _____opposite of advantage_____

18. nonskid _____without sliding or skidding_____

19. involuntary _____not voluntary_____

20. prejudge _____to judge in advance_____

Vocabulary and Spelling

▶ **Exercise 2** Write in the blank a word with a prefix that means the same as the words in parentheses.

Achim was chosen to _____preview_____ the new movie. (view in advance)

1. His actions were very _____unkind_____. (not kind)

2. Mara's homework was _____incomplete_____. (not complete)

3. When playing this card game, after each turn you must _____discard_____. (remove a card from your hand)

4. Harold completed the job in one _____nonstop_____ session. (without stopping)

5. Does your mother always _____preapprove_____ the books that you read? (approve in advance)

6. Juan helped Teresa _____defrost_____ the refrigerator. (remove the frost)

7. Detectives often travel in _____unmarked_____ cars. (no markings)

8. The man used _____indirect_____ quotations in his speech. (not direct)

9. We agree to _____disagree_____. (not agree)

10. The sauce was made with _____nonfat_____ milk. (fat removed)

11. Mr. Alvarez was very thin during his _____preteen_____ years. (before teenage)

12. Passengers may _____deplane_____ at gate forty-two. (remove themselves from the airplane)

13. The items at the bake sale were _____unpriced_____. (not priced)

14. The puppy was a victim of _____inhumane_____ treatment. (not humane)

15. The chilly wind added to his _____discomfort_____. (lack of comfort).

▶ **Writing Link** Write a paragraph about a relaxing Saturday afternoon. Use at least three words with prefixes and underline them.

_____

_____

_____

_____

_____

_____

Vocabulary and Spelling

Lesson 88
Building Vocabulary: Suffixes

A **suffix** is a word part that is added to the end of a word and changes its part of speech and its meaning. Adding the suffix -er to *read* (a verb) makes *reader* (a noun). Adding -less to *face* (a noun) makes *faceless* (an adjective).

SUFFIX	MEANING	EXAMPLE	MEANING
-er	one who	bak**er**	one who bakes
	that which	dic**er**	a device that chops or dices vegetables
	more	strong**er**	more strong
-or	one who	debt**or**	one who owes a debt
-ist	one who	clarinet**ist**	one who plays a clarinet
-less	without	change**less**	without change
-able	can be	wash**able**	can be washed
	having the quality of	valu**able**	having value
-ible	can be	deduct**ible**	can be deducted
	having the quality of	sens**ible**	having sense
-ness	quality of	gentle**ness**	quality of being gentle
	state of being	great**ness**	state of being great

▶ **Exercise 1** Write the word that is formed by adding the given suffix to each word. Then write a basic meaning of the new word. Be careful to check the spelling of the new word.

win + -er	winner	one who wins
1. fault + -less	faultless	without fault
2. advise + -or	adviser	one who advises
3. make + -er	maker	one who makes
4. like + -able	likable	can be liked
5. piano + -ist	pianist	one who plays the piano
6. ready + -ness	readiness	the state of being ready
7. kind + -ness	kindness	the quality of being kind

Vocabulary and Spelling

8. freeze + -*er*	freezer	that which freezes something
9. depend + -*able*	dependable	can be depended on
10. terror + -*ible*	terrible	having the quality of terror
11. weak + -*er*	weaker	more weak
12. mow + -*er*	mower	that which mows
13. match + -*less*	matchless	without match or equal
14. admire + -*able*	admirable	can be admired
15. good + -*ness*	goodness	quality of being good
16. resist + -*ible*	resistible	can be resisted
17. defense + -*ible*	defensible	can be defended
18. aware + -*ness*	awareness	state of being aware
19. grant + -*or*	grantor	one who grants or gives
20. type + -*ist*	typist	one who types
21. wrestle + -*er*	wrestler	one who wrestles
22. laugh + -*able*	laughable	can be laughed at
23. sure + -*er*	surer	more sure
24. calm + -*ness*	calmness	state of being calm
25. force + -*ible*	forcible	having the quality of force
26. burn + -*er*	burner	that which burns something
27. thin + -*er*	thinner	more thin
28. cycle + -*ist*	cyclist	one who rides cycles
29. ill + -*ness*	illness	state of being ill
30. honor + -*able*	honorable	having the quality of honor
31. write + -*er*	writer	one who writes
32. fast + -*er*	faster	more fast, speedier
33. damp + -*ness*	dampness	state of being damp
34. sleep + -*less*	sleepless	without sleep
35. teach + -*er*	teacher	one who teaches

Vocabulary and Spelling

Lesson 89
Synonyms and Antonyms

Synonyms are words that have similar meanings. Knowing synonyms can help you understand new words. Some dictionaries list synonyms with the definition of a word. A thesaurus is a special dictionary that lists all synonyms. Because each synonym has a slightly different meaning, choosing the right one can help you say exactly what you mean.

The cat **sprang** at the ball of yarn. (Substituting a synonym such as *jumped* or *leaped* could help in understanding the unfamiliar word *sprang*.)
The man **walked** to the store. (*Ambled* and *trudged* are synonyms for walked. Using one of these synonyms would give a slightly different meaning to the sentence.)

Antonyms are words that have opposite or nearly opposite meanings. Knowing antonyms can also help you understand unfamiliar words. Common ones are *hot-cold*, *large-small*, and *love-hate*. Many antonyms can be formed by adding a prefix meaning *not*. Adding *un-* to *bending* makes *unbending*, the antonym to *bending*.

▶ **Exercise 1 Circle the best synonym for each italicized word. Use a dictionary if necessary.**

Maria enjoyed the *placid* atmosphere of the library.
plastic   (quiet)   studious   stressed

1. The band has an *immense* following.
   (large)   intense   crude   silly

2. Francisco *pleaded* with his mother for a new skateboard.
   pulled   argued   asked   (begged)

3. If you want to *acquire* fame, do something better than anyone else.
   buy   (get)   know   allow

4. Most birds go to roost at *dusk*.
   bedtime   night   (twilight)   afternoon

5. Alan took good care of his *molars*.
   clippers   binoculars   moles   (teeth)

6. Rabbits shed their *coats* four times a year.
   jackets   skin   (fur)   nails

Vocabulary and Spelling

7. Micah went shopping for sports *apparel*.
   (clothing)   equipment   cards   item

8. At the end of the race, Ke Min was *exhausted*.
   happy   upset   (tired)   last

9. Kim was proud of her *raven* hair.
   brown   blonde   (black)   red

10. Yoshin loved the *scent* of roses.
    price   beauty   (smell)   color

11. Renee has great *affection* for Pedro.
    falsehood   dislike   candy   (love)

12. I witnessed his *solemn* vow.
    sad   (serious)   fame   silent

13. The *mariner* prized his blue parrot.
    (seaman)   cook   preacher   master

14. How will you *conclude* that story for English class?
    (end)   produce   copy   write

15. Grandpa spent his entire life in *agronomy*.
    pain   teasing   (farming)   astronomy

▶ **Exercise 2** **Write an antonym for each word by adding the proper prefix. Use a dictionary to check meaning and spelling.**

happy _____unhappy_____

1. appear ____disappear____
2. direct ____indirect____
3. complete ____incomplete____
4. true ____untrue____
5. sense ____nonsense____
6. equal ____unequal____
7. own ____disown____
8. root ____uproot____
9. hook ____unhook____
10. join ____disjoin____

11. compress ____decompress____
12. infect ____disinfect____
13. support ____nonsupport____
14. dress ____undress____
15. pack ____unpack____
16. mount ____dismount____
17. activate ____deactivate____
18. essential ____nonessential____
19. place ____displace____
20. welcome ____unwelcome____

Lesson 90
Homonyms

Homonyms are words that sound alike but have different meanings. Homonyms may have the same spelling or different spellings. Those that have different spellings can be tricky when writing. Be careful to choose the correct word for the meaning you want to use.

HOMONYM	MEANING
here	this place
hear	listen
through	in one side, out the opposite
threw	tossed
its	belonging to it
it's	contraction for *it is* or *it has*
to	in the direction of
too	also, in addition to
two	the number
principal	one in charge of a school
principle	a rule, guideline, or law
their	belonging to them
there	in that place
they're	contraction for *they are*
your	belonging to you
you're	contraction for *you are*

▶ **Exercise 1** Underline the homonym in parentheses that best completes each sentence.

Katya wrote a letter (<u>while</u>, wile) Lu Chan talked on the phone.

1. The (<u>knight</u>, night) wore shining armor.

2. Mrs. Chin (new, <u>knew</u>) that yesterday was my birthday.

3. I had eight (<u>right</u>, write, rite) answers out of ten.

4. Jason (through, <u>threw</u>) his jacket on the couch.

5. A blue jay perched on the lowest (<u>bough</u>, bow) of the tree.

6. Who will be the first to (<u>break</u>, brake) the piñata?

7. The tomato vines were tied to wooden (steaks, <u>stakes</u>).

8. Would you like a (peace, <u>piece</u>) of pie?

Vocabulary and Spelling

9. The man wore (wholly, holey, holy) gloves.

10. When (your, you're) all alone, the sound of the wind is frightening.

11. Aggie couldn't wait to (hear, here) the results of the election.

12. Billy and An-Li lost (there, their) homework.

13. (Its, It's) a wonderful story.

14. My brother likes going (too, to, two) the fair.

15. The contest was guided by the (principles, principals) of fair play.

16. (Who's, Whose) notebook is on the floor?

17. How many times does the (tied, tide) rise each day?

18. Carlos sanded his bicycle frame to the (bear, bare) metal.

19. Did Consuelo (tare, tear) her sleeve?

20. The wild (boar, bore) is a dangerous animal.

21. The storm delayed her departure for an (our, hour).

22. The cabin was located on a (hi, high) mountain.

23. The (cent, scent) reminded me of the woods.

24. Is that the (sight, site, cite) of the new mall?

25. Will Myra's apology (lesson, lessen) Merle's pain?

26. This discussion makes no (scents, cents, sense).

27. My quarter rolled off the curb and through the sewer (great, grate).

28. Does the fireplace need more (would, wood)?

29. Beethoven was (borne, born) on December 16, 1770.

30. I put a (pear, pair) in my backpack for a snack.

▶ **Writing Link** **Write two or more sentences with homonym pairs.**

_____

_____

_____

_____

Vocabulary and Spelling

Lesson 91
Basic Spelling Rules I

SUFFIXES AND THE SILENT *E*

When adding a suffix that begins with a consonant to a word that ends with a silent *e*, keep the *e*. When adding a suffix that begins with *a* or *o* to a word that ends with *ce* or *ge*, keep the *e*. When adding a suffix that begins with a vowel to a word that ends in *ee* or *oe*, keep the *e*.

love + -*ly* = lovely   knowledge + -*able* = knowledgeable
canoe + -*ing* = canoeing

When adding -*ly* to a word that ends with an *l* plus a silent *e*, drop the *e*.

When adding a suffix that begins with a vowel or *y* to a word that ends with a silent *e*, usually drop the *e*.

terrible + -*ly* = terribly   shine + -*ing* = shining   nose + -*y* = nosy

SUFFIXES AND THE FINAL *Y*

When a word ends in a consonant + *y*, change the *y* to *i*. When the suffix begins with an *i*, do not change the *y* to *i*. When a word ends in a vowel + *y*, keep the *y*.

fry + -*ed* = fried   cry + -*ing* = crying   relay + -*ed* = relayed

SPELLING *IE* AND *EI*

Put *i* before *e* except after *c* and when sounded like *a*, as in *neighbor* and *weigh*. Some exceptions to this rule are *height, seize, leisure, either, efficient*.

belief   deceive   eight

▶ **Exercise 1** **Write the word that is formed when the suffix given is added to each word.**

try + -*ed* _____tried_____

1. try + -*ing* _____trying_____   8. awe + -*some* _____awesome_____

2. admire + -*able* _____admirable_____   9. probable + -*ly* _____probably_____

3. home + -*ly* _____homely_____   10. manage + -*able* _____manageable_____

4. cry + -*ed* _____cried_____   11. muddy + -*ing* _____muddying_____

5. state + -*ment* _____statement_____   12. fry + -*ing* _____frying_____

6. foresee + -*able* _____foreseeable_____   13. like + -*ness* _____likeness_____

7. annoy + -*ing* _____annoying_____   14. gentle + -*ly* _____gently_____

15. change + -*able* _____changeable_____   **18.** mercy + -*ful* _____merciful_____

16. play + -*ful* _____playful_____   **19.** craze + -*y* _____crazy_____

17. shoe + -*ing* _____shoeing_____   **20.** merry + -*ment* _____merriment_____

▶ **Exercise 2** **Write the word in the blank that is formed by adding *ei* or *ie* to the incomplete word in each sentence.**

_____lei_____   The Hawaiians gave me a necklace of flowers called a l__ .

_____belief_____   **1.** Ms. Kang will not stray from her bel__f.

_____receipt_____   **2.** Wally did not bring his rec__pt with him.

_____vein_____   **3.** The v__n of ore ran for nearly three miles.

_____conceive_____   **4.** How could anyone conc__ve of such a thing?

_____achieve_____   **5.** Dowana worked hard to ach__ve honor-roll status.

_____freight_____   **6.** In the distance, we heard the whistle of a fr__ght train.

_____chief_____   **7.** Mr. Suzuki was appointed ch__f of staff.

_____priest_____   **8.** Father O'Brien had been a parish pr__st for forty years.

_____eight_____   **9.** Mario had __ght years of piano lessons.

_____retrieve_____   **10.** Duke learned to retr__ve a stick in only three days.

_____receive_____   **11.** Is Pam well enough to rec__ve visitors?

_____height_____   **12.** Our sunflowers grew to a h__ght of eleven feet.

_____eight_____   **13.** I read __ght books this month.

_____conceited_____   **14.** Sue's brother is conc__ted.

_____grieve_____   **15.** How long did Alice gr__ve after Alejandra moved to Texas?

_____ceiling_____   **16.** What color shall we paint the c__ling?

_____veil_____   **17.** What kind of lace did Jana choose for her v__l?

_____deceit_____   **18.** Be careful that his promises contain no dec__t.

_____sleigh_____   **19.** We went for a sl__gh ride.

_____weight_____   **20.** Athletes must maintain a certain w__ght.

Lesson 92
Basic Spelling Rules II

When a word ends in a single consonant following one vowel, double the final consonant if the word is one syllable. Also double the final consonant if the last syllable of the word is accented and the accent stays there after the suffix is added.

sit + -*ing* = sitting   slap + -*ed* = slapped   sad + -*er* = sadder
refer + -*ed* = referred   occur + -*ence* = occurrence   deter + -*ing* = deterring

Do not double the final consonant if the suffix begins with a consonant, if the accent is not on the last syllable, or if the accent moves when the suffix is added.

hurt + *ful* = hurtful   pain + -*less* = painless   great + -*ly* = greatly
envelop + -*ed* = enveloped   govern + -*ing* = governing   motor + -*ize* = motorize
refer + -*ence* = reference   confer + -*ence* = conference

Do not double the final consonant if two vowels come before the final consonant or if the word ends in two consonants.

drain + -*ed* = drained   moan + -*ing* = moaning   keep + -*ing* = keeping
start + -*er* = starter   belong + -*ing* = belonging   apart + -*ment* = apartment

When adding -*ly* to a word that ends in *ll*, drop one *l*.

dull + -*ly* = dully   full + -*ly* = fully

When forming compound words, keep the original spelling of both words.

soap + box = soapbox   fly + wheel = flywheel   back + pack = backpack

▶ **Exercise 1** **Write the word that is formed when the suffix given is added to each word.**

fan + -*ing*   fanning

1. pat + -*ed*   patted
2. expel + -*ing*   expelling
3. full + -*ly*   fully
4. rain + -*ing*   raining
5. admit + -*ance*   admittance
6. shut + -*er*   shutter
7. civil + -*ize*   civilize

8. confer + -*ence*   conference
9. glad + -*est*   gladdest
10. main + -*ly*   mainly
11. equip + -*ed*   equipped
12. sharp + -*ly*   sharply
13. layer + -*ing*   layering
14. pad + -*ing*   padding

15. rebel + -ed _____rebelled_____   **18.** tip + -ing _____tipping_____

16. loan + -ed _____loaned_____   **19.** smart + -est _____smartest_____

17. plant + -ed _____planted_____   **20.** begin + -er _____beginner_____

▶ **Exercise 2 Write the compound word formed from the words in parentheses. If the sentence is correct, write *C* in the blank.**

___screwdriver___   Please hand me the smallest (screw driver).

___C___   **1.** What did you use for a (steering wheel) on your go-cart?

___bedroom___   **2.** Micah does his studying in his (bed room).

___C___   **3.** Marisha is proud of her (table manners).

___beehive___   **4.** Yesterday, our class was a (bee hive) of activity.

___C___   **5.** With a huge leap, Katarina caught the (line drive).

___bookkeeper___   **6.** Does your mother hire a (book keeper)?

___earthquake___   **7.** No one in our class has ever experienced an (earth quake).

___C___   **8.** Mr. Sanchez wore gray (dress pants) with his blue blazer.

___anybody___   **9.** Achim finished the test before (any body) else.

___C___   **10.** Did you remember to bring your (fishing pole)?

___snowstorm___   **11.** How many hours did the (snow storm) last?

___C___   **12.** Do you think Mimi would like a (jewelry box) for her birthday?

___somewhere___   **13.** I know that book is (some where) in this room.

___C___   **14.** Ms. Yedon has the most beautiful (flower garden) in the neighborhood.

___strawberry___   **15.** My favorite part of the meal was the (straw berry) and banana dessert.

___C___   **16.** Please bring some (light bulbs) when you come home.

___C___   **17.** Elijah has a new (sport coat) to wear to the program.

___warehouse___   **18.** Dad purchased our new television directly from the (ware house).

___C___   **19.** Our (bird feeder) needs to be refilled.

___windshield___   **20.** I was scared when the stone flew against the (wind shield).

Vocabulary and Spelling

Lesson 93
Basic Spelling Rules III

Many English words form plurals by specific rules.

If the noun ends in *s, ch, sh, x,* or *z* (including proper names), add *-es.*

grass, grasses   catch, catches   fox, foxes   Lopez, Lopezes

If the noun ends in a consonant + *y,* change the *y* to *i* and add *-es.*

carry, carries   mercy, mercies   puppy, puppies

If the noun ends in *o* or a vowel + *y,* add *-s.*

rodeo, rodeos   piano, pianos   key, keys   boy, boys
Exceptions: potato, potatoes   echo, echoes

If the noun ends in *f* or *ff,* add *-s.*

beef, beefs   clef, clefs   cuff, cuffs
Exceptions: sheaf, sheaves   loaf, loaves (change *f* to *v* and add *-es*)

If the noun ends in *lf* or *fe,* change the *f* to *v* and add *-es.*

calf, calves   shelf, shelves   life, lives

One-word compound nouns follow the general rules for plurals. For compound nouns of more than one word or hyphenated words, make the most important word plural.

grandmother, grandmothers   lady-in-waiting, ladies-in-waiting
ice cream, ice creams   chief of staff, chiefs of staff

Some nouns have irregular plurals and follow no rules.

man, men   foot, feet   child, children

Some nouns do not change spelling for the plural.

deer, deer   sheep, sheep   series, series

Vocabulary and Spelling

▶ **Exercise 1,** **Write the correct plural form of each word.**

watch ___watches___

1. dress ___dresses___   3. factory ___factories___

2. Aldrich ___Aldriches___   4. goof ___goofs___

5. joy	joys	23. stress	stresses
6. broomstick	broomsticks	24. toy	toys
7. loaf	loaves	25. Jones	Joneses
8. glass	glasses	26. buzz	buzzes
9. box	boxes	27. latch	latches
10. wish	wishes	28. moose	moose
11. editor in chief	editors in chief	29. mother-in-law	mothers-in-law
12. Truax	Truaxes	30. dish	dishes
13. folly	follies	31. kangaroo	kangaroos
14. crutch	crutches	32. berry	berries
15. woman	women	33. Martinez	Martinezes
16. beach	beaches	34. wedding ring	wedding rings
17. McCandlish	McCandlishes	35. cuff	cuffs
18. proof	proofs	36. mouse	mice
19. knife	knives	37. wife	wives
20. fifty	fifties	38. handkerchief	handkerchiefs
21. secretary-general	secretaries-general	39. stereo	stereos
22. echo	echoes	40. half	halves

▶ **Writing Link** **Write a paragraph about a group of people. Use at least four plural words.**

_____

_____

_____

_____

_____

_____

_____

_____

Vocabulary and Spelling

Lesson 94
Often Misspelled Words

Some words do not follow basic spelling rules. This can make them hard to spell. One way to learn how to spell difficult words is to make a personal word list. List the words that you find especially difficult or that you often misspell.

Study the correct spellings. Use these words in your writing to remember how to spell them.

▶ **Exercise 1** **Underline the word in parentheses that is spelled correctly.**

Brad could become a famous (athelete, <u>athlete</u>) someday.

1. Julia will (<u>recommend</u>, reccommend) a song for the celebration.

2. The Mayfield Middle School soccer team (garantees, <u>guarantees</u>) a victory in tomorrow's game.

3. Our school (chior, <u>choir</u>) practices three times a week.

4. Tanya found it difficult to choose a video because the store had such a wide (<u>variety</u>, vareity).

5. Steve and Jose ate lunch in the (cafiteria, <u>cafeteria</u>).

6. We are waiting for the committee to announce (<u>definite</u>, defanite) plans.

7. Mrs. Kwan introduced her (<u>niece</u>, neice) to the class.

8. Have you filled out your (skedule, <u>schedule</u>) for next semester yet?

9. Margaret painted a picture of a (beatiful, <u>beautiful</u>) sunset while on vacation in South Carolina.

10. The well-known scientist gave us a tour of her (labertory, <u>laboratory</u>).

11. Mom was (truely, <u>truly</u>) pleased with the birthday present.

12. Randy had several books to return to the (libary, <u>library</u>).

13. I hope Billy doesn't do anything to (embarass, <u>embarrass</u>) me.

14. Katrina is going to read her (<u>original</u>, orignal) story to us.

15. The festival will begin at twelve o'clock (<u>Wednesday</u>, Wenesday).

16. Todd's (abcense, <u>absence</u>) made it impossible for us to rehearse the play.

17. According to the weather forecaster, it will (probably, probablely) rain tomorrow.

18. The entire family is going to Little Rock to see Uncle Luigi, who will be (fourty, forty) years old this Saturday.

19. Jake saw a (humerous, humorous) program on television.

20. Rachel and Joan have (similar, simaler) taste in clothing.

▶ **Exercise 2 Complete each word by filling in the missing letters.**

accident _a_ _l_ ly (happening by accident)

1. traff _i_ _c_ (movement of cars along a road)

2. de _s_ _c_ end (to go from a higher place to a lower one)

3. rest _a_ _u_ rant (a place where people eat)

4. us _u_ _a_ lly (most of the time)

5. for _e_ _i_ gn (outside one's own country)

6. ne _c_ e _s_ sary (needed; required)

7. perm _a_ n _e_ nt (lasting; without change)

8. gramm _a_ r (the study of words and sentences)

9. advi _s_ _e_ r (a person who gives information or recommendations)

10. n _e_ _i_ ghborhood (the area in which one lives)

11. jew _e_ _l_ ry (rings, bracelets, necklaces)

12. li _c_ en _s_ e (a permit to do something)

13. bus _i_ n _e_ ss (a company or type of work)

14. immed _i_ _a_ te (right away; now)

15. h _e_ _i_ ght (the distance from the bottom to the top of something)

16. te _c_ _h_ nology (new knowledge or a new way of doing something)

17. rec _o_ _g_ nize (to know or be familiar with)

18. sep _a_ r _a_ te (distinct; apart)

19. ball _e_ _t_ (a classical dance)

20. gove _r_ _n_ ment (an organization formed to run a country)

Lesson 95
Easily Confused Words

Some words are often confused because they sound similar, even though they have different spellings and meanings.

desert, dessert When the accent is on the first syllable, *desert* means "a dry, barren region." When the accent is on the second syllable, *desert* means "to abandon."
Dessert is a sweet course served at the end of a meal.

lessen, lesson *Lessen* means "to shrink in size or degree." *Lesson* means "something to learn."

passed, past *Passed* means "to have moved on or ahead." *Past* means "time gone by" or "existed earlier."

quiet, quite *Quiet* means "little or no sound." *Quite* means "wholly, completely."

weather, whether *Weather* means "the daily conditions of temperature, moisture, wind, and so on." *Whether* is a conjunction often used in indirect quotations.

▶ **Exercise 1** **Underline the word that best completes each sentence.**

The doctor advised Mr. Wilson to (<u>lessen</u>, lesson) his intake of fat.

1. Jim's cousins offered to show him (<u>their</u>, there) secret clubhouse.

2. Tina finished reading that story in one (<u>hour</u>, our).

3. Mom likes to drink English breakfast (<u>tea</u>, tee).

4. Louis cannot decide (weather, <u>whether</u>) to practice baseball or soccer.

5. Kim's kite sailed (<u>higher</u>, hire) into the air than Bill's kite.

6. Once the assembly began, everyone grew (<u>quiet</u>, quite).

7. Uncle Simon took pictures of his trip through the (<u>desert</u>, dessert).

8. Ling said the movie was so dull that he couldn't (bare, <u>bear</u>) to watch it.

9. This book is about a poor girl who becomes (air, <u>heir</u>) to a fortune.

10. Calid (<u>passed</u>, past) Mr. Sokol on his way home from school.

Vocabulary and Spelling

11. Dad refused to let Tommy (peak, <u>peek</u>) at his birthday gifts before the party.

12. Mrs. Jenkins and her husband cooked (stake, <u>steak</u>) for the winners of the spelling bee.

13. Sara will (right, <u>write</u>) a letter to her friend after dinner.

14. Jean was (holy, <u>wholly</u>) surprised when she won the contest.

15. Dividing fractions was today's math (lessen, <u>lesson</u>).

16. Poloma ate the last (peace, <u>piece</u>) of blueberry pie.

17. Don't forget to bring (<u>your</u>, you're) camera.

18. My cat might (brake, <u>break</u>) that vase if I leave it on the windowsill.

19. Ramon (<u>blew</u>, blue) the trumpet, but no sound came out.

20. Jermaine saw several (dear, <u>deer</u>) in the park yesterday.

21. Grandmother (cent, <u>sent</u>) each of us a beautiful sweater.

22. Anne (wood, <u>would</u>) like to learn how to dance.

23. Larry bought a new computer game because it was on (sail, <u>sale</u>).

24. The bright sun cast (it's, <u>its</u>) rays across the meadow.

25. The Watsons are planning a vacation by the (<u>sea</u>, see).

26. What kind of ice cream do you want for (desert, <u>dessert</u>)?

27. The speaker began by stating her (<u>main</u>, mane) purpose.

28. Kendra borrowed (for, <u>four</u>) videotapes from Roger.

29. David went to the store to buy (<u>meat</u>, meet) and potatoes.

30. Belinda likes to (<u>read</u>, reed) historical novels.

31. Of all the people who live on our street, Ms. Romanoff receives the most (<u>mail</u>, male).

32. The gemstones we discovered in the treasure chest were (<u>real</u>, reel).

33. That comedian is very entertaining; he could never be a (boar, <u>bore</u>).

34. Kyle was extremely (soar, <u>sore</u>) after the hockey game.

35. Aunt Rita is in the kitchen making (moor, <u>more</u>) popcorn.

Lesson 96
Review: Building Vocabulary

▶ **Exercise 1** **Write the definition of the word in italics. If there are clue words, circle them.**

The cooler's *buoyancy,* (that is) its ability to float, saved the man from drowning.

ability to float

1. Jim works in a *haberdashery.* He sells men's shirts, socks, belts, and other accessories.

 a store that specializes in men's clothing and accessories

2. The pine tree is a *conifer—* (that is) it bears cones.

 a tree that produces cones

3. Roses are *perennials,* (which means) that they live for many years.

 plants that live for many years

4. The loser created a *spectacle.* He pouted, stamped his feet, and slammed his hat on

 the ground. something viewed as unusual

5. Juan is a *statistician,* (in other words) he keeps track of data.

 a person who collects and analyzes data

6. Reiko is *bilingual,* (which means) that she speaks two languages.

 able to speak two languages

7. Diane shows traits of an *extrovert.* She makes friends easily, she participates in many

 activities, and the presence of strangers doesn't bother her.

 a person who is outgoing and friendly

8. In case of an emergency, our home has two *auxiliary* heating systems, (including) a

 wood stove and a kerosene heater. extra, supplementary

9. Elaine practices excellent *hygiene—* (that is) she is always neat and clean.

 cleanliness for the prevention of disease

10. Mrs. Tadashi's greenhouse is full of *tropical* plants (such as) palms, orchids, and

 African violets. relating to a climate that supports year-round plant growth

11. The *dais* was well decorated, (including) the platform, the seats for the speakers, and the podium. <u>a raised platform used by speakers, honored guests, and the like</u>

12. Having published the life stories of three movie stars, Miss Suzuki became a well known *biographer.* <u>a person who writes an account of another person's life</u>

13. Mr. Green is a valuable *custodian.* Our building is always clean, and its equipment is maintained regularly. <u>one in charge of cleaning and maintaining a building</u>

14. Some people believe they can break the law with *impunity*; (that is), they believe they will never be punished. <u>freedom from punishment</u>

15. That couch is called a *divan* (because) it has no back. <u>a long backless couch</u>

16. Amodahy's father repairs major *appliances* (such as) refrigerators, washers, and dryers. <u>electrical machines designed for household use</u>

17. Covering nearly three acres, the *concourse* was filled with people awaiting the arrival of *Air Force One.* <u>a large gathering area</u>

18. A little arrow, (known as) a *cursor*, is moved by a mouse to select items on a personal computer. <u>an electronic symbol that identifies the place of activity</u>

19. Watching television is a *secondary* activity for Timothy. Completing his homework is more important. <u>second in importance</u>

20. Barely six inches wide, the *miniatures* on the wall depicted covered bridges of Pennsylvania. <u>very small paintings or objects</u>

▶ **Exercise 2** Write *synonyms*, *antonyms*, or *homonyms* to describe each pair of words.

quick, fast	synonyms		
1. terror, fright	synonyms	**7.** hour, our	homonyms
2. start, finish	antonyms	**8.** behold, look at	synonyms
3. weave, we've	homonyms	**9.** like, dislike	antonyms
4. ebony, black	synonyms	**10.** meat, mete	homonyms
5. hay, hey	homonyms	**11.** important, unimportant	antonyms
6. zip, unzip	antonyms	**12.** light, featherweight	synonyms

Vocabulary and Spelling

Lesson 97
Review: Basic Spelling Rules

▶ **Exercise 1** **Correct each misspelled word. Write *C* in the blank if the word is spelled correctly. Use a dictionary if necessary.**

	allys	allies
1.	terriblely	terribly
2.	deciet	deceit
3.	keyes	keys
4.	relyance	reliance
5.	fullly	fully
6.	kittens	C
7.	potatos	potatoes
8.	changable	changeable
9.	brother-in-laws	brothers-in-law
10.	partly	C
11.	joiful	joyful
12.	muffes	muffs
13.	referrence	reference
14.	lonly	lonely
15.	swimer	swimmer
16.	pianoes	pianos
17.	riegn	reign
18.	offerring	offering
19.	soft drinks	C
20.	concieve	conceive
21.	neighbor	C
22.	friing	frying

Vocabulary and Spelling

23. leafs   leaves

24. losses   C

25. releif   relief

26. neither   C

27. childs   children

28. trainnable   trainable

29. sheeps   sheep

30. liesure   leisure

31. preist   priest

32. moveing   moving

33. halfs   halves

34. serieses   series

35. containning   containing

36. flurrys   flurries

37. oxes   oxen

38. freing   freeing

39. vien   vein

40. watchs   watches

41. toeing   C

42. crispper   crisper

43. peanut   C

44. crazyer   crazier

45. eighteen   C

46. boxs   boxes

47. maping   mapping

48. wieghtier   weightier

49. chief of staffs   chiefs of staff

50. pigpen   C

Vocabulary and Spelling

Unit 13 Review

▶ **Exercise 1 Underline the word in parentheses that best completes each sentence.**

We studied (<u>prewar</u>, postwar) America—that is, America before the war.

1. No one can rely on Randy's (<u>changeable</u>, changeless) personality.

2. The auditorium had a sufficiently (<u>large</u>, small) stage for the big production.

3. Julian (<u>threw</u>, through) his cap in the air.

4. Laura and Harry could not (beleive, <u>believe</u>) they had won the doubles tournament.

5. The book you are looking for is (siting, <u>sitting</u>) on a shelf.

6. This movie shows the (lifes, <u>lives</u>) of several famous people.

7. Dr. Kotlinski's (neice, <u>niece</u>) will accompany us to the museum.

8. Sheila and her mother are making cheesecake for (desert, <u>dessert</u>).

9. When I learn Spanish, I will be bilingual; that is, I will speak (<u>two</u>, three) languages.

10. The happy people sang a (joiful, <u>joyful</u>) song as they worked.

11. The tickets have to be paid for in advance, which means we must (<u>prepay</u>, postpay).

12. Early in the morning, the beach is a placid, or (loud, <u>quiet</u>), place.

13. Jennifer adored the characters, so I think she (<u>liked</u>, disliked) the play.

14. If George didn't run to the park, maybe he (raced, <u>walked</u>).

15. (There, <u>They're</u>) planning to go to the zoo on Saturday.

16. Everyone agreed it was a (<u>lovely</u>, lovly) day for a picnic.

17. Uncle Keith is attending a (<u>conference</u>, conferrence) in New Orleans.

18. The Carleys have three (radioes, <u>radios</u>) in their house.

19. Miki is a scholar and an (athelete, <u>athlete</u>).

20. The (<u>weather</u>, whether) will change greatly next week.

21. Dad asked the tailor to change the (<u>cuffs</u>, cuffes) on his shirt.

22. Two former (<u>secretaries of state</u>, secretary of states) attended the meeting.

Vocabulary and Spelling

Cumulative Review: Units 1–13

► **Exercise 1** Write the part of speech above each italicized word: *N* (noun), *V* (verb), *pro.* (pronoun), *adj.* (adjective), *adv.* (adverb), *prep.* (preposition), *conj.* (conjunction), or *int.* (interjection).

               V   N

Georgia *visits* the lakeshore in the *summer.*

             N   prep.

1. Uncle *Andrew* is famous *for* his roses.

      conj.   prep.

2. Sam *and* Patrick are working *on* a science fair project.

      adj.   adv.

3. A *red* cardinal flew *gracefully* over the trees.

     int.   adj.

4. *Wow!* Look at that *beautiful* rainbow.

             pro.   N

5. Celeste gave *them* a tour of the radio *station.*

           V   adj.

6. The story *began* with a trip to an *unusual* castle.

                          conj.   adj.

7. Rachel often meets Marta in the park, *and* they fly *their* kites there.

                 adv.   prep.

8. The baseball player *quickly* ran *around* the bases.

     pro.   N

9. *She* hopes to play the *piano* in the spring talent show.

     int.   adj.

10. *Whew!* It's *very* hot today.

          V   conj.

11. Carter *will* demonstrate his new invention, *but* we cannot touch it.

      adj.   V

12. A *silvery* brook *ran* down the mountainside.

           conj.   pro.

13. Either Tyler *or* Rick will meet *us* at the ice cream shop.

           N   adj.

14. The drama *club* is presenting a *funny* play next week.

       V   adj.

15. Sun *drenched* the *sandy* beach.

   pro.   prep.

16. *He* borrowed three books *from* the library.

        V   adv.

17. We are *going* to the pet store *tomorrow.*

      N   N

18. *Grandfather* told us about his *adventures* at the carnival.

          pro.   adj.

19. Last night *I* had a *strange* dream.

    N   prep.

20. *Dad* is making lasagna *for* dinner.

▶ **Exercise 2** **Underline the word in parentheses that best completes each sentence.**

I hope our team does not (loose, <u>lose</u>) the game.

1. The cat lost control of (<u>its</u>, it's) ball of yarn.

2. Sven (all ready, <u>already</u>) programed the videocassette recorder.

3. The members of the group brought (<u>too</u>, two) many desserts to the meeting.

4. Janna will (<u>choose</u>, chose) which song to play first.

5. Geoff hopes to (<u>learn</u>, teach) German from his great-aunt.

6. No one (accept, <u>except</u>) Michael would try the new amusement park ride.

7. It is Carol's turn to (<u>raise</u>, rise) the school flag.

8. (Beside, <u>Besides</u>) field hockey, Keshia also likes to play tennis.

9. Does anyone know (who's, <u>whose</u>) jacket this is?

10. Peter can't decide (among, <u>between</u>) the cherry pie and the peach pie.

11. Dr. Skybo is (all together, <u>altogether</u>) certain nothing is wrong.

12. (<u>Lay</u>, Lie) the newspaper on the kitchen table.

13. The guests moved from the living room (in, <u>into</u>) the dining room.

14. Where should we (set, <u>sit</u>) for the picnic?

15. After buying the magazine, Tamara had (a lot of, <u>sixteen</u>) dollars left.

16. The bus will (<u>leave</u>, let) at one o'clock.

17. (Its, <u>It's</u>) amazing how much we accomplished in such a short time.

18. Mr. Lombardo doesn't know what time (<u>their</u>, they're) plane arrives.

19. Are you going (<u>to</u>, too) the theater tonight?

20. First mix the batter; (than, <u>then</u>) pour it into the cake pans.

▶ **Exercise 3** **Add any missing punctuation to each sentence.**

Clara, of course, was the director's first choice for the role of Anna.

1. Mom asked us to buy bread, milk, and tomatoes.

2. Watch out for that falling tree limb!

3. In the last scene of the movie, the hero saves the planet.

4. Green is Louie's favorite color; purple is Taylor's favorite color.

5. The following issues will be discussed: goals, costs, and publicity.

6. Carlo, did you see the eclipse?

7. "My dream," Katia said, "is to have my own store."

8. Take these pictures to Mrs. Jackson's office.

9. Forty-seven persons volunteered to help with the project.

10. March 18, 1995, is a day I will never forget.

▶ **Exercise 4** **Complete each word by filling in the missing letters.**

bel _i_ _e_ ve (to have faith)

1. tr _i_ _e_ d (attempted)

2. lov _e_ _l_ y (beautiful)

3. hop _i_ ng (longing)

4. knowledg _e_ _a_ ble (full of knowledge)

5. cano _e_ _i_ ng (rowing)

6. fr _i_ _e_ s (plural of *fry*)

7. sa _y_ _i_ ng (to say)

8. repl _i_ _e_ d (answered)

9. n _i_ _e_ ce (the daughter of one's brother or sister)

10. rec _e_ _i_ ve (to be given something)

11. _e_ _i_ ght (4 + 4)

12. tri _p_ _p_ ed (stumbled)

13. deligh _t_ ful (full of delight)

14. trai _n_ ing (teaching)

15. catcher _s_ (plural of *catcher*)

16. cherr _i_ _e_ _s_ (plural of *cherry*)

17. radio _s_ (plural of *radio*)

18. shel _v_ _e_ _s_ (plural of *shelf*)

19. Thomas _e_ _s_ (plural of *Thomas*)

20. secretar _i_ _e_ _s_ (plural of *secretary*)

21. Mary _s_ (plural of *Mary*)

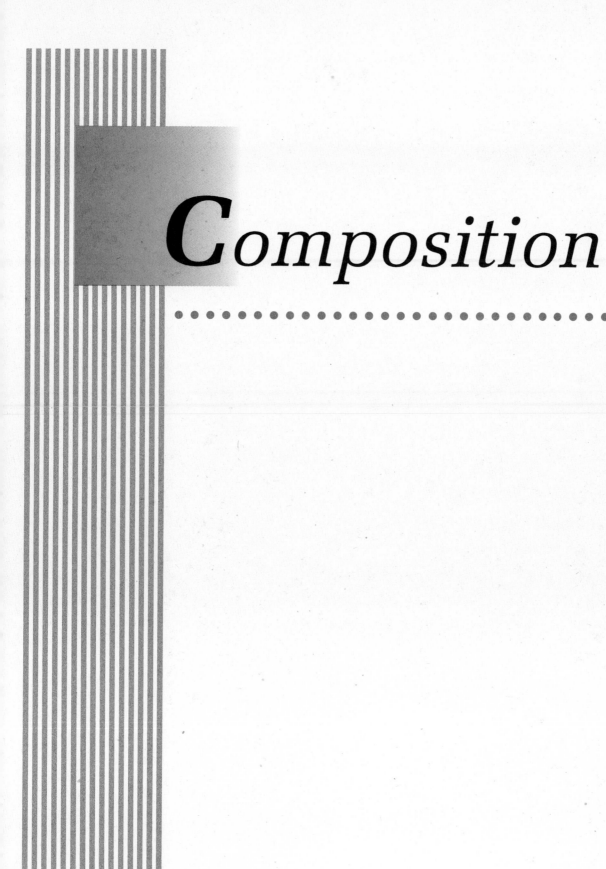

Composition

Unit 14: Composition

Lesson 98
The Writing Process: Prewriting I

During the prewriting stage, you plan what you will write. You choose a topic, or subject about which you will write. You can get ideas for topics in any of the following ways:

- *Freewrite* Write for several minutes, nonstop, about whatever comes into your mind.
- *Collect information* Gather facts and information from various sources.
- *Make a list* of events, experiences, people, or ideas that interest you.
- *Ask questions* Think of a question that you would like to answer.

The topic you select may cover too much information for you to use in one piece of writing. When that is the case, you continue to ask questions or group the information into related items. When the information is cut down to a more suitable size, your topic will be narrow enough to write about.

▶ **Exercise 1 Spend five minutes prewriting. Continue writing the entire time. Then look over your freewriting and circle any ideas that you might use as writing topics.**

_____

_____

_____

_____

_____

_____

_____

_____

_____

_____

_____

Composition

Name _____ Class _____ Date _____

▶ **Exercise 2** **For each general topic, list two narrower topics related to it that interest you.**

Volunteering _Why do people like to volunteer?_____

_Volunteering at the cat shelter._____

1. Dancing _____

_____

2. Junk food _____

_____

3. Your community _____

_____

4. Pets _____

_____

5. Math _____

_____

6. Privacy _____

_____

7. Self-confidence _____

_____

8. Field trips _____

_____

9. Movies _____

_____

10. Computers _____

_____

11. Jokes _____

_____

12. Winter _____

_____

Lesson 99
The Writing Process: Prewriting II

During prewriting, you also choose a **purpose**—the goal you want to accomplish by writing about your topic. Your purpose might be to inform, to persuade, to entertain, to create a work of art, or perhaps a combination of these. Finally, you select and analyze your **audience**, those who will read or hear your work. Knowing your audience will help you decide what information to include and what writing style to use, such as formal or informal.

▶ **Exercise 1** **Rewrite each word, phrase, or sentence for the audience named in parentheses.**

The new rule at school really bugs me. (Rewrite for an audience of parents.)
The new rule at school is very unfair.

1. Manuel hit a homer in the bottom of the ninth inning to win the game. (Rewrite for an audience who knows nothing about baseball.) Manuel scored the winning point by hitting the ball over the fence late in the game.

2. Listen up, dudes. (Rewrite as a statement to a noisy roomful of students during a class.) Listen, everyone.

3. During the 1995 annual period, the corn crop had an extremely high yield. (Rewrite as an explanation for a fellow student.) During 1995 the corn crop was plentiful.

4. No suds. No clean duds. (Rewrite as a note for someone about to go to the laundry.) Don't forget the detergent when you wash the clothes.

5. This bread is made with 3 cups of flour, a stick of melted butter, 2 beaten eggs, 1 teaspoon of vanilla, and 2 teaspoons of cinnamon. (Rewrite as a description for someone who does not intend to make the bread.) This bread is made with flour, melted butter, eggs, vanilla, and cinnamon.

6. Give the dog some drops of this medicine in his ears. (Reword as a veterinarian's instructions to the dog's owner. Invent any missing details.) Put three drops of the medicine in each ear once a day.

Composition

7. That cap is radical, man. (Rewrite as a statement to a teacher.) __Your cap is really nice.__

_____

8. Send me some stuff about Egyptian mummies. (Rewrite for a letter to the head of the

education department at a natural history museum.) __Could you please send any printed__

__information you have about Egyptian mummies?__

▶ **Exercise 2** Write the purpose of each of the following types of writing: *to inform, to persuade, to entertain,* or *to create a work of art.* Some items may have more than one purpose.

a retelling of a funny scene from a movie __to entertain, to inform__

1. an account of what happens during one scene of a play __to inform__

2. a short story about a frog-jumping contest __to entertain__

3. several paragraphs in which the speaker pretends to be a speck of dust __to create a work__
__of art__

4. a speech you will read to a community group about why your school needs more

classrooms __to persuade__

5. a riddle __to entertain__

6. a note giving instructions on where to find a hidden object __to inform__

7. a review of a movie __to inform, to persuade__

8. a letter to a college that is sent along with an application __to persuade__

9. a poem about a historical event __to create a work of art, to inform__

10. a composition comparing funny jokes and jokes that aren't funny __to inform, to persuade__

11. a report on how different animals hibernate __to inform__

12. an announcement in a magazine about a writing contest __to inform__

13. an editorial in the school paper about student safety at school __to persuade__

14. a newspaper article about last Friday's basketball game __to inform__

15. a paragraph written for a parent explaining why the writer should get a larger

allowance __to persuade__

16. a speech made by a candidate for mayor __to persuade__

Lesson 100
The Writing Process: Drafting I

After you have decided on your topic and purpose and gathered ideas and details for writing, you can begin drafting. **Drafting** is writing about your topic in paragraph form.

The first paragraph of your draft should include a **thesis statement**, which is a sentence that presents the **theme**, or main point you want to make. The other paragraphs each develop a main idea related to the theme.

▶ **Exercise 1** Underline the thesis statement that best expresses each theme.

Theme: the appeal of computer games

Computer games can be very expensive.

My favorite computer game is Donkey Kong.

Someday I hope to design a computer game.

<u>Computer games involve the hand, the eye, and the mind.</u>

1. Theme: the benefits of some bacteria

   Some bacteria are harmful.

   <u>Many kinds of bacteria are useful to humans.</u>

   Bacteria are very tiny, single-celled organisms.

   Some helpful bacteria live in the human digestive tract.

2. Theme: the satisfactions of volunteering at the cat shelter

   Sign up at the front desk if you want to volunteer at the cat shelter.

   The cat shelter is a place where you can go to adopt a cat or kitten.

   I like cats because they are like miniature lions.

   <u>I like volunteering at the cat shelter because I know I'm helping animals as well as our community.</u>

3. Theme: the health benefits of cross-country skiing

   Cross-country skiing offers fun for people of all ages.

   <u>Cross-country skiing develops the heart and lungs as well as the body.</u>

Composition

Cross-country skiing is an extremely popular sport in Norway.

Cross-country skiing is much safer than downhill skiing.

4. Theme: the importance of wearing a bicycle helmet

Bicycle helmets are not suitable for motorcyclists.

Most bicycle helmets have a sleek shape to lower wind resistance.

Bicyclists who have their heads on straight always wear helmets.

Bicyclists who are safe riders always use hand signals when making turns.

5. Theme: the humor in a movie you saw recently

Half of the characters in the movie *Bonzo Goes Bananas* are apes.

Bonzo Goes Bananas is funnier than *Bonzo Goes Ape*.

If you like slapstick humor, you'll love the movie *Bonzo Goes Bananas*.

The movie *Bonzo Goes Bananas* won't appeal to everyone.

▶ **Exercise 2** **Underline the three main ideas that support the thesis statement provided.**

Thesis statement: My first trip in an airplane went smoother than I expected.

Main ideas: Airports are busy places these days.

I was a little nervous at first.

I spent the middle part of the trip studying the landscape far below.

The descent and landing were exciting.

1. Thesis statement: Building a bluebird house is not difficult.

Main ideas: Assemble your materials.

Construct the house.

Paint or stain the house.

Feed the bluebirds.

2. Thesis statement: This model is a replica of a medieval castle.

Main ideas: The design is typical of twelfth-century English castles.

Women in medieval society were in charge of household tasks.

The rooms are authentically furnished and decorated.

The tiny figures represent the royal family, their knights, and servants.

Lesson 101
The Writing Process: Drafting II

Each paragraph has a topic sentence which states the main idea. Other sentences in the paragraph contain details that support the main idea.

▶ **Exercise 1** **Write three related sentences that provide details to support the topic sentence.**

1. Immigrants to the United States sometimes have difficulty adjusting to their new

   country. _____

   _____

   _____

   _____

   _____

   _____

2. The Underground Railroad was a secret network that allowed slaves to travel north to

   freedom. _____

   _____

   _____

   _____

   _____

   _____

3. Sometimes a younger brother or sister can be a bother. _____

   _____

   _____

   _____

   _____

   _____

Composition

4. Native Americans are sometimes called the first Americans. _____

_____

_____

_____

_____

_____

5. A sixth grader needs to have some private time. _____

_____

_____

_____

_____

_____

6. Black Studies Week is a time to celebrate the accomplishments of African Americans.

_____

_____

_____

_____

7. Students and teachers should treat one another with respect. _____

_____

_____

_____

_____

_____

8. You can catch more flies with honey than with vinegar. _____

_____

_____

_____

_____

Composition

Lesson 102
The Writing Process: Revising I

After you complete a first draft, you will want to revise, or improve your writing. Begin by looking at each individual paragraph. The topic sentence should clearly state what the paragraph is about. Each of the other sentences should support the topic sentence and work together to develop the topic in a clear, interesting way.

If you find a sentence in your paragraph that does not support the topic, either move it to a paragraph where it would make sense or do not use it at all. If your sentences fit the topic but do not flow together smoothly, try adding a transition word such as *first, next,* or *finally.*

Greta had a busy day. She played tennis all morning. She had lunch with Aunt Susan. She visited the aquarium in the afternoon, and she called me tonight.

Greta had a busy day. **First,** she played tennis all morning. **Next,** she had lunch with Aunt Susan. She visited the aquarium in the afternoon, and, **finally,** she called me tonight.

▶ **Exercise 1 Revise the following paragraph.**

The Venus flytrap is a plant that can be grown indoors. The Venus flytrap is a plant that can move fast to catch insects. If you want help catching insects in your home, you might want to get a Venus flytrap. I have a cactus. The tip of each leaf of the Venus flytrap has two pads that hinge at the base. Each pad has sensitive hairs on its surface. When an insect lands on a pad, these hairs move slightly, causing the pads to snap shut. The long "teeth" at the edges of the pad interlock to keep the insect from escaping.

If you want help catching insects in your home, you might want to get a Venus flytrap. The Venus flytrap is a plant that can move fast to catch insects. It is also a plant that can be grown indoors. The tip of each leaf has two pads that hinge at the base. Each pad has sensitive hairs on its surface. When an insect lands on a pad, these hairs move slightly, causing the pads to snap shut. The long "teeth" at the edges of the pad interlock to keep the insect from escaping.

_____

_____

_____

Composition

▶ **Exercise 2** **Write a topic sentence for this paragraph. Then revise the paragraph to support and develop the idea in your topic sentence.**

This means that they do not have a backbone. Many kinds of animals are included in this category. Corals and sea anemones, which are both in the sea, have a plantlike appearance. Other invertebrates are agile predators. Some invertebrates are very simple animals that never move. A spider can dart quickly when attacking its prey. Crabs and lobsters can move quickly. Beetles, butterflies, and bees are all in this class. Invertebrates such as worms, snails, and starfish move at a slower pace. One of the largest classes is the insects. You can see from these examples there are many different kinds of invertebrates.

Most of the world's animals are invertebrates. This means that they do not have a backbone. Many kinds of animals are included in this category. Some invertebrates are very simple animals that never move. For instance, corals and sea anemones have a plantlike appearance. However, other invertebrates are agile predators. A spider can dart quickly when attacking its prey. Crabs and lobsters can move quickly, too. Invertebrates such as worms, snails, and starfish move at a slower pace. One of the largest classes of invertebrates is the insects. Beetles, butterflies, and bees are all in this class. You can see from these examples there are many different kinds of invertebrates.

_____

_____

_____

_____

_____

_____

_____

_____

_____

_____

_____

_____

Composition

Lesson 103

The Writing Process: Revising II

Once you have revised the content of your paragraphs, you can revise the structure. The idea is to create sentences that make your paragraphs lively and interesting to read. Each sentence should flow smoothly into the next. Varying the length of your sentences can help. Rather than writing all long sentences or all short ones, try to create a balance. Divide a long sentence into two short ones to grab a reader's attention. Combine two or three short sentences into one longer, flowing sentence by using a connecting word such as *or, and,* or *but*. Read your sentences aloud to hear how they sound. A combination of long and short sentences will form a pleasing pattern.

▶ **Exercise 1** **Combine the short sentences into one longer sentence. Divide the longer sentences into two or three short ones.**

Sue had roast beef for dinner. Sue had potatoes for dinner. _Sue had roast beef and_ _potatoes for dinner._

1. Kyle likes to play football. Kyle likes to play baseball. _Kyle likes to play football and_ _baseball._

2. We met Cindy at the park. We met Jan at the park. We met Bobby at the park.
 We met Cindy, Jan, and Bobby at the park.

3. The wind whistled through the trees while the young girl made her way through the deep, dark forest. _The wind whistled through the trees. The young girl made her way through the_ _deep, dark forest._

4. I tried strawberry ice cream. I like chocolate better. _I tried strawberry ice cream, but I like_ _chocolate better._

5. The first television program was fast-paced and exciting, and the second television program was slower and rather dull. _The first television program was fast-paced and exciting._ _The second television program was slower and rather dull._

Composition

▶ Exercise 2 **Revise the following paragraph.**

Yesterday my class visited the new zoo, and I found it far more interesting than the old zoo because of the way the animals are kept. There are no old-fashioned cages with bars. Instead, natural-looking areas with fences prevent the animals and visitors from getting hurt. You would not believe how many animals live in this zoo! I saw elephants. I saw eels. I saw cute baby koala bears. The zoo director explained how each kind of animal lives in the wild. The zoo director explained how her staff has tried to reproduce those conditions within the zoo. I thoroughly enjoyed the trip, and I hope to go back soon.

Yesterday my class visited the new zoo. I found it more interesting than the old zoo because of

the way the animals are kept. Instead of the old-fashioned cages with bars, fences surround

natural-looking areas and prevent animals and visitors from getting hurt. You would not believe

how many animals live in this zoo! I saw elephants, eels, and cute baby koala bears. The zoo director

explained how each kind of animal lives in the wild and how her staff has tried to reproduce those

conditions within the zoo. I thoroughly enjoyed the trip. I hope to go back soon.

Lesson 104
The Writing Process: Editing

After you have made a clean copy of your revised draft, you should proofread it for errors in spelling, grammar, usage, and mechanics. Check for correct subject-verb agreement, correct verb tenses, and clear pronoun references. Also check for run-on sentences and sentence fragments. Use the following proofreading marks to make corrections. If you replace words or phrases, draw a line through them and write the new words just above them.

MEANING	EXAMPLE
insert ^	one a a time
delete	thee
insert space #	blue whale
close up space	bee hive
capitalize ≡	dear sir:
make lowercase /	Mother
check spelling sp	ordnary sp
switch order	you do
new paragraph	. . . game ended. Afterward . . .

▶ **Exercise 1 Edit each sentence for correct spelling, grammar, usage, and mechanics.**

      will
What did you do tomorrow?

             is
1. To a botanist, a tomato are a fruit.

      o
2. You, to, can learn Japanese calligraphy.

3. The boy holding the white persian cat is my brother.

4. Nathaniel Jacob and play in the YMCA Basketball League.

                               changed
5. I didn't care for the television show, so I altered the channel.

              is
6. My best friend be Troy.

Composition

7. Mary watched the Experiment with great interest.

8. The car I really like is the Porsche it's very sleek.

9. Pre writing is the first stage of the writing progress.

10. Prewriting is a time for gathering writingideas.

▶ **Exercise 2** **Edit the paragraph for correct grammar and word usage.**

Last Saturday knight I went on an owl walk for the first time. February is the matingseason for Owls in this part of the state, so we herd many owls calling. If you imitate an owl's call, some times it calls back.

▶ **Exercise 3** **Proofread each sentence to correct spelling, punctuation, and capitalization errors.**

In my neighbors small orchard, you can find apples, peaches, and pears.

1. dogs seem to understand what wee say to them.

2. Ben is president of the agassiz club, our school science club.

3. Because the nightsky was so clear, we could see the constellations.

4. Do porposses swim with a sense of purpose?

5. The Great Saltlake in Utah is a beautiful place.

6. Mr. Decker's tree farm has white pines and blue spruce s.

7. Jean said, "Please, mother, let me get my ears peirced.

8. Autumn not spring, is my favorite season.

9. Tiffanys swaeter matches our school colors.

10. I looked for the lost key on my dresser in the car and in my cote pockets.

Composition

Lesson 105
The Writing Process: Presenting

When you have completed a piece of writing, you may decide to present your work to others. How you will present your writing depends on the audience you selected during prewriting and the nature of the material.

An outlet for presenting your writing to a specific audience is called a *market*. Many different markets are available to sixth-grade students. Among these are school newspapers and classroom presentations; community groups, newspapers, and radio stations; local and national contests; and magazines that feature the work of young people. *The Market Guide for Young Writers,* available in many libraries, can give you some ideas for marketing your work.

To decide how to present your piece, analyze your audience; then search for an outlet that serves that audience. Some outlets, such as radio programs or speech contests, offer a chance for oral presentation. In these cases, visual aids may add to your presentation.

▶ **Exercise 1** **Suggest an outlet or market for each piece of writing described below.**

a poem about school spirit _school newspaper_

1. a speech about democracy _community group meeting, school assembly_

2. an opinion piece about the quality of school lunches _school paper_

3. an essay about how the first day of spring makes you feel _magazine contest, the school_ newspaper

4. words for a song _school talent contest, sheet music publishing company_

5. a set of ten tongue twisters _class presentation, young writers' magazine_

6. a one-page short story _school literary magazine, young writers' magazine_

7. a scary story with numerous sound effects _campfire presentation, local radio program_

8. a book review _class presentation, local public television spot_

9. an opinion piece about whether community basketball courts should be repaired _local newspaper, letter to city council_

10. a poem about a historical event _school assembly, classroom presentation_

Composition

► **Exercise 2** **Suggest a visual aid that could increase the effectiveness of each presentation below.**

1. a speech to a science class about the 1994 flood of the Mississippi River __large map__ __showing river before flood and flooded area__

2. a profile of your school for new students __photographs of different school activities and__ __facilities__

3. an original cowboy song presented at a school talent show __a cowboy outfit, guitar for__ __accompaniment__

4. an oral reading of a poem that has animal characters __animal masks__

5. a classroom presentation about smoking among teenagers __a graph showing the recent__ __trend, illustrations or photographs of lung damage__

6. an oral presentation about foods from India __samples of food, photographs__

7. an original speech by Sir Winston Churchill __a suit like that worn by Churchill, an__ __illustration or photograph of him__

8. a report on how lawn mowers contribute to air pollution __a labeled diagram of a lawn__ __mower engine or chart showing what percentage of pollution comes from lawn mowers__

► **Exercise 3** **Think of an idea for a piece of writing intended for a specific audience. Then, in a short paragraph, describe how you would present the piece.**

Idea: nursery rhymes rewritten with new, humorous endings
Intended audience: students in grades 2–6
Form of presentation: The rhymes will be presented as short plays. Then the narrator will recite the poem while the actors mime their parts. The characters will carry a simple prop or wear an article of clothing that identifies them. The plays would be presented in individual classrooms at different grade levels.

Idea: _____

Intended audience: _____

Form of presentation: _____

_____

_____

_____

Composition

Lesson 106
Outlining

During prewriting you generate ideas. **Outlining** gives you a way to organize those ideas before you begin drafting. One way to make an outline is to write pieces of information from your prewriting material on index cards. You can then arrange the cards by *main topic* and *supporting details.* When writing an outline, use roman numerals for the main topics. Use capital letters for subtopics. Under each topic, list details using regular numerals. If you include details for a topic or subtopic, always give at least two items. An outline for an account of a rafting trip might look like this:

I. Beginning
   A. Floating calmly
   B. Sights along river
      1. Birds fishing
      2. Fish jumping
II. Middle
   A. Shooting the rapids
      1. Quick reactions of guide
      2. Excitement of passengers
   B. Stopping for picnic lunch

▶ **Exercise 1** **Organize the following subtopics and details into an outline for a paragraph about a trip in a hot air balloon. The main topics are provided.**

Ended near Calgary, Canada   Flight lasted four days
Length of trip   Balloonist endured zero temperatures
More than 6,000 miles   Started in Seoul, South Korea
Two heaters failed   Route of trip

I. First solo balloon flight across Pacific Ocean

  A. _Route of trip_____

    1. _Started in Seoul, South Korea_____

    2. _Ended near Calgary, Canada_____

  B. _Length of trip_____

    1. _More than 6,000 miles_____

    2. _Flight lasted four days_____

Composition

II. Hardships of trip

A. <u>Two heaters failed</u>

B. <u>Balloonist endured zero temperatures</u>

▶ **Exercise 2 Use the outline below to write a paragraph about types of feathers on birds.**

   I. Body feathers
     A. Used for insulation
     B. Used for display
       1. Bright colors
       2. Distinct markings
  II. Tail feathers
     A. Important for steering in flying
     B. Used for balance on ground
 III. Flight feathers
     A. Used for flight
     B. Side of feather toward wing is usually narrower
     C. Broader side bends easily to let air move through wing

    You might have known that a bird can have feathers of different colors, but did you know that all birds have different feathers with different purposes? All birds need three kinds of feathers: body feathers, tail feathers, and flight feathers. Colorful body feathers insulate the bird's body and also serve as distinctive markings. Tail feathers are important for steering in flying. They also help the bird keep its balance on the ground. Flight feathers are, of course, used for flight. The side of the feather toward the wing is usually narrower. The broader side bends easily to let air move through the wing.

Composition

Lesson 107
Writing Effective Sentences I

Here are some tips for making your sentences more effective.

- **Vary the length of your sentences.** Avoid using all long sentences or all short sentences.
- **Vary the structure of your sentences.** Avoid using the same pattern for all sentences.

▶ **Exercise 1** **Combine the repetitious short sentences into a longer, more interesting sentence. Reword as needed.**

a. The sun was setting.

b. It was setting behind the barn.

c. The barn is red.

d. The swallows began to feed.

The sun was setting behind the red barn as the swallows began to feed.

1. a. Fumio plays on a team.

b. The team is a soccer team.

c. Fumio is the goalie.

d. The team's name is the "Jets."

Fumio is the goalie on a soccer team called the "Jets."

2. a. Fall is a beautiful time of year.

b. Fall is a somewhat sad time, too.

c. The trees will soon be bare.

d. The grass will turn brown.

Fall is a beautiful, but somewhat sad, time of year because the trees will soon be bare and the grass

will turn brown.

Composition

3. a. Alice is a curious girl.

   b. She is intelligent.

   c. Alice is the main character in *Alice in Wonderland*.

   d. Her adventures in a make-believe world are humorous.

> **Alice, the main character in *Alice in Wonderland*, is a curious and intelligent girl who has many**
>
> **humorous adventures in a make-believe world.**

4. a. This fable is by Aesop.

   b. The title is "The Lion and the Mouse."

   c. The story is about good deeds.

   d. In the story a good deed is rewarded.

> **Aesop's fable "The Lion and the Mouse" is a story about how good deeds bring rewards.**

5. a. Nils keeps a journal.

   b. He uses a blue pen for all journal entries.

   c. The journal is a notebook.

   d. The notebook is spiral-bound.

> **Nils keeps his journal in a spiral-bound notebook and always writes in it with a blue pen.**

▶ **Exercise 2** **Rewrite the paragraph, changing some of the sentence patterns.**

Lek and I had nothing to do. We rode our bikes down the street. We came to the old park. We used to play baseball in the old park. We saw a shed in the old park. The shed looked empty. We looked into a window of the shed. We saw a mother dog and her puppies on the floor. We opened the door to the shed. We went in. We played with the dogs. Finally, we went home.

> **Possible answer: One afternoon my friend Lek and I could think of nothing to do. After riding our**
>
> **bikes around town for a while, we came to the old park where we used to play baseball. We saw an**
>
> **empty-looking shed and peeked into a window. Imagine our surprise when we saw a mother**
>
> **dog and her pups! We spent the rest of the afternoon playing with the dogs.**

Composition

Lesson 108
Writing Effective Sentences II

- **Lead with an interesting topic sentence.** Word the sentence so that it "hooks" your readers and makes them want to read on.

- **Use active verbs primarily.** In a sentence with an active verb, the subject performs the action (e.g., He speaks). In a passive-verb sentence, the subject is acted upon (e.g., He is spoken to). Active verbs generally make a stronger impression than passive verbs. Use a passive verb when the "doer" of an action is unknown or unimportant.

▶ **Exercise 1** Underline the topic sentence that best hooks the reader.

Toonia, my new pen pal, lives with her grandmother in Bangkok, Thailand.

Having a pen pal is one way to learn about another country.

I know more about Thailand than I used to know.

Amid the bright colors and noisy streets of Bangkok lives my new pen pal, Toonia.

1. That stubborn girl who prefers MegaMedia over the new MultiMedia is none other than my sister!

   My sister and I never agree on anything.

   My sister and I like two different, but similar, stores that sell books and tapes.

   I like the new store MultiMedia, but my sister prefers MegaMedia.

2. Twelve inches of snow fell yesterday, but it all melted today.

   Not the usual one or two inches of snow fell yesterday.

   How could we have ever guessed that twelve whole inches of snow would disappear almost overnight?

   Due to temperatures rising to 60°, all the snow that fell yesterday melted today.

3. Here is what I think about smoking: Kids shouldn't smoke because smoking is bad for their health and it becomes a habit that is nearly impossible to break.

   Kids shouldn't smoke because it is bad for their health and it is a hard habit to break.

   Coughing every few minutes and pausing for an extra gasp of air, the speaker warned students about the dangers of smoking.

Composition

4. The water in the river was rough, and the water bounced the raft around.

If you are going out on the water, you should wear a life jacket.

When the rough water bounced the raft around, we were glad that we were wearing life

jackets.

Here's why you should wear a life jacket when you are on a boat.

▶ **Exercise 2** **Rewrite the following passage, changing passive verbs to active verbs
where appropriate.**

The last scene in the movie is packed with action. Tex Carlson, the sheriff, is chased
into a dead-end canyon by a band of nasty-looking outlaws. A way out is found by Tex,
though, at the last minute. He scrambles up the cliff like an agile mountain goat, just as his
deputy is arriving.

> The last scene in the movie is packed with action. A band of nasty-looking outlaws chases Tex
>
> Carlson, the sheriff, into a dead-end canyon. Tex finds a way out at the last minute, though. He scrambles
>
> up the cliff like an agile mountain goat, just as his deputy is arriving.

Composition

Lesson 109
Writing Effective Sentences III

- **Create special effects.** You can repeat certain words or phrases for emphasis or to create a certain effect. You can also use interruption for emphasis. A sudden break in thought can call attention to an important point. Another way to emphasize is to use a different kind of sentence that stands out from all the others.

▶ **Exercise 1** **Use the list to identify how the sentence or sentences below were made more effective. Some may have more than one answer.**

interesting topic sentence	repetition for emphasis
varied sentence length	varied sentence structure
interruption for emphasis	unusual sentence for special effect

1. Did you know that 1 in 3 families today has a single parent? The situation was very different 25 years ago. At that time, only about 1 in 10 families had a single parent.
   interesting topic sentence, varied sentence structure
   _____
   _____

2. Some people think that if you don't learn how to ride a bike when you're a child that you can never learn. It's not true. My father learned to ride when he was 33 years old.
   varied sentence length
   _____
   _____
   _____

3. I don't have a ride. I don't have any money. How can I possibly go to the concert?
   repetition for emphasis
   _____
   _____
   _____

Composition

4. When you go out in the pasture, be sure to wear rubber boots. The ground is very soggy

and the little stream is swollen. It is April, after all. __varied sentence length, varied sentence__

__structure__

_____

5. Who-o-o-o-o-o-o-o-o! I heard the owl call again. __unusual sentence for special interest__

_____

_____

6. My stomach tells me—oops, there it goes, growling again—that it's time for lunch.

__interruption for emphasis__

_____

_____

▶ **Exercise 2 Rewrite the paragraph below using effective sentences.**

The school bus was racing up the twisty mountain road. There was a tree in the road. It

fell there. It happened suddenly. The tree blocked the path of the bus. Then there was

thunder. Then it began to rain in buckets. Night was falling. The busload of children

wondered what would happen next.

__The school bus was racing up the twisty mountain road. Suddenly, it screeched to a halt. A tree had__

__fallen across the road, blocking the way. As the children stared at the tree, they heard thunder. Rain__

__came down in buckets. They realized that night was falling. The children had only one thought: what__

__would happen next?__

_____

_____

_____

_____

_____

_____

Lesson 110
Building Paragraphs I

You can arrange the supporting details in a paragraph in several ways. One way is based on time. Chronological order places events in the order in which they happened. An easy way to order chronologically the events you are writing about is first to make a timeline of them. Make use of words that signal chronological order. These include the following: *first, while, then, after, when, immediately, suddenly, finally,* and *last.* Notice some of these words in the following paragraph:

I took my usual walk in the park today with Fifi. First we strolled through the rose garden. Then we stopped at the green bench for a brief rest. After resting a while, we walked all the way around the pond and back down Plum Street. Eventually we became hungry, so we stopped for a lunch break under a big elm tree. Feeling full and content, I lay down for a nap in the grass. When Fifi's barking woke me suddenly, I sat up, rubbed the sleep from my eyes, and looked around. The sun was setting, signaling that it was time to go home. Once again, Fifi and I took off walking. This time, however, we headed straight for the park entrance. Walking quickly down the sidewalk, we finally arrived at our apartment.

▶ **Exercise 1** **Write the words that signaled chronological order in the paragraph above.**

First, Then, After, Eventually, When, Once again, finally
_____

_____

▶ **Exercise 2** **Write the following list of events in paragraph form. Be sure the chronological order makes sense.**

The water felt cold.
Then we took off our shoes and shorts.
First we put on our bathing suits under our shorts.
Once we got used to the water, we played in it for about an hour.
Then we walked to the beach.
Finally, it was time to go home.
While walking barefoot on the beach, we noticed seashells.
When we arrived, we spread out our towels.
On our walk home, we talked about the wonderful day.
After collecting shells, we waded into the water.

Composition

First, we put on our bathing suits under our shorts. Then we walked to the beach. When we arrived, we spread out our towels. Then we took off our shoes and shorts. While walking barefoot on the beach, we noticed seashells. After collecting shells, we waded into the water. The water felt very cold! Once we got used to the water, we played in it for about an hour. Finally, it was time to go home. On our walk home, we talked about the wonderful day.

_____

_____

_____

_____

_____

▶ **Exercise 3** **Write a paragraph about what you did last weekend. Be sure events are in chronological order.**

_____

_____

_____

_____

_____

_____

_____

_____

_____

_____

_____

_____

_____

Lesson 111
Building Paragraphs II

Another way to order details in a paragraph is by using spatial order. When you use spatial order, you arrange details by their location or position. There are different ways to arrange details in spatial order. For example, your description may go from near to far, left to right, or low to high.

Some words that help show spatial order include the following: *next to, on, below, above, across, near, far, out, by, through, over, between, away, left,* and *down.* These words may appear as prepositions, adjectives, or adverbs.

The teapot **on** the stove whistled. (preposition)
The dog ran **in** a **nearby** field. (preposition, adjective)

The following paragraph is arranged in spatial order.

As I sat in the park on the green bench, I looked at Fifi to my right. Her paws were muddy from the dirt around the bench. She started barking when she noticed a German shepherd in the nearby field. The dog approached us and sat in front of the bench. I threw a stick and both dogs went running across the field. I watched them for a while from the bench, waiting to see which would return with the prize.

▶ **Exercise 1** **Write the words that signaled spatial order in the above paragraph.**

in, on, at, to, around, nearby, in front of, across, from
_____

_____

▶ **Exercise 2** **Write the following details in paragraph form. Use spatial order that moves from near to far.**

Farther to the right was the audio-visual section.
Near the entrance to the left was the circulation desk.
I stood at the entrance to the library.
At the end opposite the library's entrance were stairs leading down to the nonfiction books and up to the magazine area.
Just beyond the stairs was the back entrance, filled with works of art by local patrons.
To the right of the front door was the children's room.
Past the circulation desk on the left were the reference room and the reading room.
Behind the circulation desk was the librarian's office.

I stood at the entrance to the library. Near the entrance to the left was the circulation desk. Past the

circulation desk were the reference room and the reading room. Behind the circulation desk was the

librarian's office. To the right of the front door was the children's room. Farther to the right was the

audio-visual section. At the end opposite the library's entrance were stairs leading down to the non-

fiction books and up to the magazine area. Just beyond the stairs was the back entrance, filled with

works of art by local patrons.

_____

_____

_____

_____

_____

▶ **Exercise 2** **Write a paragraph describing the room you are in now. Use spatial order.**

_____

_____

_____

_____

_____

_____

_____

_____

_____

_____

_____

_____

_____

_____

Composition

Lesson 112
Building Paragraphs III

In **compare/contrast** order, present details about two subjects by describing their similarities and differences. This can be done in two ways. You can discuss all the details about one subject and then about the other subject:

Fifi is a small black poodle. She has very short, curly hair. She is very quiet and stays away from people. She loves to be lazy and lie outside in the sun. Rex is a large brown and white collie. He has long, thick fur. He is very friendly and barks loudly. He loves to play fetch with a stick in the backyard.

Or you can do comparisons detail-by-detail, writing about both subjects at the same time:

While Fifi is a small black poodle, Rex is a large brown and white collie. Fifi has short curly hair and Rex has long thick fur. Fifi is very quiet and stays away from people. Rex is very friendly and barks loudly. While Fifi loves to be lazy and lie in the sun, Rex prefers to play fetch with a stick.

▶ **Exercise 1 Write the following details in paragraph form. Use compare/contrast order.**

Bony fish are more common.
Fish can be divided into two groups: bony fish and cartilage fish.
Cartilage fish have skeletons made of cartilage.
The end of your nose is cartilage.
Bony fish have skeletons like human bones.
Both kinds of fish have fins and gills.
Only the teeth of cartilage fish are calcified like bones.

Fish can be divided into two groups: bony fish and cartilage fish. Bony fish are more common. They

have skeletons like human bones. Cartilage fish, on the other hand, have skeletons made of cartilage,

like the end of your nose. Only the teeth of cartilage fish are calcified like bones. Both kinds of fish have

fins and gills.

_____

_____

_____

_____

_____

Composition

Grandma Nora is quiet and dignified.
Grandma Hazel plays the piano.
Grandma Hazel works for a political organization.
Grandma Nora sings with a band.
Grandma Hazel is talkative and fun.
Grandma Hazel lives in Phoenix.
Grandma Nora lives in Chicago.
Grandma Nora works for a government agency.

Grandma Nora lives in Chicago. She works for a government agency and sings with a band. She is quiet and dignified. Grandma Hazel lives in Phoenix. She works for a political organization and plays the piano. She is talkative and fun.

_____

_____

_____

_____

_____

▶ **Exercise 2** Write a paragraph that compares and contrasts your own interests and abilities with those of a friend.

_____

_____

_____

_____

_____

_____

_____

_____

_____

_____

Lesson 113
Paragraph Ordering

Just as you needed to choose an order for your sentences, you need to choose an order for the paragraphs in your writing. When you are revising, check that each sentence tells something about the topic of that paragraph. Cross out any sentences that do not. Be sure your paragraphs follow one another in a way that makes sense. Finally, check that you have transition words between the last sentence of one paragraph and the first sentence of the following paragraph.

FIRST DRAFT:

The second day we went to the beach. The sun came out, the water was cool, and we had a great time. The sky was blue. We made huge sand castles. We went swimming and waterskiing.

The first day of our vacation was a big disappointment.We had to stay indoors. It rained all day long. There were thunder and lightning, too.

The weather was perfect the rest of the week. I'm glad I didn't go home after the first day!

REVISED DRAFT:

The first day of our vacation was a big disappointment. It rained all day long. There were thunder and lightning, too, so we had to stay indoors.

The second day we went to the beach. The sky was blue, and the sun came out. First we made huge sand castles; then we went swimming and waterskiing. We had a great time.

The weather was perfect the rest of the week. I'm glad I didn't go home after the first day!

▶ Exercise 1 Write *1*, *2*, or *3* in the blank in front of each paragraph to show how the three paragraphs should be ordered.

__3__   Finally, Aunt Susan offered to bake some of her famous cherry pies. With all

that food to sell, we were certain to raise enough money to go to Toronto.

__1__   My soccer team was invited to play in a tournament in Toronto, Canada.

Unfortunately, we did not have enough money to rent a bus to take us there. We

really wanted to go, so we decided to have a bake sale to raise some of the money.

_____2_____ The morning of the bake sale, we realized we did not have enough food. Kelly, who was in charge of donations, was especially upset. Since she was scheduled to work at the sale all morning, she didn't know how she was going to get more food. I called my friend Lois, who was not scheduled to work until afternoon. She said she and her grandfather could make another four dozen cookies. Then I called my sister Kate. She asked the owner of the bakery where she works if he would donate some pastries. Meanwhile, I went home to bake two more cakes.

▶ **Exercise 2 Revise the following paragraphs. Rewrite them in the space provided.**

Admission is free, but seating is limited—so come early and enjoy! Polk Middle School is announcing its spring production, *Images.* It includes songs, dances, and sketches of life as a sixth grader. This is a new play written by the students themselves.

There will also be an afternoon performance at 2:00 P.M. on June 2. Everyone in the community is invited to attend. The play will be performed at 8:00 P.M. June 1 and 7:30 P.M. June 2.

Polk Middle School is announcing its spring production, *Images.* This is a new play written by the students themselves. It includes songs, dances, and sketches of life as a sixth grader.

Everyone in the community is invited to attend. The play will be performed at 8:00 P.M. June 1 and 7:30 P.M. June 2. There will also be an afternoon performance at 2:00 P.M. on June 2. Admission is free, but seating is limited—so come early and enjoy!

_____

_____

_____

_____

_____

_____

Composition

Lesson 114
Personal Letters I

A **personal letter** is an informal letter to a person that you know well. Personal letters have a tone similar to friendly conversation. They describe recent events in your life and your reactions to them. They also ask the recipient of the letter for news. In a personal letter, the heading and the closing are usually indented, as is each paragraph in the body of the letter.

▶ **Exercise 1 Read the following personal letter. Answer each question.**

> 2496 Harrison Avenue
> Worthington, Ohio 43085
> March 3, 1996

Dear Yvonne,

    I was really happy to get your last letter. What a funny family you have. I laughed out loud when I read about how you and your dad had to carry a ladder on the subway to your new apartment.

    Things have been pretty quiet here, but I do have one piece of news. Our jump rope team entered the all-school jump rope competition, and we came in second! Boy, were we nervous. But we kept our cool and just kept jumping. The next time you visit I'll show you our routine.

    When you come, be sure to bring your swimsuit. The new community pool is finally finished. By the way, how did you ever get that ladder up seven flights of stairs?

> Your good friend,
> *Angie*

1. Who is Yvonne? _a friend of Angie's_

_____

2. What lines show that Angie is interested in what is happening in Yvonne's life?

first paragraph and the question in the last paragraph

_____

3. Which paragraph gives Yvonne some news about what Angie has been doing?

second

4. What do you notice about the placement of the heading and the closing? _They are_

positioned to the far right and indented the same amount.

_____

5. Would you describe the tone of the letter as formal or informal? Explain.

The letter is informal and friendly. The writer eagerly anticipates her friend's next visit. The language

is generally casual, using slang as well as sentence fragments.

_____

▶ **Exercise 2 Write a letter to a friend about your summer activities.**

Students' letters should be informal in tone and written in indented form. The letter should include

information about recent events in the writer's life and ask questions about events in the recipient's life.

_____

_____

_____

_____

_____

_____

_____

_____

_____

_____

_____

_____

_____

_____

Composition

Lesson 115
Personal Letters II

Personal letters can also take the form of invitations and thank-you notes. For example, you might write a thank-you note to a naturalist who gave a talk to your class. You might write a letter inviting your grandmother to visit you at your home. These two kinds of personal letters are usually semiformal, avoiding the slang and sentence fragments that you might use in a postcard to a friend. The heading and the closing are usually indented, as is each paragraph in the body of the letter.

► Exercise 1 **Write a thank-you note to an adult relative. In your letter express your appreciation for something nice that he or she did for you.**

Letters should be semiformal, probably avoiding slang, and should comment in some positive way on

what the relative did. Letters should use indented elements and have an appropriate closing.

_____

_____

_____

_____

_____

_____

_____

_____

_____

_____

_____

_____

_____

_____

_____

_____

_____

Composition

▶ **Exercise 2** Write a letter inviting the parents of students in your class to attend a poetry reading by members of the class.

Letters should use the salutation "Dear Parents" and a closing such as "Sincerely." The body of the letter should explain the event. The style should be informal and the tone enthusiastic. Paragraphs should be indented, and the heading and closing should align.

_____

_____

_____

_____

_____

_____

_____

_____

_____

_____

_____

_____

_____

_____

_____

_____

_____

_____

_____

_____

_____

_____

_____

Composition

Lesson 116
Personal Letters III

If you want to write to an author or a performer that you admire, you should write a **personal letter**. When you write to a celebrity, use a respectful tone and a semiformal writing style. Be sure to state clearly how the author's work has affected you. Celebrities cannot respond to each and every letter. However, if your letter catches the author's interest, you might receive a letter in return.

▶ **Exercise 1** **Read the following letter. Then answer each question.**

Dear Jean,

    Mrs. Fritz, I have read all your books. The book I like best is the one about growing up in China. The things you wrote about China made me want to visit it some day. I understood how homesick you felt because once I had to spend the entire summer in Arizona, far away from my family in New Jersey.

    I've learned a lot about United States history from your biographies. I feel as if I have met each of your subjects in person. Could you please send me an autographed copy of one of your books? It doesn't matter which one.

Your friend,

Janine Janiewicz

1. Did the writer use an appropriate salutation? Why or why not? **No. A respectful**
salutation for an adult who is not a close friend would be "Dear Mrs. Fritz" or "Dear Jean Fritz." A
correct salutation would make "Mrs. Fritz" in the first line unnecessary.

_____

_____

2. Was the writer clear about which book she admires the most? Explain. **Stating the title of**
the book would make it clearer.

_____

3. Explain whether the style and tone of the first paragraph is appropriate. **Generally, the**
style and tone is semiformal and appropriate.

_____

Composition

4. In the second paragraph, what unrealistic request does the writer make? <u>She asks the</u>

<u>author to sign and mail a book back to her.</u>

_____

5. In what lines does the writer of the letter explain how the author's work has affected

her? <u>in the last sentence of paragraph 1 and the first two sentences of paragraph 2</u>

_____

_____

6. Is the closing appropriate? Explain. <u>A more appropriate closing would be "Sincerely" or</u>

<u>"Yours truly" since the writer and recipient do not have a close personal relationship.</u>

_____

▶ **Exercise 2** **Write a personal letter to an author or performer you admire.**

<u>Letters should be semiformal, use indented style, and make specific comments about the author or</u>

<u>performer's effect on the writer.</u>

_____

_____

_____

_____

_____

_____

_____

_____

_____

_____

_____

_____

_____

Composition

Lesson 117
Business Letters: Letters of Request or Complaint

Business letters are letters sent to an organization to achieve a specific purpose. One common type of business letter is the letter of request. A letter of request asks for information or service. In this type of letter, begin by identifying yourself. Then explain what information you need and why you need it. Also, be clear about where the information should be sent. Since you are asking for a favor, always show courtesy in your request.

Business letters are usually written in block form or semiblock form. In block form, all parts of the letter are lined up at the left margin. In semiblock form, the heading, closing, and signature are aligned on the right side of the page. The recipient of a business letter is usually a stranger, so the letter should be formal in style and respectful in tone.

▶ **Exercise 1 Read the following letter of request. Then answer each question below.**

Dear Mr. Holbrook:
　　I am a sixth grader at Horatio Alger Middle School. Could you send me some information about the national parks in the West? Thanks tons.
　　　　　　　　　　　　　　　　　　　　Sincerely,
　　　　　　　　　　　　　　　　　　　　Pramode Pirakh

1. Are the salutation and closing appropriate? _yes_____

2. Does the letter writer identify himself? _yes_____

3. Does the letter writer explain why he needs the information? _no_____

4. Is the writer specific enough about the information he wants? _no_____

5. Is the letter courteous in tone? _no—it is rather brief_____

6. Is the letter appropriately formal in style? _no—the last line in particular is too casual_

▶ **Exercise 2 Rewrite the above letter to make it better. Refer to your evaluation, and add new information as needed. Sign your own name to the letter.**

Students should expand the letter. The request for information should be more specific than in the

sample, the tone should be courteous, and the style should be formal or semiformal. A heading and an

inside address should be included.

Composition

Another common type of business letter is the letter of complaint. A letter of complaint informs someone about a problem and usually requests some type of action. In your letter state the problem and how it has affected you. Use supporting details to explain the problem. End your letter by stating what you want done. Be firm but polite. If you let your anger burst out, you are less likely to get help in solving the problem.

▶ **Exercise 3 Read the following letter of complaint. List three weak points of the letter below.**

Dear Sir or Madam:
    The other day I decided I finally needed a new daypack, so I went to three different stores at the mall. Then I saw your daypacks and bought one. Your daypacks are really crummy. I bought the daypack two weeks ago and the back pocket is already coming off! I use the pocket to hold little things like my eraser and pencil sharpener and house key. Yesterday my key fell out because of the hole in the seam of the pocket! I shouldn't have to mend a new pack. I demand a full refund of my money!

The money or else . . .
Inez Garcia

1. The letter has an angry tone. _____

2. The letter is not brief and to the point. _____

3. The letter does not have an appropriate closing. _____

▶ **Exercise 4 Rewrite the letter of complaint above to make it more effective.**

Letters should be concise and state the problem at the beginning of the letter. The tone should be firm

but polite. An acceptable business closing, such as "Sincerely," should be used. A heading and an inside

address should be included.

_____

_____

_____

_____

_____

_____

Composition

Lesson 118
Business Letters: Letters of Opinion

A letter of opinion is a letter that voices your thoughts and ideas on a particular issue. You might write a letter of opinion to the school newspaper about a new policy or program. You might write to a public official to comment on a community or national issue. Or you might write to a magazine to react to a recent article.

Here are some guidelines for writing a good letter of opinion.

- Try to put your main idea into a single sentence.

- Provide details to support your opinion.

- If possible, suggest a solution to the problem.

- Use a courteous tone: avoid name-calling or broad generalizations.

▶ **Exercise 1** **Read the following letter of opinion. Then answer the questions that follow.**

Dear Mayor Farmer:

The downtown recreation center is a great idea, but the plan for it could be improved. According to the current plan, there will be room for four basketball courts, which can also serve as volleyball courts. It's true that the youth basketball leagues need more space for their games. However, our city does not have a single indoor tennis court. More than two hundred young people take part in summer tennis tournaments in Mount Airy, but they have no place to practice during the winter. Many adults fill the five outdoor courts in summer. They, too, would benefit from an indoor facility. The new recreation center should appeal to many different groups in our community. I strongly urge you to include at least one tennis court in the plan for the new facility.

Sincerely,
Demar Johnson

1. What sentence states the specific problem the writer is addressing? __Our city does not__ have a single indoor tennis court.

2. What details does the writer include to support his point of view? __Many young people__ and adults who play tennis have nowhere to practice in winter. The recreation center should appeal to many different groups in the community.

3. What solution does the writer propose to the problem? <u>Include one indoor tennis court in</u>

<u>the new recreation center.</u>

4. How would you describe the tone of the letter? <u>calm and polite</u>

_____

▶ **Exercise 2** **Write a letter of opinion to your school or community paper about an issue that is important to you, or choose one of the following topics. Use the guidelines above in drafting your letter.**

a change in a school rule   safety in your community
a needed facility at your school   a way to beautify your community

<u>Letters should state the problem clearly near the beginning of the letter and offer a solution. Supporting</u>

<u>details should be included to illustrate the problem and/or justify the solution offered. The tone of the</u>

<u>letter should be courteous.</u>

_____

_____

_____

_____

_____

_____

_____

_____

_____

_____

_____

_____

_____

Composition

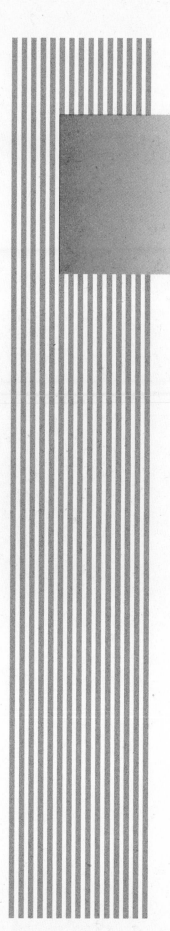

*I*ndex

Index

A

A, *an, the* (articles), 7, 121
Abbreviations, correct use of, 18, 255, 257
Abstract nouns, defined, 4
Accept, except, 12, 197
Action verbs, defined, 4, 75, 79
Active voice, explained, 6, 319
  in writing, 319
Adjective clauses, 9, 40
  nonessential, 40
Adjective phrases
  as participial phrases, 10
  as prepositional phrases, 10, 155
Adjectives, defined, 7–8, 119
  articles as, 7, 121
  comparative forms of, 8, 123, 125
    avoiding errors in, 36–37
  demonstrative, 121
  diagraming, 185
  distinguishing from adverbs, 139, 141
  hyphen in compound, 18
  predicate, 3, 81, 119, 139, 183
  proper, 7, 15, 44, 119, 225, 227
  superlative, 8, 123, 125, 135
    avoiding errors in, 36–37
Adverb clauses, 9, 40
  commas with, 40
Adverb phrases
  as prepositional phrases, 10, 155
Adverbs, defined, 8, 131
  comparative forms of, 8, 135, 137
  conjunctive, 9, 16
  diagraming, 185
  distinguishing from adjectives 139, 141
  distinguishing from prepositions, 157
  modifying adjectives and adverbs, 8, 133
  modifying verbs, 8, 131
  negative words as, 8, 143
Agreement
  pronoun-antecedent, 7, 34, 109
  subject-verb, 4, 11, 28–31, 67, 167, 169, 171, 173
    and collective nouns, 4, 67
    and compound subjects, 11, 30–31, 173
    and subject pronouns, 11, 29, 169
    and prepositional phrases, 11, 28, 171

    and indefinite pronouns, 11, 29, 113
    in inverted sentences, 11, 28–29, 171
    with titles of works, 11
All ready, already, 12, 197
All together, altogether, 12, 197
A lot, alot, 12, 197
Already, all ready, 12, 197
Altogether, all together, 12, 197
Among, between, 12, 199
Antecedents, defined, 7, 109
  agreement of pronouns with, 7, 109
  clear pronoun reference, 7, 34, 109
Antonyms, 275
Apostrophes, rules for using, 17–18, 41–43, 251
  in contractions, 18, 43, 251
  in possessive nouns and pronouns, 17, 41–43, 251
  in special plurals, 17, 42, 251
Appositive phrases, 10, 16, 39
Appositives, 10, 16, 39
Articles, 7, 121
Audience, choosing, 20, 301, 313
Auxiliary (helping) verbs, defined, 4, 87, 89, 91

B

Bad, worse, worst, 36, 125
Beside, besides, 12, 199
Between, among, 12, 199
Block form for letters, 21, 337
Bring, take, 12
Business letters, 21–22, 337–339
  letters of complaint, 338
  letters of opinion, 22, 339
  letters of request, 22, 337
But, coordinating conjunction, 9, 159

C

Can, may, 12
Capitalization, rules for, 14–15, 44, 213, 215, 217, 219, 221, 223, 225, 227
  in direct quotations, 14, 44, 213
  in family names and titles of persons, 15, 217, 219

Proper adjectives, 8, 15, 44, 119, 225, 227
Proper nouns, defined, 3, 63
Punctuation rules. *See specific types*
Purpose, choosing in writing, 20, 301

Q

Question marks, 15, 233
  and quotation marks, 17, 247
Quiet, quite, 13
Quotation marks, 17, 247
  with colons or semicolons, 17
  with commas or periods, 17, 38–39, 247
  in direct quotations, 17, 247
  within a quotation, 17
  with question marks or exclamation points,
    17, 247
  with titles of short works, 17, 249
Quotations, capitalizing, 14, 44, 213

R

Raise, rise, 13, 203
Reflexive pronouns, 6
Regular verbs, 4–6, 85
Relative pronouns, 6
Request, letters of, 22, 337
Revising, 20, 307, 309
  sentence variety, 20, 309
  topic sentences, 307
  transition words, 307
Rise, raise, 13, 203
Roots of words, 19
Run-on sentences, 26–27, 59

S

Semiblock form of letters, 21, 337
Semicolons, 16–17, 245
  to correct run-on sentences, 26, 59
Sentence, defined, 47
Sentence fragments, 24–25, 57
Sentence structure, 9–10, 55
  complex, 10
  compound, 10, 55
  simple, 10, 55
Sentences, effective, 309, 317, 319, 321
  active voice, 6, 319
  passive voice, 319
  special effects, 321

  topic sentence, 319
  varied length, 317
  varied structure, 317
Sentences, kinds of
  declarative, 10, 47
  exclamatory, 10, 49
  imperative, 10, 49
  interrogative, 10, 47
Sentences, run-on, 26–27, 59
Series
  commas in, 16, 38, 235
  colon before, 17, 245
Set, sit, 14, 203
Simple predicates, defined, 3, 51
Simple sentences, defined, 10, 55
Simple subjects, defined, 3, 51
Singular nouns, 3, 65
Sit, set, 14, 203
Spatial order, 20, 325
Spelling
  adding *-ly*, 20, 281
  doubling the final consonant, 19, 281
  of easily confused words, 287
  forming compound words, 20, 281
  of often misspelled words, 285
  of plural nouns, 20, 283
  of prefixes, 19
  of suffixes, 19, 279
  of *ie* and *ei,* 19, 279
  of unstressed vowels, 19
Subject-verb agreement, 4, 11, 28–31, 67, 167,
    169, 171, 173
  and collective nouns, 4, 67
  and compound subjects, 11, 30–31, 173
  and intervening expressions, 11, 28, 171
  and prepositional phrases, 11, 28, 171
  and indefinite pronouns, 11, 29, 113
  in inverted sentences, 11, 28–29, 171
  with subject pronouns, 11, 29, 169
  with titles of works, 11
Subjects
  agreement of verb with, 4, 11, 28–31, 67,
    167, 169, 171, 173
  complete, 3, 51
  compound, 3, 30–31, 53, 173
  pronouns as, 34–35, 105, 107, 169
  simple, 3, 51
Subordinate (dependent) clauses, 9–10
Subordinating conjunctions, 9

Unit 1: Subjects, Predicates, and Sentences

▶ **Subtest 1** Write *dec.* in the blank before each declarative sentence, *int.* before each interrogative sentence, *exc.* before each exclamatory sentence, and *imp.* before each imperative sentence. Add the correct punctuation mark at the end of each sentence.

_____ 1. My brother turned sixteen last week

_____ 2. That was an unbelievable shot

_____ 3. Has anyone seen my notebook

_____ 4. Please don't move that

_____ 5. I wonder if all mammals have fur

_____ 6. Listen to this song

_____ 7. Tina's mom won the lottery

_____ 8. Do all insects have six legs

_____ 9. March has thirty-one days, but February has only twenty-eight days except in

leap years

_____ 10. Where did you buy that backpack

▶ **Subtest 2** Write *S* before each simple sentence, *C* before each compound sentence, *F* before each sentence fragment, and *RO* before each run-on sentence.

_____ 1. Have you read that book I didn't think so.

_____ 2. I can meet you at the airport, or you can take a taxi.

_____ 3. Has your brother tried out for the baseball team?

_____ 4. Doesn't enjoy playing volleyball.

_____ 5. Mom liked the play, but Dad didn't care for it.

_____ 6. Jeremy brought his gerbil to class, everyone loved it.

_____ 7. Out of the fog appeared the great detective.

_____ 8. The friend of my next-door neighbor.

_____ 9. In autumn birds fly south, and leaves fall from the trees.

_____ 10. About three times a week.

▶ **Subtest 3** Draw a line under each compound subject. Circle each compound predicate.

1. My sister and I enjoy cross-country skiing.

2. Hildy wanted my lunch and offered me a dollar for it.

3. The guitarist and the drummer bowed and left the stage.

4. Bears and raccoons are not closely related animals.

5. Seashells and starfish washed up on the shore and lay on the beach.

6. The barber cut the customer's hair and then gave him a shave.

7. Basketball and soccer are two of my favorite sports.

8. Bees collect nectar from flowers and pollinate them.

9. Finches and chickadees sang and twittered high in the trees.

10. My uncle and his friend took a trip to Canada.

▶ **Subtest 4** Draw one line under each simple subject. Draw two lines under each simple predicate.

1. Nobody would believe such a story.

2. Over the years Steven has worked at several jobs.

3. Fountain pens are not very common.

4. My best friends will visit me in the hospital.

5. The senator gave a rousing speech at the convention.

6. The huge silver airplane landed at the airport.

7. The weather forecaster predicted rain for the weekend.

8. The new chef served delicious ham sandwiches for lunch.

9. The football fans cheered wildly.

10. A single yellow crocus peeped from under the snow.

Unit 2: Nouns

• •

▶ **Subtest 1** Write *P* above each proper noun, *C* above each common noun, and *col.* above each noun that is both common and collective.

1. The team sold candy to raise money for a trip to Chicago.

2. Aunt Jane brought her famous pie to the picnic.

3. The crowd groaned when Matt missed his shot.

4. I would love to ride on a dogsled.

5. The red truck skidded around the curve.

6. Our class voted to donate money to the victims of the hurricane.

7. That group won a Grammy for the best classical performance.

8. Roberta emphasized the accomplishments of our band.

9. My mom and dad built a patio.

10. A gigantic flock of birds landed in the field across the road.

11. The board voted to allow the meeting.

12. The cast of the play included Maria and Hakim.

13. Tod and his family saw a herd of wild buffalo on their trip to Montana.

14. Close the curtains if it's too light in the room.

15. Would anyone be interested in starting a social club?

16. My brother plays a trombone in the marching band.

17. The program described a trip to the Himalaya Mountains in Nepal.

18. The jury returned to the courtroom with solemn looks on their faces.

19. Samantha needs new glasses.

20. Donyel had never seen such a pleased audience.

▶ **Subtest 2** Write the form of the noun indicated in parentheses.

1. Max (possessive) _____

2. tax (plural) _____

3. players (possessive) _____

4. wishes (singular) _____

5. fox (plural) _____

6. Ms. Alvarez (possessive) _____

7. babies (singular) _____

8. piano (plural) _____

9. nurses (possessive) _____

10. turkeys (singular) _____

11. movie (plural) _____

12. family (plural) _____

13. democracy (possessive) _____

14. bus (plural) _____

15. leaves (singular) _____

16. kittens (possessive) _____

17. echo (plural) _____

18. pilot (possessive) _____

19. jackets (possessive) _____

20. key (plural) _____

21. Charles (possessive) _____

22. hero (possessive) _____

23. match (plural) _____

24. penny (plural) _____

Unit 3: Verbs

•••

▶ **Subtest 1** Circle each action verb. If there is a direct object, draw one line under it. If there is an indirect object, draw two lines under it.

1. The player for the Lakers shot the ball well.

2. Kristy gave Amy a pair of gloves.

3. My brother's dog ate quickly.

4. The farmer plants soybeans on his farm.

5. The new store at the mall offers customers many choices.

6. Michelle tossed Ian the foam ball.

7. Curtis bought a book of old photographs.

8. Would you bring me that newspaper, please?

9. Kristina called a while ago.

10. The lifeguard will teach us water safety.

▶ **Subtest 2** Circle each linking verb. Write *PN* above each predicate noun and *PA* above each predicate adjective.

1. My mother looked very pretty for her date last night.

2. The situation seemed hopeless for the hero of the movie.

3. Brittany will become president of the Math Club next month.

4. The puppy was tired after its walk.

5. I was feeling responsible for the team's defeat.

6. Coach Rodriguez was coach of the year.

7. Jason looked proud of his achievement.

8. These flowers smell fabulous!

9. Your eyes appear blue in certain kinds of light.

10. My locker mate is the best player on the junior varsity volleyball team.

▶ **Subtest 3** Write *pres. prog.* in the blank if the verb in italics is present progressive, *past prog.* if it is past progressive, *pres perf.* if it is present perfect, and *past perf.* if it is past perfect.

_____ 1. Iris and Robin *had gone* to the beach.

_____ 2. The robins *were singing* in the trees outside Allison's window.

_____ 3. Many ships *have sunk* in that area.

_____ 4. We *are planning* our presentation.

_____ 5. *Had* Suzanne ever *eaten* Korean food before last night?

_____ 6. The buckskin horse *is trotting* across the pasture.

_____ 7. The soldiers *were following* their orders.

_____ 8. The 49ers *have won* five Super Bowls.

_____ 9. The maple trees *had lost* all their leaves.

_____ 10. This pen *is running* out of ink.

_____ 11. Shelley's grandmother *has collected* figurines for fifty years.

_____ 12. Felice *was buying* groceries for her family.

_____ 13. My dad *had wanted* to attend the play.

_____ 14. Chapa and Kai *are visiting* their cousins in New Mexico.

_____ 15. Nguyen *has* just *moved* here from Denver.

_____ 16. I *was wondering* about that part of the movie.

_____ 17. Most birds *have flown* south by the beginning of December.

_____ 18. *Is* Luisa *coming* to the game tonight?

_____ 19. The neighbor's dog Mitzi *had run* out into the street.

_____ 20. The cowboy *was putting* on his spurs.

▶ **Subtest 4** Draw a line under each helping verb. Circle each main verb.

1. The dog had eaten all the meat loaf!

2. Basir's mother was applying for a new job.

3. Michael Jordan did attend the University of North Carolina.

4. Have you seen Ms. Maldonado this afternoon?

5. The screen door is banging in the wind.

6. Ahmed has never ridden on a roller coaster.

7. Do gerbils make interesting pets?

8. The leaves are blowing all over the yard.

9. His parents were discussing the problem.

10. Does their computer have a CD-ROM drive?

11. You should pass a water tower and a gas station.

12. Could Marissa take me to the pool today?

13. Duane will participate in Sunday's walk-a-thon.

14. Will you have this project ready by Friday?

15. How high can Alfred jump?

▶ **Subtest 5** Write in the blank the tense of the verb indicated in parentheses.

1. The detective _____ clues to the crime. (*seek*, future)

2. The sea otters _____ near the rocks. (*swim*, past progressive)

3. Ricardo _____ his new tie to the meeting. (*wear*, past)

4. The team members _____ the ice water by the bench. (*drink*, present progressive)

5. Shannon _____ the secret to herself for now. (*keep*, present progressive)

6. Our committee _____ that decision in a few days. (*make*, future)

7. Mr. Chang _____ the advanced English class. (*teach*, past progressive)

8. Erika _____ the ball in front of the fence. (*catch*, past)

9. I _____ to wonder about his attitude. (*begin*, present progressive)

10. Ms. Clancy _____ social studies for twenty years. (*teach*, past perfect)

11. People _____ on these park benches every day. (*sit*, present)

12. My dad _____ not _____ well. (*feel*, present progressive)

13. The white horse _____ the parade. (*lead*, future)

14. We _____ this song before in choir. (*sing*, present perfect)

15. Thomas was so tired he _____ until eleven o'clock. (*sleep*, past)

16. Ms. Singh _____ her performance with a song. (*begin*, past)

17. Michael _____ his homework early. (*do*, past perfect)

18. The Diaz twins _____ brownies to the party. (*bring*, present perfect)

19. The new car model _____ not _____ very well.

    (*sell*, present progressive)

20. Daneene _____ twelve bags of nuts would be enough. (*think*, past

    perfect)

21. T. J. and his brother _____ a calf to raise for the state fair. (*buy*, past)

22. Martin _____ the papers on the teacher's desk. (*lay*, past progressive)

23. Cheetahs _____ faster than any other animals. (*run*, present)

24. LaToyah _____ the answer before anyone else. (*know*, past perfect)

25. The dead branch _____ dangerously. (*swing*, present progressive)

26. Randall _____ his book bag in the gym. (*leave*, past)

27. I _____ to the market early in the morning. (*go*, past perfect)

28. On the camping trip they _____ dried food. (*eat*, future)

29. Matt _____ to Omaha with his sister. (*fly*, past)

30. This dishwasher _____ a good value for the money. (*be*, present)

Name _____ Class _____ Date _____

Unit 4: Pronouns

● ●

▶ **Subtest 1** Draw a line under the word in parentheses that correctly completes the sentence. Write *S* in the blank if the word is a subject pronoun. Write *O* if it is an object pronoun.

_____ 1. The person at the door is (she, her).

_____ 2. Maria and (I, me) are going to the game together.

_____ 3. Did you ask (they, them) about the time of the meeting?

_____ 4. (We, Us) don't agree with you on that issue.

_____ 5. Mr. Singh sent (she, her) the book.

_____ 6. The sheep watched (we, us) and finally ambled away.

_____ 7. (They, Them) will meet us at the entrance.

_____ 8. The woman at the International Foods Festival offered (he, him) some

Japanese candy.

_____ 9. Jeannetta gave (me, I) some helpful advice.

_____ 10. When the tree fell, (it, they) made a great crashing sound.

▶ **Subtest 2** Draw a line under each personal pronoun. Draw an arrow from the pronoun to its antecedent.

1. Martin watched the new television show. He really enjoyed it.

2. Rachel asked Robin to call José and Shannon. Did she call them?

3. When the cardinal looked under the birdbath, it saw the cat.

4. My dad and mom were at the play. They thought it was funny.

5. Wait a minute, Terri! You forgot to pick up the letter!

6. Those glasses belong to Ms. Armstrong. Please give them to her.

7. Erin has an Irish name, and she is very proud of it.

8. The Bears are the best team in the league. No one can beat them!

9. The computer Rick has isn't working properly. It is giving him much trouble.

10. If your parents attend the school festival, they will have a good time.

▶ **Subtest 3** Write an appropriate possessive pronoun in the blank.

1. We all laughed as the monkey scratched _____ ear.

2. I believe that green skirt is _____.

3. The history teachers claim that _____ are the most popular classes.

4. I built the model, and I feel it should be _____.

5. Have you found _____ softball glove yet?

6. Jeremy presented _____ report this afternoon.

7. Mom, Dad, and I think the biggest garden in the neighborhood is _____.

8. Carla sent in _____ application for summer art school.

9. I finished my lunch before you finished _____.

10. The salt shaker has lost _____ lid.

▶ **Subtest 4** Draw a line under each indefinite pronoun. Draw two lines under the verb in parentheses that best completes the sentence.

1. Everybody (has, have) friends.

2. Many of the animals on the list (is, are) in danger of becoming extinct.

3. No one (has, have) signed up for volunteer work in the library.

4. Each of the teams (was, were) wearing red uniforms.

5. Some of the students (wastes, waste) their time in study hall.

6. Both of the contestants (knows, know) the answer.

7. Others (has, have) learned to drive in a few weeks.

8. Someone (calls, call) every night at seven.

9. Neither of the girls (gets, get) any kind of exercise.

10. Several of our neighbors (works, work) downtown.

Unit 5: Adjectives

• •

▶ **Subtest 1** Underline each adjective. Above the word write *P* if it is a proper adjective, *art.* if it is an article, and *dem.* if it is a demonstrative adjective.

1. Those fishing boots are English.

2. The koala is a fascinating creature.

3. The class studied gorgeous Nigerian fabrics.

4. These new slippers are made of Australian sheepskin.

5. We wandered for hours along the small country roads.

6. Grandmother enjoys listening to fiction books on tape.

7. The African sunsets are especially beautiful.

8. That tall boy plays on the soccer team.

9. Looking at the spectacular scenery is an important part of a trip to Colorado.

10. Robert built an anemometer to study the weather.

11. Have you tried any of those delicious strawberries?

12. The little sisters sleep in bunk beds.

13. These mushrooms have green mold on them.

14. The garden club helped Mr. Sung plant a vegetable plot.

15. Doug has a Mexican peso and a Swedish krona.

16. This sunflower is the biggest one I've ever seen!

17. Mrs. Ito bought the little brick house at the end of the road.

18. The Amazon forest is in danger from farming and logging.

19. The crossword puzzles in that book are harder than the puzzles in this book.

20. Can you name an Italian dish?

▶ **Subtest 2** **Fill in the blank with the correct form of the adjective in parentheses.**

1. The rust on that shovel is _____ than I thought. (bad)

2. The unabridged dictionary is the _____ book in the school library. (large)

3. Few dogs are _____ than the collie. (beautiful)

4. Nino's makes the _____ pizza in town. (good)

5. This is the _____ pair of boots I've ever owned. (sturdy)

6. Jamal found the study of owls _____ than he had expected. (fascinating)

7. She'll have to do _____ work than she is doing now if she expects to get an A in that class. (much)

8. Denali is the _____ mountain in the United States. (high)

9. Kanya collected _____ signatures on her petition than I did. (many)

10. That was the _____ meat loaf I have ever tasted! (bad)

11. Mr. Morton's parrot is the _____ bird I've ever seen. (tame)

12. Most of our class think apples taste _____ than pears. (good)

13. I have never sat in a _____ chair! (uncomfortable)

14. Danitra has _____ milk in her glass than Tina does. (little)

15. Which person in the class has the _____ brothers and sisters? (many)

16. The detective said that the situation would only become _____ until the thief was caught. (bad)

17. The dangerous mountain pass was the _____ path the pioneers had yet seen. (narrow)

18. Paul annoys his friends by doing the _____ amount of work he can. (little)

19. Is there anything _____ than a ripe peach? (delicious)

20. I have prepared _____ posters than anyone else. (many)

Unit 6: Adverbs

● ●

▶ **Subtest 1** Draw a line under each adverb. Draw an arrow from the adverb to the word or words it modifies.

1. Tamara and her parents often play table tennis.

2. The elderly man stood up and slowly walked away.

3. Put the groceries there.

4. I have never been so surprised in my life!

5. The poodle and the golden retriever were barking loudly.

6. My dad usually cooks dinner for our family.

7. Kia sang the national anthem beautifully.

8. My friends and I seldom disagree about movies.

9. There are several good films in the theaters now.

10. You can put your casserole dish here on the table.

11. Philip nearly choked on a piece of chicken.

12. Your cat is behaving oddly.

13. I will see you later, Sharon.

14. The baby babbled cutely as the adults watched and smiled.

15. Grandfather was very grateful for the birthday presents he received.

▶ **Subtest 2** Underline the first adverb in each sentence. Write *V* if it modifies a verb, *adj.* if it modifies an adjective, and *adv.* if it modifies another adverb.

_____ 1. Our English class is meeting temporarily in the cafeteria.

_____ 2. Pete almost never fails to complete his homework.

_____ 3. Unbelievably, the woodpecker landed on the windowsill.

_____ 4. My great-grandmother speaks quite often of her childhood in Hungary.

_____ 5. The race car entered the dangerous curve rather slowly.

_____ 6. The members of the church donated freely to the emergency fund.

_____ 7. The governor was totally shocked by the result of the election.

_____ 8. The soccer team played badly but eventually tied the game.

_____ 9. Soto felt quite honored to receive the prize for the best essay.

_____ 10. My brother is really proud of his science project.

_____ 11. The horse ran the race in the very fast time of two minutes and one second.

_____ 12. Do you think you did very well on the math exam?

_____ 13. The page was so old that the print was barely readable.

_____ 14. Michael wants to come to the movie, too.

_____ 15. Let's walk to the shopping center together.

_____ 16. The explorer was extremely glad to escape from the snowdrift.

_____ 17. Store the two chemicals absolutely separately to prevent an explosion.

_____ 18. My mom is somewhat disappointed in my grade report this term.

_____ 19. I hardly knew what to think about her comment yesterday.

_____ 20. Natalie is feeling well now after her illness.

▶ **Subtest 3 Supply the correct form of the adverb in parentheses.**

1. Nick's team played _____ than Angela's. (well)

2. The expedition traveled _____ into the desert than any previous explorers had gone. (far)

3. Of all my relatives I have visited _____ with Aunt Jo and Uncle Karl. (long)

4. Winona knows she could succeed if she tried _____. (hard)

5. Because she didn't study, Mindy scored _____ of all the students who took the spelling test. (badly)

6. Try playing the piece _____ than you did last time. (slowly)

7. This parrot talks _____ than my mynah bird. (little)

8. Container A came to a boil _____ than Container B. (rapidly)

9. The little boy answered the queen _____ of all. (politely)

10. Do you feel you know Alex _____ than you know his brother? (well)

11. Felix climbed the rope _____ the second time than the first time. (easily)

12. Rex studies _____ of anyone in the class, but he gets good grades anyway! (little)

13. I've seen *The Lion King* _____ than I've seen *The Dark Crystal*. (recently)

14. Sopranos, please sing your part _____ than usual. (softly)

15. Lawrence's buddy at summer camp swam _____ than anyone else in his cabin. (badly)

▶ **Subtest 4 Draw a line under the word in parentheses that best completes each sentence.**

1. That brand of compact-disc player (almost, most) never breaks.

2. The new paint job on your bike looks (good, well).

3. The red fox darted (quick, quickly) out of sight.

4. Winning the first place trophy (sure, surely) is a thrill!

5. Please don't feel (bad, badly); it wasn't your fault.

6. When Nina's name wasn't called, she turned around and (sad, sadly) walked toward the door.

7. The old engine on our lawn mower doesn't burn gasoline very (efficient, efficiently).

8. Reynaldo runs long distances faster than anyone else in our grade, but he's a (slow, slowly) sprinter.

9. We could tell Mom wasn't feeling very (good, well).

10. Having the second-place lamb at the county fair is a (real, really) accomplishment.

11. Seán's grandmother fell on the ice and hurt herself (bad, badly).

12. The amaryllis is certainly a (strange, strangely) plant.

13. (Surprising, Surprisingly), no one in our class has seen the movie yet.

14. When rock climbing, it's important to get a (sure, surely) grip on the ledge.

15. Our neighbors' car was (total, totally) destroyed in an accident.

16. When asking for information, it's important not to be (rude, rudely).

17. Jonathan said that (almost, most) of the members would attend the meeting.

18. It was (unusual, unusually) to see three woodpeckers in one tree.

19. How (good, well) did you do on the history quiz?

20. If you're (real, really) sure this is what you want, go ahead.

▶ **Subtest 5** **Place a check (✔) beside each correct sentence.**

_____ **1.** Dad said nothing about going to the ice cream store after dinner.

_____ **2.** They hadn't never expected us to win the league championship.

_____ **3.** She wanted to borrow some money from me, but I said I didn't have none.

_____ **4.** I didn't tell no one about the secret gift.

_____ **5.** The librarian had nothing to say to the detective when he questioned him.

_____ **6.** You can't tell my dog Prince nothing about being obedient.

_____ **7.** Don't expect him to listen to no rock music.

_____ **8.** We won't ever have a better vacation than the time we went to Disney World.

_____ **9.** David couldn't find his soccer shoes nowhere.

_____ **10.** There isn't anyone in Greek legends who did more good deeds than Hercules.

_____ **11.** I haven't never stayed up so late before.

_____ **12.** Georgie didn't spend any money at the mall.

_____ **13.** Wasn't anyone prepared for the math quiz Wednesday?

_____ **14.** Don't stop to talk with nobody on the way.

_____ **15.** I can't get anything done today.

Unit 7: Prepositions, Conjunctions, and Interjections

● ●

▶ **Subtest 1** **Draw one line under each prepositional phrase and two lines under its object.**

1. Aviva saw the baby bird above the large window.

2. Expect the visitors at seven in the evening.

3. The cows suddenly ran down the steep hill.

4. In the photo I'm standing in front of Deon and Tracie.

5. The football players burst through the paper sign.

6. We decided to meet at the pizza shop after the show.

7. Dad always puts a gold star on top of the tree.

8. The telephone call was for Mr. Olivero.

9. The squirrel jumped onto the roof from the oak tree.

10. My little brother found a worm under a rock.

11. Aside from my mom everyone in my family has red hair.

12. Would you like french fries with your hamburger?

13. The scientist poured the liquid into the beaker.

14. When you're camping, it's good to have a tent roof over your head.

15. The dog ran away from the girl.

16. Darcie signed up for the drama club instead of hockey.

17. He found the softball among the weeds by the stream.

18. Angie squeezed against the wall behind the door.

19. Charles took a stopwatch out of his pocket.

20. The submarine traveled thousands of miles beneath the surface of the sea.

21. The vice president of the club spoke to the parents' group.

22. According to this book, that's not the right answer.

23. We had our picnic beneath the large maple tree.

24. Ms. Van Houten received a letter from her sister.

25. My grandfather immigrated to America during the Vietnam War.

▶ **Subtest 2 Draw a line under the pronoun in parentheses that best completes each sentence.**

1. For (who, whom) is that letter intended?

2. What did Donna say about Lori and (I, me)?

3. During the dinner I sat across from (she, her).

4. Do you recognize the woman standing beside (we, us)?

5. (Who, Whom) requested that song?

6. Let's keep this a secret between you and (I, me).

7. The tall tree near (he, him) is a sycamore.

8. The package was addressed to my uncle and (I, me).

9. The decorations were finished by the art club and (they, them).

10. To (who, whom) was your father speaking just now?

▶ **Subtest 3 Write in the blank *adj.* if the prepositional phrase functions as an adjective phrase or *adv.* if it functions as an adverb phrase. Circle the word it modifies.**

_____ **1.** The outlook for victory seemed doubtful without the star player.

_____ **2.** The boy ran past the drugstore.

_____ **3.** The painting by the Danish artist is probably my favorite.

_____ **4.** The driver raced his car around the track.

_____ **5.** According to Johan that song was number one.

_____ **6.** The two men trudged slowly across the burning desert sands.

_____ **7.** We found our cat behind the sofa.

_____ **8.** All of the students signed the letter.

_____ **9.** Pineapples are important to the economy of Hawaii.

_____ **10.** The dog under the tree is a spaniel.

_____ **11.** Instead of Jordan the teacher chose Marcie.

_____ **12.** The house near the river belongs to the Lopezes.

_____ **13.** My mother hadn't seen her sister since 1991.

_____ **14.** Laurie read a newspaper article about the new factory.

_____ **15.** The hummingbird was hovering above the feeder.

_____ **16.** The cows were mooing before the storm.

_____ **17.** During halftime, we can get a hot dog.

_____ **18.** The edge of the bikepath is slippery.

_____ **19.** The important highway runs east out of town.

_____ **20.** Indiana is located between Illinois and Ohio.

_____ **21.** I want the white shirt with the blue stripes.

_____ **22.** Thomas ran farther along the forest edge.

_____ **23.** A snowball whizzed past my ear.

_____ **24.** The American flag on top of the fort waved proudly.

_____ **25.** Those flowers are rare in mountain regions.

▶ **Subtest 4** Write *prep.* in the blank if the italicized word is used as a preposition. Write *adv.* if it is used as an adverb.

_____ **1.** I'm sure Monica's lost kitten will turn *up* soon.

_____ **2.** The plant our science class was growing fell *out* the open window.

_____ **3.** A sea bird was building a nest *below* the edge of the cliff.

_____ **4.** Kara thought she had her wristwatch *on.*

_____ **5.** Everyone at the picnic ran *inside* when it started to rain.

_____ **6.** Butterflies were fluttering in the sun *above* my head.

_____ **7.** If you don't know the meaning of a word, look it up *in* a dictionary.

_____ **8.** The scout leader hiked first, with the rest of the scouts following *behind.*

_____ **9.** The cavalry charged *down* the hill.

_____ **10.** I'm afraid we'll have to do our report *over.*

▶ **Subtest 5** Write *conj.* above each conjunction and *int.* above each interjection.

1. Hey! That's my jacket!

2. Oh! Are dolphins and whales mammals?

3. Oswaldo is talkative and friendly, but his sister is quiet and reserved.

4. Rats! Paula missed the shot!

5. Well, I could go with you to the bowling alley.

6. At Lucia's party, she served ice cream, peanuts, and birthday cake.

7. For my second period class next year, I plan to take Spanish or Latin.

8. Both Roberto and Kazu finished the test early.

9. Mom just hit her thumb with a hammer. Ouch!

10. Do you prefer your hot dog with mustard or with ketchup?

11. Oops, I knocked the birthday cake onto the floor.

12. Hurray! Our team has won the state championship!

13. Julie likes her new dwarf frog, but it eats the young guppies.

14. Either I ride my bike to the park, or I get a ride with my sister.

15. Both Yuri and Tina want to be astronauts.

16. Camilla would love to study painting, but she doesn't have time for it.

17. Phew! That vinegar has an awfully strong odor.

18. Neither Baron Reginald nor Countess Vanessa had considered the consequences.

19. Both Clare and Justin volunteered immediately, but Nicole remained silent.

20. What! You borrowed my grammar book and left it at home!

21. Alas, the hero died of a broken heart.

22. I have never taken riding lessons, but I would love to ride a horse.

23. The children asked for water or juice to drink.

24. Not only George but also Yoshi said the movie was great.

25. Wow, that's a real three-winged World War I fighter airplane!

Unit 8: Subject-Verb Agreement

▶ **Subtest 1** Underline the simple subject in each sentence. Circle the correct form of the verb in parentheses. Some sentences may have compound subjects.

1. Neither Canada nor the United States (is, are) a crowded country.

2. (Does, Do) all kinds of birds fly south for the winter?

3. Animals in the zoo (is, are) enjoyed by thousands of people each day.

4. Dametri and you (has, have) the best grades in the class.

5. There (is, are) many reasons for my silence on this matter.

6. Corey (collects, collect) baseball cards.

7. Both sheep and cows (grazes, graze) in that pasture over there.

8. Students at our school (helps, help) with playground maintenance.

9. Here (is, are) the answers to your questions.

10. Tim or his parents (plans, plan) to attend the neighborhood festival.

11. (Has, Have) your cousins ever visited a foreign country?

12. There (was, were) not any people sitting in the last row of the balcony.

13. Our picnic under the trees (was, were) delightful.

14. Both tulips and hyacinths (is, are) popular spring flowers.

15. The important test on World Wars I and II (determines, determine) half of our grade in history.

16. (Does, Do) the racer use gasoline to run his car?

17. Here (goes, go) the prize-winning kites!

18. Either math or science (is, are) Lisa's best subject.

19. (Was, Were) you thinking about entering the drama contest?

20. Something (needs, need) to be done about the litter around the school.

21. The gerbil and a white rat (is, are) attracting a lot of attention at the pet show.

22. The different acts during the telethon (was, were) entertaining.

23. No one (has, have) found my earring yet.

24. Mr. Garcia or his brothers (hopes, hope) to read that book next.

25. Both the maples and the red oak (turns, turn) lovely colors in the autumn.

26. Weasels (is, are) surprisingly small creatures.

27. Deena's aunt and cousins (lives, live) in Dallas.

28. Under the table (is, are) the missing cards.

29. Here (ends, end) the legends about the great hero.

30. (Is, Are) we invited to the party or not?

31. Either Mitchell or the De Grassi twins (is, are) going to perform next.

32. There (wasn't, weren't) any reason for the traffic jam.

33. Gerald's mice and guinea pig (stays, stay) in cages in the basement.

34. (Does, Do) Zora want to join the Math Club?

35. Michael (has, have) everything needed to complete the project.

36. Both carrots and celery (tastes, taste) good raw or cooked.

37. Here (is, are) the tickets you requested.

38. The tables beside the flower bed (is, are) already taken.

39. (Was, Were) you asked to take part in the school cleanup campaign?

40. Neither rain nor snow (prevents, prevent) the delivery of the mail.

Unit 9: Diagraming Sentences

● ●

▶ **Subtest 1** **Diagram each sentence.**

1. Pete caught the ball and quickly threw it back.

2. Give this plate of food to your sister.

3. Have you and your family visited your cousins in Guatemala?

4. Marci offered Dawn the extra tickets.

5. The sky is becoming clear and the heavy rain has stopped.

6. Lisa was the tallest girl in the sixth grade.

7. Pablo and I washed and dried the dishes.

10. The flowers in Judy's garden are quite beautiful.

8. Gwen was elected treasurer of the club.

11. The new ceiling fans cool this room nicely.

9. The contestants eagerly waited for the judges' decision.

12. The O'Hara's basement flooded again.

Unit 10: Usage Glossary

• •

▶ **Subtest 1** **Choose the best word from the list and write it in the blank. Use each word only once.**

accept	two	lay	then
already	chose	lie	to
all ready	except	loose	too
among	its	lose	who's
between	it's	than	whose

1. First the squirrel collected the walnuts; _____ it buried them.

2. Paul walked across the stage to _____ his prize.

3. My favorite restaurant has changed _____ menu.

4. Does Nikki know _____ basketball this is?

5. Ms. Montgomery asked for _____ volunteers.

6. Ask Allan _____ coming to the movie with us.

7. Just _____ the pie pan on the counter.

8. The Wisemans got a ticket because their dog ran _____ .

9. Nina got an A in every course _____ history.

10. If your sister isn't feeling well, she ought to _____ down.

11. What time are you going _____ the cafeteria today?

12. If Taini doesn't close her purse, she's going to _____ something important.

13. A cheetah can run faster _____ any other animal.

14. We think _____ a shame Toby had to miss the play.

15. If you order the special, you get an egg roll, _____ .

16. The committee will decide _____ the three options suggested.

17. Kara has _____ finished her homework.

18. The camera club cannot decide _____ a contest and an exhibition.

19. My brother _____ to take geometry.

20. Our class is _____ for the field trip.

▶ **Subtest 2** **Underline the word in parentheses that best completes each sentence.**

1. When (their, they're) playing well, the Dolphins are one of the NFL's best teams.

2. Please (sit, set) that plate of brownies on the table.

3. When the room grew too hot, Dad asked me to (raise, rise) the window.

4. Did your plane (leave, let) on time last night?

5. When Regina arrived, I was (all ready, already) to go.

6. Put the chair (beside, besides) Chris.

7. Dad is having a hard time deciding (between, among) the chicken and the fish.

8. Which movie would you (choose, chose) to see on your birthday?

9. Uncle Frank isn't (all together, altogether) sure about his decision.

10. Dogs (learn, teach) simple tricks very quickly, but cats don't.

11. (Leave, Let) me help you with those grocery bags.

12. The bus had (all ready, already) left when we reached the bus stop.

13. Our neighbors let (their, they're) dog bark all night long.

14. Which fantasy books have you read (beside, besides) *The Hobbit?*

15. Martin (choose, chose) not to play in last week's chess tournament.

16. The work will go fast if we divide it (between, among) Randall, Lena, you, and me.

17. Jessica wants to (sit, set) next to William at the assembly.

18. The almanac will tell us when the sun will (raise, rise).

19. My dad can (learn, teach) you how to paddle a canoe.

20. We will have more fun if we go (all together, altogether) to the basketball game.

Unit 11: Capitalization

• •

▶ **Subtest 1** Mark each letter that should be capitalized by drawing three lines under it. Mark each letter that should be lowercase by drawing a slash (/) through it.

1. The Police Officer said, "may I see your driver's license, please?"

2. The high school band sponsored an ice-cream social on labor day.

3. Both Ronald Reagan and George Bush were members of the republican party.

4. erica's Grandmother was born in lithuania.

5. I saw that actress's picture in *people.*

6. The picture on the next page is of the lincoln memorial in washington, d.c.

7. Both oldsmobiles and pontiacs are made by general motors corporation.

8. Phil's Father explained that He would pick him up at Five o'clock.

9. Carol Mosely Braun is the first african american woman to serve in the Senate.

10. The ship sailed South under a broiling Sun.

11. Patricia Alexander was elected Governor in the last Election.

12. The speaker at the graduation ceremony was general Colin Powell.

13. Marlon is camping this week with the boy scouts.

14. Her appointment with the Dentist for next tuesday was canceled.

15. A boat sailing East across the atlantic ocean from new york would reach portugal.

16. I can't believe we won second prize, a genuine bouncemaster trampoline!

17. During the war Jan's Grandfather was stationed in africa.

18. Many of the fastest-growing cities in the United States are in the southwest.

19. Ms. Geldis is reading to us from *huckleberry finn.*

20. The civil war was fought between the North and the south.

21. "Don't forget the most important thing," mom added. "have fun."

22. The winds were Westerly at a speed of ten Miles Per Hour.

23. Does Ken griffey jr. still play for the seattle Mariners?

24. "Yes, major," the soldier replied, "The cavalry is ready to attack."

25. Vicki's family stopped at the grand canyon on their way East.

26. The knox county 4-H club is having a bake sale to raise Money.

27. The explorer stated, "the Continent of Australia is yet to be fully explored."

28. dear dr. Andreas,

29. Did deon say that Nobody would be admitted late?

30. Sanibel island is in the gulf of mexico south of tampa.

31. The part of the State where we live, Western ohio, is quite flat.

32. Monique's birthday is in the Fall, in either october or november.

33. "Few students," the principal explained, "Have ever scored this high."

34. My older brother is learning to speak chinese at the university of wisconsin.

35. the sign on the door read Linda Dodds, m.d.

36. The basketball players all drank powerblitz sports drink.

37. The company whose catalog i received is in san antonio, texas.

38. The city of new orleans is at the mouth of the mississippi river.

39. Michael replied, "not everyone on the west coast is a surfer, you know."

40. For his birthday dinner, dad chose a korean restaurant.

41. sincerely yours, Shawna Martinez

42. "don't believe everything you read in that magazine," Sandie said with a laugh. "in fact, don't believe anything!"

43. Ruben wondered If the baby lamb might be injured.

44. My Grandparents sent us a postcard of an italian church built during the renaissance.

45. The old Office Building on main street burned down last night.

Unit 12: Punctuation

• •

▶ **Subtest 1 Add end punctuation and commas where necessary.**

1. Oh, my gosh

2. Margaret would you hand Joan this pen?

3. Yes the Florida Everglades are a fascinating place to visit.

4. Heather's favorite animals at the zoo were the elephants the pandas and the electric eels.

5. My dad enjoys reading fiction but my mom prefers nonfiction.

6. At first I was unsure which game to choose

7. Please don't close the window

8. Instead of apples peaches were served at the picnic

9. Dear Aunt Sylvia

10. William Tecumseh Sherman is a famous general from Ohio too.

11. The fetlock as you know is the part of a horse's leg just above the hoof.

12. Does the new term begin in August 1997

13. Kristy Yamaguchi won the Olympic gold medal in figure skating and Mary Lou Retton won in gymnastics.

14. Grandpa's new address is 912 Adams Street Owings Mills Maryland 21117.

15. Norma Lawton M.D. will perform the eye surgery.

16. No I've never known anyone who raised pigeons.

17. What an amazing shot

18. The two teams represented Oshkosh Wisconsin and Derry New Hampshire in the tournament.

19. After the Civil War Reconstruction began in the South.

20. Dr. Santiago I don't know how to thank you for your help.

21. Where did your grandparents go on vacation

22. That pitcher can throw a fastball a curveball and a change-up.

23. We can see the Native American exhibits first or we can look at the antique cars.

24. Franklin's birth date is December 2 1984.

25. Except for Michael Jake is probably my best friend.

26. My three favorite colors are cherry red shocking pink and royal purple.

27. Your friend Tina

28. In the bushes behind the garage Maria saw a ferret.

29. "Don't begin" cautioned the coach "until I blow my whistle."

30. The police officer wondered if she should give the driver a ticket

▶ **Subtest 2 Add punctuation and italics (underline) where necessary.**

1. Frederick's flight was scheduled to leave at 618 P.M.

2. The painting at the museum Doug said was of a Pueblo village

3. Its too bad we couldnt go scuba diving.

4. Joe DiMaggio was a great baseball player for the New York Yankees his career stretched from 1936 to 1951.

5. Katies family has lived in Dallas, New York, and Miami.

6. My favorite of Edgar Allan Poes stories is The Pit and the Pendulum

7. Does your sister in law have a dachshund?

8. The film director threw down his clipboard in disgust and yelled Cut

9. The dingo is a wild dog found in Australia explained the speaker.

10. Rex loves Robert Frosts poem The Road Not Taken

11. Mandy read a story to the childrens group at the library.

12. Ms. Randolph whispered Be as quiet as you can

13. The math test will cover fractions decimals percentages multiplication and division.

14. If youre looking for Mr. Menendezs apartment, its across the street.

15. Thai food is usually very spicy Japanese food often is not.

16. Mr. Maxwell and I planted the following herbs parsley, dill, basil, marjoram, and sage.

17. My grandmothers mother in law was the first female dentist in the state.

18. The farmer said The calf is limping badly on its injured leg

19. Stephanie shouted Wait for me!

20. Juanita and I read about alligators and crocodiles in Natural History magazine.

21. The girls basketball team lost a close game to Moorehead Middle School.

22. Dominica is a tiny country in the West Indies Christopher Columbus landed there in 1493.

23. Fifty eight boats were tied to the dock.

24. Did Kenneth say I'm not interested

25. Which one of Pearl Jams albums do you like best

26. Kias favorite book is A Night to Remember its about the Titanic.

27. Arent those ice skates hers?

28. Next year, hes taking math, history, Spanish, and science.

29. Dear Manager of Customer Relations

30. Felipe asked What's the assignment for Monday

▶ **Subtest 3** **Place a check beside each sentence that uses abbreviations correctly.**

_____ **1.** The football season begins in Aug. and ends in Jan.

_____ **2.** Jason's uncle is an F.B.I. agent in California.

_____ **3.** Send your sweepstakes entry to P.O Box 125, San Diego, Ca 92109.

_____ **4.** Dr. Brian witnessed a car accident on Valleyview Ave.

_____ **5.** The special guest at the dinner was Mr. Harold MacGinnity.

_____ **6.** A French army invaded England in 1066 a.d.

_____ **7.** Hiroki Fukuzawa, MD, has opened an office in the medical center.

_____ **8.** The eclipse will begin at 1:39 P.M.

_____ **9.** Oh, my gosh, that vulture must be four ft. long!

_____ **10.** A famous battle was fought near the Greek island of Salamis in 480 B.C.

_____ **11.** Next Tuesday, an astronaut is coming to our school to talk about NASA.

_____ **12.** I set my alarm for 6:00 AM, but I didn't get up until 7:00 AM.

_____ **13.** DR Samantha Willis is our family doctor.

_____ **14.** Is Mrs. Lesoto entered in the next race?

_____ **15.** John D. Rockefeller Jr. was the father of an unelected vice president of the United States.

▶ **Subtest 4 Underline the term in parentheses that best completes the sentence.**

1. More than (sixty-four percent, 64 percent) of the voters supported the school levy.

2. The (three, 3) longest rivers in the world are the Nile, the Amazon, and the Yangtze.

3. (Two hundred eighty-six, 286) pigs were entered in the fair.

4. Frieda was so happy she hugged the (first, 1st) person who walked through the door.

5. The government spent more than (680 million, 680,000,000) dollars on the project.

6. Matt and Ethan will meet us at the pool at (7, seven) o'clock.

7. The vote at the business meeting was (eleven, 11) in favor and 268 opposed.

8. We signed up to work at the recycling station on April (21, twenty-first).

9. The airplane flew (three thousand six hundred seventy-one, 3,671) miles before landing in Tokyo.

10. Reynaldo's dad called to say he would pick him up at (5:15, five fifteen) P.M.

11. The winning candidate received (fifty-one, 51) percent of the vote.

12. The buffet included three main courses and (ten, 10) side dishes.

13. Cathy's room number is (four hundred seventy-five, 475).

14. Jason became the (fifth, 5th) student to choose Thailand as the topic of his report.

15. There were only (14,000, fourteen thousand) fans in the huge stadium.

16. The concert will begin at (eight, 8) o'clock this evening.

17. A survey showed that 230 of the (three hundred, 300) students preferred pizza for lunch.

18. Aunt Elizabeth is getting married on May (fifteenth, 15).

19. Only (two hundred twenty-four, 224) days remain until our trip to Greece.

20. Because of parent-teacher conferences school will end at (one-thirty, 1:30) P.M. today.

Unit 13: Vocabulary and Spelling

• •

▶ **Subtest 1 Circle the best answer to each question.**

1. Andrew is quite outgoing, but his brother Matt is reserved.
   Which word is a synonym of *reserved?*

   loud   tall   quiet   nervous

2. At the canine house at the zoo, we saw wolves, coyotes, and Australian dogs.
   Which animal is also a canine?

   cat   gorilla   mouse   dog

3. Our last goal attempt in the soccer match was disallowed by the referee, so our team lost.
   What does the prefix in *disallowed* mean?

   not   before   without   too much

4. "Hey, Ryan," said Jon, "why are you looking so glum? You should be thrilled."
   Which word is an antonym of *glum?*

   sad   happy   disappointed   tired

5. Grandfather said that he would like to come to the concert, too.
   Which word is a homonym of *too?*

   also   very   tool   two

6. I was surprised by the man's rudeness when I asked for directions.
   What does the suffix in *rudeness* mean?

   quality of   without   person belonging to   one who

7. Jan was apprehensive about her choir audition, but when she started singing, all her
   fears vanished.
   Which word is a synonym for *apprehensive?*

   anxious   serious   happy   understanding

8. The waiter at the fancy restaurant answered all our questions thoroughly and cordially.
   Which word is not a synonym of *cordially?*

   politely   courteously   graciously   angrily

9. Ty threw the ball to first base.
   Which work is a homonym of *threw?*

   tossed   true   through   held

10. I don't know why that man misunderstood the clear and simple directions. Which word is an antonym of *misunderstood?*

   misinterpreted   understood   mistook   confused

▶ **Subtest 2** **Underline the word that best completes each sentence.**

1. Dad found the radio on top of the (bookkcase, bookcase).

2. The boxer (trained, trainned) more than six months for the championship fight.

3. The Martinezes will be (stayying, staying) with relatives in El Paso.

4. The truck that (passed, past) us on the freeway was carrying oranges and lemons.

5. We watched as the mother fox took food to the baby (foxes, foxxes).

6. Juan was (to, too) tired to watch television.

7. The climate here in Oregon is very (changeable, changable).

8. A tin roof sundae is definitely my favorite (dessert, desert)!

9. Erica brought her radio-(controlled, controled) car to my house.

10. Because she has been married twice, my mom has had two (father-in-laws, fathers-in-law).

11. Rae Anne is (fully, fullly) aware of her responsibilities.

12. Ask your sister if she (received, recieved) the invitation to my party.

13. Our (nieghborhod, neighborhood) is foll of friendly and helpful people.

14. The hospital nursery was filled with (babys, babies), each one crying loudly.

15. I (spotted, spoted) a beautiful goldfinch sitting on a branch in that tree.

16. We study history so we won't repeat the mistakes of the (past, passed).

17. Katya scooped up a (handdful, handful) of the tiny seashells.

18. Jacob (denies, denys) it, but I know he put the frog in the camp counselor's sleeping bag.

19. The oak tree was the only one with any (leafs, leaves) left on it.

20. Kerstin missed the slumber party because she (developed, developped) tonsillitis.

Name _____ Class _____ Date _____

Unit 14: Composition

●●

▶ **Subtest 1** Edit the following paragraphs. Then rewrite the paragraphs based on your editing marks.

Last week our music class go on an interesting Field Trip. We took a tour of Great Sounds Recordding Studio. 1 of the engineers, ms. tanaka, showed us how a recording studio works, there was one room for the musicians and another room four the engineers. Them, could see each other threw a large glass window and talk to each other through an intercom.

After the musicians recorded the music; a singger arrived to record the vocals. she wore headphones. The engineers plaied the newly recorded music through the headphones and recorded the singers' voice as she sing the song. Ms. Tanaka explaned, that the voice and music would be combined electronically so that the song would sound really good. When I grow up; i defanately want to work in a recording studio.

_____

_____

_____

_____

_____

_____

_____

_____

▶ **Subtest 2** Rewrite each topic sentence to make it more interesting. Add supporting details.

1. The park was filled with people.

_____

_____

2. One book remained on the shelf.

_____

_____

_____

3. I heard a noise.

_____

_____

4. The sand felt warm.

_____

_____

5. Kelly could smell something baking.

_____

_____

_____

6. The building was empty.

_____

_____

7. Keith wrote a letter.

_____

_____

8. Jennifer helped her teacher.

_____

_____

_____

9. The movie seemed funny.

_____

_____

10. Federico received a package.

_____

_____

_____

▶ **Subtest 3 Read the letter, and then answer the questions that follow.**

Dear Miki,

   I am so excited about having you as a pen pal! I hope you are excited, too. There are so many things to tell you about life in the United States.

   I live in Silver Spring, Maryland, which is close to Washington, D.C., our nation's capital. Sometimes my class takes field trips to visit the monuments and museums. The Smithsonian Institution is a museum with all kinds of interesting exhibits. They even have props from famous movies and television shows. If you ever come to the United States, that is one place you will definitely want to visit.

   Please write soon and tell me what else you would like to know about life in the United States. What is life like in Japan? What is your neighborhood like? What do you do for fun? I like to play soccer and computer games.

Your pen pal,

Kelly

1. Who is Miki?

_____

2. Why is Kelly writing to Miki?

_____

_____

3. Is this a good example of a pen pal letter? Why or why not?

_____

_____

_____

4. How could this letter be improved?

_____

_____

_____

_____

_____

▶ **Subtest 4** **Answer the following questions about this opinion letter.**

Dear Editor of *YP*:

   What were you thinking of? How could you put an article as stupid as "Cards to Collect" in your magazine? Everyone knows which baseball cards are valuable. Seeing pictures of the cards I want but can't get is depressing. Why don't you put good stories in your magazine instead? Of course, if you do, I won't see them. I am never buying your magazine again!

Sincerely,

Josh Mularsky

1. Who is Josh Mularsky?

   _____

2. Why is he writing to the Editor of *YP* magazine?

   _____

   _____

3. Is this a good example of an opinion letter? Why or why not?

   _____

   _____

   _____

   _____

4. How could this letter be improved?

   _____

   _____

   _____

   _____

Answer Key to Testing Program

UNIT 1: SUBJECTS, PREDICATES, AND SENTENCES

Subtest 1 (type of sentence; end punctuation)
1. dec; .
2. exc.; !
3. int.; ?
4. imp.; .
5. dec.; .
6. imp.; .
7. exc.; ! *or* dec.; .
8. int.; ?
9. dec.; .
10. int.; ?

Subtest 2
1. RO
2. C
3. S
4. F
5. C
6. RO
7. S
8. F
9. C
10. F

Subtest 3 (compound subject; *compound predicate*)
1. sister, I
2. *wanted, offered*
3. guitarist, drummer; *bowed, left*
4. Bears, raccoons
5. Sea shells, starfish; *washed, lay*
6. *cut, gave*
7. Basketball, soccer
8. *collect, pollinate*
9. finches, chickadees; *sang, twittered*
10. uncle, friend

Subtest 4 (simple subject; *simple predicate*)
1. Nobody; *would believe*
2. Steven; *has worked*
3. pens; *are*
4. friends; *will visit*
5. senator; *gave*
6. airplane; *landed*
7. forecaster; *predicted*
8. chef; *served*
9. fans; *cheered*
10. crocus; *peeped*

UNIT 2: NOUNS

Subtest 1
1. team, col.; candy, C; money, C; trip, C; Chicago, P
2. Aunt Jane, P; pie, C; picnic, C
3. crowd, col.; Matt, P; shot, C
4. ride, C; dogsled, C
5. truck, C; curve, C
6. class, col.; money, C; victims, C; hurricane, C
7. group, col.; Grammy, P; performance, C
8. Roberta, P; accomplishments, C; band, col.
9. mom, C; dad, C; patio, C
10. flock, col.; birds, C; field, C; road, C
11. board, col.; meeting, C
12. cast, col.; play, C; Maria, P; Hakim, P
13. Tod, P; family, col.; herd, col.; buffalo, C; trip, C; Montana, P
14. curtains, C; room, C
15. anyone, C; club, col.
16. brother, C; trombone, C; band, col.
17. program, C; trip, C; Himalaya Mountains, P; Nepal, P
18. jury, col.; courtroom, C; looks, C; faces, C
19. Samantha, P; glasses, C
20. Donyel, P; audience, col.

Subtest 2
1. Max's
2. taxes
3. players'
4. wish
5. foxes
6. Ms. Alvarez's
7. baby
8. pianos
9. nurses'
10. turkey
11. movies
12. families
13. democracy's
14. buses
15. leaf
16. kittens'
17. echoes
18. pilot's
19. jackets'
20. keys
21. Charles's
22. hero's
23. matches
24. pennies

UNIT 3: VERBS

Subtest 1 (verb, *indirect object*, **direct object**)
1. shot, **ball**
2. gave, *Amy*, **pair**
3. ate
4. plants, **soybeans**
5. offers, *customers*, **choices**
6. tossed, *Ian*, **ball**
7. bought, **book**
8. Would bring, *me*, **newspaper**
9. called
10. will teach, *us*, **safety**

Subtest 2 (verb, *predicate noun*, **predicate adjective**)
1. looked, **pretty**
2. seemed, **hopeless**
3. will become, *president*
4. was, **tired**
5. was feeling, **responsible**
6. was, *coach*
7. looked, **proud**
8. smell, **fabulous**
9. appear, **blue**
10. is, *player*

Subtest 3
1. past perf.
2. past prog.
3. pres. perf.
4. pres. prog.
5. past perf.
6. pres. prog.
7. past prog.
8. pres. perf.
9. past perf.
10. pres. prog.
11. pres. perf.
12. past prog.
13. past perf.
14. pres. prog.
15. pres. perf.
16. past prog.
17. pres. perf.
18. pres. prog.
19. past perf.
20. past prog.

Subtest 4 (helping verb **main verb**)
1. had **eaten**
2. was **applying**
3. did **attend**
4. Have **seen**
5. is **banging**
6. has **ridden**
7. Do **make**
8. are **blowing**
9. were **discussing**
10. Does **have**
11. should **pass**
12. Could **take**
13. will **participate**
14. Will **have**
15. Can **jump**

Subtest 5
1. will seek
2. were swimming
3. wore
4. are drinking
5. is keeping
6. will make
7. was teaching
8. caught
9. am beginning
10. had taught
11. sit
12. is feeling
13. will lead
14. have sung
15. slept
16. began
17. had done
18. have brought
19. is selling
20. had thought

21. bought
22. was laying
23. run
24. had known
25. is swinging
26. left
27. had gone
28. will eat
29. flew
30. is

UNIT 4: PRONOUNS

Subtest 1

1. she, S
2. I, S
3. them, O
4. We, S
5. her, O
6. us, O
7. They, S
8. him, O
9. me, O
10. it, S

Subtest 2 (pronoun, *antecedent*)

1. He, *Martin;* it, *show*
2. she, *Robin;* them, *José and Shannon*
3. it, *cardinal*
4. They, *dad and mom;* it, *play*
5. You, *Terri*
6. them, *glasses;* her, *Ms. Armstrong*
7. she, *Erin;* it, *name*
8. them, *Bears*
9. It, *computer;* him, *Rick*
10. they, *parents*

Subtest 3 (Answers may vary.)

1. its
2. hers
3. theirs
4. mine
5. your
6. his
7. ours
8. her
9. yours
10. its

Subtest 4 (indefinite pronoun, verb)

1. Everybody, has
2. Many, are
3. No one, has
4. Each, was
5. Some, waste
6. Both, know
7. Others, have
8. Someone, calls
9. Neither, gets
10. Several, work

UNIT 5: ADJECTIVES

Subtest 1 (adjective, type)

1. Those, dem.; fishing; English, P
2. The, art.; a, art.; fascinating
3. The, art.; gorgeous; Nigerian, P
4. These, dem.; new; Australian, P
5. the, art.; small; country
6. fiction
7. The, art.; African, P; beautiful
8. That, dem.; tall; the, art.; soccer
9. the, art.; spectacular; an, art.; important; a, art.
10. an, art.; the, art.
11. those, dem.; delicious
12. The, art.; little; bunk
13. These, dem.; green
14. The, art.; garden; a, art.; vegetable
15. a, art.; Mexican, P; a, art.; Swedish, P
16. This, dem.; the, art.; biggest
17. the, art.; little; brick; the, art.; the, art.
18. The, art.; Amazon, P
19. The, art.; crossword; that, dem.; the, art.; this, dem.
20. an, art.; Italian, P

Subtest 2

1. worse
2. largest
3. more beautiful
4. best
5. sturdiest
6. more fascinating
7. more
8. highest
9. more
10. worst
11. tamest
12. better
13. more uncomfortable
14. less
15. most
16. worse
17. narrowest
18. least
19. more delicious
20. more

UNIT 6: ADVERBS

Subtest 1 (adverb, *word modified*)

1. often, *play*
2. up, *stood;* slowly, away, *walked*
3. there, *Put*
4. never, *have been;* so, *surprised*
5. loudly, *were barking*
6. usually, *cooks*
7. beautifully, *sang*
8. seldom, *disagree*
9. now, *are*
10. here, *can put*
11. nearly, *choked*
12. oddly, *is behaving*
13. later, *will see*
14. cutely, *babbled*
15. very, *grateful*

Subtest 2

1. temporarily, V
2. almost, adv.
3. Unbelievably, V
4. quite, adv.
5. rather, adv.
6. freely, V
7. totally, V
8. badly, V
9. quite, adj.
10. really, adj.
11. very, adj.
12. very, adv.
13. so, adj.
14. too, V
15. together, V
16. extremely, adj.
17. absolutely, adv.
18. somewhat, adj.
19. hardly, V
20. now, V

Subtest 3

1. better
2. farther
3. longest
4. hard *or* harder
5. worst
6. more slowly
7. less
8. more rapidly
9. most politely
10. better
11. more easily
12. least
13. more recently
14. more softly
15. worse

Subtest 4

1. almost
2. good
3. quickly
4. surely
5. bad
6. sadly
7. efficiently
8. slow
9. well
10. real
11. badly

12. strange
13. Surprisingly
14. sure
15. totally
16. rude
17. most
18. unusual
19. well
20. really

Subtest 5
Checked sentences are 1, 5, 8, 10, 12, 13, and 15.

UNIT 7: PREPOSITIONS, CONJUNCTIONS, AND INTERJECTIONS

Subtest 1 (prepositional phrase, object)
1. above the large **window**
2. at **seven**; in the **evening**
3. down the steep **hill**
4. In the **photo**; in front of **Deon** and **Tracie**
5. through the paper **sign**
6. at the pizza **shop**; after the **show**
7. on top of the **tree**
8. for **Mr. Olivero**
9. onto the **roof**; from the oak **tree**
10. under a **rock**
11. Aside from my **mom**; in my **family**
12. with your **hamburger**
13. into the **beaker**
14. over your **head**
15. from the **girl**
16. for the **drama club**; instead of **hockey**
17. among the **weeds**; by the **stream**
18. against the **wall**; behind the **door**
19. out of his **pocket**
20. of **miles**; beneath the **surface**; of the **sea**
21. of the **club**; to the parents' **group**
22. According to this **book**
23. beneath the large maple **tree**
24. from her **sister**
25. to **America**; during the **Vietnam War**

Subtest 2
1. whom
2. me
3. her
4. us
5. Who
6. me
7. him
8. me
9. them
10. whom

Subtest 3
1. adj., outlook; adv., doubtful
2. adv., ran
3. adj., painting
4. adv., raced
5. adv., was
6. adv., trudged
7. adv., found
8. adj., All
9. adv., important; adj., economy
10. adj., dog
11. adv., chose
12. adj., house; adv., belongs
13. adv., had seen
14. adj., article
15. adv., was hovering

16. adv., were mooing
17. adv., can get
18. adj., edge
19. adv., runs
20. adv., is located
21. adj., shirt
22. adv., ran
23. adv., whizzed
24. adj., flag
25. adv., rare

Subtest 4
1. adv.
2. prep.
3. prep.
4. adv.
5. adv.
6. prep.
7. prep.
8. adv.
9. prep.
10. adv.

Subtest 5 (conjunction, *interjection*)
1. *Hey*
2. *Oh;* and
3. and; but; and
4. *Rats*
5. *Well*
6. and
7. or
8. Both, and
9. *Ouch*
10. or
11. *Oops*
12. *Hurray*
13. but
14. Either, or
15. Both, and
16. but
17. *Phew*
18. Neither, nor
19. Both, and; but
20. *What;* and
21. *Alas*
22. but
23. or
24. Not only, but also
25. *Wow*

UNIT 8: SUBJECT-VERB AGREEMENT

Subtest 1 (subject; *verb form*)
1. Canada, United States; *is*
2. kinds; *Do*
3. Animals; *are*
4. Dametri, you; *have*
5. reasons; *are*
6. Corey; *collects*
7. sheep, cows; *graze*
8. Students; *help*
9. answers; *are*
10. Tim, parents; *plan*
11. cousins; *Have*
12. people; *were*
13. picnic; *was*
14. tulips, hyacinths; *are*
15. test; *determines*
16. racer; *Does*
17. kites; *go*
18. math, science; *is*
19. you; *Were*
20. Something; *needs*
21. gerbil, rat; *are*
22. acts; *were*
23. No one; *has*
24. Mr. Garcia, brothers; *hope*
25. maples, oak; *turn*
26. Weasels; *are*
27. aunt, cousins; *live*
28. cards; *are*
29. legends; *end*
30. we; *Are*

31. Mitchell, twins; *are*
32. reason; *wasn't*
33. mice, guinea pig; *stay*
34. Zora; *Does*
35. Michael; *has*
36. carrots, celery; *taste*
37. tickets; *are*
38. tables; *are*
39. you; *Were*
40. rain, snow; *prevents*

UNIT 9: DIAGRAMING SENTENCES

Subtest 1

1.
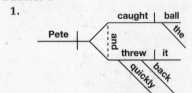

2.
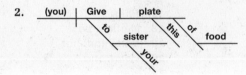

3.
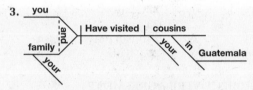

4.
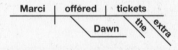

5.
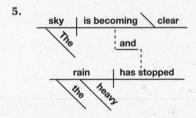

6.
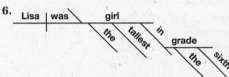

7.
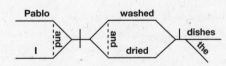

8.
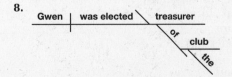

9.
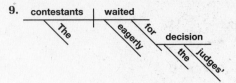

10.
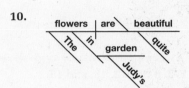

11.
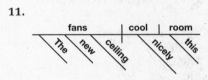

12.
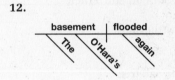

UNIT 10: USAGE GLOSSARY

Subtest 1

1. then
2. accept
3. its
4. whose
5. two
6. who's
7. lay
8. loose
9. except
10. lie

11. to
12. lose
13. than
14. it's
15. too
16. among
17. already
18. between
19. chose
20. all ready

Subtest 2

1. they're
2. set
3. raise
4. leave
5. all ready
6. beside
7. between
8. choose
9. altogether
10. learn

11. Let
12. already
13. their
14. besides
15. chose
16. among
17. sit
18. rise
19. teach
20. all together

UNIT 11: CAPITALIZATION

Subtest 1 (Uppercase; lowercase)

1. May; police officer
2. Labor Day
3. Republican
4. Erica's, Lithuania; grandmother
5. *People*
6. Lincoln Memorial, Washington, D.C.
7. Oldsmobiles, Pontiacs, General Motors Corporation
8. father, he, five
9. African American
10. south, sun
11. governor, election

12. General
13. Boy Scouts
14. Tuesday; dentist
15. Atlantic Ocean, New York, Portugal; east
16. Bouncemaster
17. Africa; grandfather
18. Southwest
19. *Huckleberry Finn*
20. Civil War, South
21. Mom, Have
22. westerly, miles per hour
23. Griffey, Jr., Seattle
24. Major; the
25. Grand Canyon; east
26. Knox County, Club; money
27. The; continent
28. Dear, Dr.
29. Deon; nobody
30. Island, Gulf, Mexico, Tampa
31. Ohio; state, western
32. October, November; fall
33. have
34. Chinese, University, Wisconsin
35. The, M.D.
36. Powerblitz
37. I, San Antonio, Texas
38. New Orleans, Mississippi River
39. Not, West Coast
40. Dad, Korean
41. Sincerely
42. Don't, In
43. if
44. Italian; Renaissance; grandparents
45. Main Street; office building

UNIT 12: PUNCTUATION

Subtest 1

1. Oh, my gosh!
2. Margaret, would you hand Joan this pen?
3. Yes, the Florida Everglades are a fascinating place to visit.
4. Heather's favorite animals at the zoo were the elephants, the pandas, and the electric eels.
5. My dad enjoys reading fiction, but my mom prefers nonfiction.
6. At first I was unsure which game to choose.
7. Please don't close the window.
8. Instead of apples, peaches were served at the picnic.
9. Dear Aunt Sylvia,
10. William Tecumseh Sherman is a famous general from Ohio, too.
11. The fetlock, as you know, is the part of a horse's leg just above the hoof.
12. Does the new term begin in August 1997?
13. Kristy Yamaguchi won the Olympic gold medal in figure skating, and Mary Lou Retton won in gymnastics.
14. Grandpa's new address is 912 Adams Street, Owings Mills, Maryland 21117.
15. Norma Lawton, M.D., will perform the eye surgery.
16. No, I've never known anyone who raised pigeons.
17. What an amazing shot!

18. The two teams represented Oshkosh, Wisconsin, and Derry, New Hampshire, in the tournament.
19. After the Civil War, Reconstruction began in the South.
20. Dr. Santiago, I don't know how to thank you for your help.
21. Where did your grandparents go on vacation?
22. That pitcher can throw a fastball, a curveball, and a change-up.
23. We can see the Native American exhibits first, or we can look at the antique cars.
24. Franklin's birth date is December 2, 1984.
25. Except for Michael, Jake is probably my best friend.
26. My three favorite colors are cherry red, shocking pink, and royal purple.
27. Your friend, Tina
28. In the bushes behind the garage, Maria saw a ferret.
29. "Don't begin," cautioned the coach, "until I blow my whistle."
30. The police officer wondered if she should give the driver a ticket.

Subtest 2

1. Frederick's flight was scheduled to leave at 6:18 P.M.
2. "The painting at the museum," Doug said, "was of a Pueblo village."
3. It's too bad we couldn't go scuba diving.
4. Joe DiMaggio was a great baseball player for the New York Yankees; his career stretched from 1936 to 1951.
5. Katie's family has lived in Dallas, New York, and Miami.
6. My favorite of Edgar Allan Poe's stories is "The Pit and the Pendulum."
7. Does your sister-in-law have a dachshund?
8. The film director threw down his clipboard in disgust and yelled, "Cut!"
9. "The dingo is a wild dog found in Australia," explained the speaker.
10. Rex loves Robert Frost's poem, "The Road Not Taken."
11. Mandy read a story to the children's group at the library.
12. Ms. Randolph whispered, "Be as quiet as you can."
13. The math test will cover fractions, decimals, percentages, multiplication, and division.
14. If you're looking for Mr. Menendez's apartment, it's across the street.
15. Thai food is usually very spicy; Japanese food often is not.
16. Mr. Maxwell and I planted the following herbs: parsley, dill, basil, marjoram, and sage.
17. My grandmother's mother-in-law was the first female dentist in the state.
18. The farmer said, "The calf is limping badly on its injured leg."
19. Stephanie shouted, "Wait for me!"
20. Juanita and I read about alligators and crocodiles in *Natural History* magazine.
21. The girls' basketball team lost a close game to Moorehead Middle School.

22. Dominica is a tiny country in the West Indies; Christopher Columbus landed there in 1493.
23. Fifty-eight boats were tied to the dock.
24. Did Kenneth say "I'm not interested"?
25. Which one of Pearl Jam's albums do you like best?
26. Kia's favorite book is *A Night to Remember;* it's about the *Titanic.*
27. Aren't those ice skates hers?
28. Next year, he's taking math, history, Spanish, and science.
29. Dear Manager of Customer Relations:
30. Felipe asked, "What's the assignment for Monday?"

Subtest 3
Checked sentences are 4, 5, 8, 10, 11, 14, and 15.

Subtest 4
1. 64 percent
2. three
3. Two hundred eighty-six
4. first
5. 680 million
6. seven
7. 11
8. 21
9. 3,671
10. 5:15
11. 51
12. ten
13. 475
14. fifth
15. fourteen thousand
16. eight
17. 300
18. 15
19. 224
20. 1:30

UNIT 13: VOCABULARY AND SPELLING

Subtest 1
1. quiet
2. dog
3. not
4. happy
5. two
6. quality of
7. anxious
8. angrily
9. through
10. understood

Subtest 2
1. bookcase
2. trained
3. staying
4. passed
5. foxes
6. too
7. changeable
8. dessert
9. controlled
10. fathers-in-law
11. fully
12. received
13. neighborhood
14. babies
15. spotted
16. past
17. handful
18. denies
19. leaves
20. developed

UNIT 14: COMPOSITION

Subtest 1
Last week our music class went on an interesting field trip. We took a tour of Great Sounds Recording Studio. One of the engineers, Ms. Tanaka, showed us how a recording studio works. There was one room for the musicians and another room for the engineers. They could see each other through a large glass window and talk to each other through an intercom.

After the musicians recorded the music, a singer arrived to record the vocals. She wore headphones. The engineers played the newly recorded music through the headphones and recorded the singer's voice as she sang the song. Ms. Tanaka explained that the voice and music would be combined electronically so that the song would sound really good. When I grow up, I definitely want to work in a recording studio.

Subtest 2 (Answers will vary.)
1. By the time the fireworks display was supposed to start, the city park was filled with people.
2. Kyle eagerly reached for the one King Arthur book that remained on the shelf.
3. Just as I was entering my tent, I heard a creepy noise.
4. The sand felt warm as I stretched out beneath my beach umbrella.
5. As she approached Grandma's house, Kelly could smell oatmeal raisin cookies baking.
6. The building the treasure map pointed to was completely empty.
7. As soon as he found out he had won the science award, Keith wrote a thank-you letter to the panel of judges.
8. Jennifer helped her teacher organize the class spelling bee.
9. After a long Saturday afternoon of chores, the movie we went to see seemed extremely funny.
10. Federico received a mysterious package from Switzerland on his birthday.

Subtest 3 (Answers will vary.)
1. Miki is Kelly's pen pal from Japan.
2. Kelly is writing to tell Miki about her life and about life in the United States.
3. Yes, this is a good example of a pen pal letter. Kelly tells something about her life and asks questions about Miki's life.
4. Kelly could give more details about Silver Spring and her daily life—school, family, friends, and so on. Also, she could describe her interests in the second paragraph, which is about her life, rather than in the third paragraph, which asks for information about Miki's life.

Subtest 4 (Answers will vary.)
1. Josh Mularsky is a reader of *YP* magazine.
2. He is writing to the Editor to complain about an article called "Cards to Collect" that appeared in the magazine.
3. No, this is not a good example of an opinion letter. This letter is rude, insulting, unclear, and illogical.
4. This letter could be improved by making it polite and respectful, by giving examples to explain what Josh considers "good" stories, and by acknowledging the fact that other readers may have enjoyed the article "Cards to Collect."